MARKETING INFORMATION SYSTEMS

MARKETING INFORMATION SYSTEMS

Chandra Sekhar Gotlagunta

KALPAZ

Marketing Information Systems

ISBN : 978-81-7835-915-1

Published in 2012 in India by
Kalpaz Publications
C-30, Satyawati Nagar,
Delhi - 110052
E-mail: kalpaz@hotmail.com
Ph.: 9212729499

Lasser Type Setting : Rajender Vashist, Delhi
Printed at : Chawla Offset Printers, Delhi

To my beloved parents

Contents

List of Figures, Exhibits and Tables 9
Preface 19
Acknowledgements 21

1. Marketing Information Systems: A Conceptual Frame work **25**

2. Literature Survey, Objectives and Methodology 56

3. Marketing Information System in Core Sector **103**

3.1 MKIS in CPCL 103
3.2 MKIS in VSP 126
3.3 MKIS in ACC Cement 151
3.4 Summary 172

4. Marketing Information System in Chemicals Sector **175**

4.1 MKIS in Neuland Laboratories Limited 175
4.2 MKIS in Erythro Pharma Pvt. Limited 196
4.3 MKIS in Bilogical E. Limited 216
4.4 Summary 235

5. Marketing Information System in Services Sector **237**

5.1 MKIS in Antrix 237
5.2 MKIS in Medinova 259
5.3 Summary 277

6. Summary of Findings and Suggestions **279**

Appendices 307

1. Questionnaire-1 307
2. Questionnaire-2 311

Index 325

List of Figures, Exhibits and Tables

LIST OF FIGURES

1.1 The Marketing Management Process and Information Flow 28

1.2 Marketing Information Systems 29

1.3 Antecedents of Marketing Problem Solving Modes 31

1.4 Matching MPSMS and MMSSS 31

1.5 A General Marketing Information System 34

2.1 An Analytical Model of Information System Effectiveness 93

3.1.1 Organisation chart of CPCL 106

3.2.1 Organisation chart of VSP 128

5.1.1 Organisation chart of ISRO – Antrix 238

5.1.2 Organisation chart of Antrix 239

6.1 An Analytical Model of Information System Effectiveness 281

LIST OF EXHIBITS

1.1 Support of MKIS to Marketing Mix 35

1.2 Support of MKIS to Marketing Decisions: Level-Wise. 37

6.1 Research Organisations 282

6.2 Profile of the Respondents 283

6.3 Comparative Analysis of MKIS - Core Sector 285

6.4 Reports in Core Sector 286

6.5 Comparative Evaluation of MKIS - Core Sector 287

6.6 Comparative Analysis of MKIS - Chemicals Sector 288

6.7 Reports in Chemicals Sector 289
6.8 Comparative Evaluation of MKIS – Chemicals Sector 290
6.9 Comparative Analysis of MKIS – Services Sector 292
6.10 Reports in Service Sector 292
6.11 Comparative Evaluation of MKIS – Services Sector 293
6.12 Marketing Information System – A Comparative View 295
6.13 Functional Effectiveness of MKIS 296
6.14 Change Orientation of MKIS 297
6.15 User Friendliness of MKIS 297
6.16 Cost Effectiveness of MKIS 298
6.17 Information Systems Management Effectiveness 299

TABLES

1.1 The Four Subsystems of Kotler 30
1.2 Key Words Characterising The Different Types of MMSS's 32
1.3 Benefits of MKIS 39
1.4 Enterprise IT Spend (growth Rate) 50
1.5 Using IT : Insurance Leads The Pack 50
1.6 Effect of IT on Various Functions of Business Organisations 54
2.1 Concept and Components of MKIS 74
2.2 Importance of MKIS 76
2.3 Development of MKIS 79
2.4 Evaluation of MKIS 82
3.1.1 Profile of Respondents 109
3.1.2 Reporting Relationships of Respondents 109
3.1.3 Perceived Role Clarity of Respondents 110
3.1.4 Dependence on Decision, Decision Making and Implementation 111
3.1.5 Perception about Information Received 112
3.1.6 Conference / Workshops Attended by 113

the Respondents
3.1.7 Source of Information Used to Keep Updated 114
3.1.8 Use of Marketing Research in Decision Making 114
3.1.9 System Management Evaluation 115
3.1.10 System Management Evaluation - Leadership 116
3.1.11 System Management Evaluation - Plans 116
3.1.12 System Management Evaluation - Controls 116
3.1.13 System Management Evaluation - Security 119
3.1.14 System Management Evaluation - Change Management 120
3.1.15 Evaluation of Information System Management 121
3.1.16 Evaluation of Information System Management - System Elements 121
3.1.17 People Evaluation 122
3.1.18 People Evaluation Details 122
3.1.19 Evaluation of System Outcomes 123
3.1.20 Evaluation of System Outcomes - Information and Output 123
3.1.21 Evaluation of System Outcomes - User Friendliness 124
3.1.22 Evaluation of System Outcomes - Decision Support 125
3.1.23 Evaluation of System Outcomes - Benefits and Satisfaction 125
3.1.24 Overall Evaluation of Information System 126
3.2.1 Profile of Respondents 131
3.2.2 Reporting Relationships of Respondents 130
3.2.3 Perceived Role Clarity of Respondents 133
3.2.4 Dependence on Decision, Decision Making and Implementation 134
3.2.5 Perception about Information Received 138
3.2.6 Conference / Workshops Attended by the Respondents 138

3.2.7 Source of Information Used to Keep Updated 138
3.2.8 Use of Marketing Research in Decision Making 139
3.2.9 System Management Evaluation 140
3.2.10 System Management Evaluation – Leadership 140
3.2.11 System Management Evaluation – Plans 141
3.2.12 System Management Evaluation – Controls 142
3.2.13 System Management Evaluation – Security 143
3.2.14 System Management Evaluation – Change Management 144
3.2.15 Evaluation of Information System Management 145
3.2.16 Evaluation of Information System Management – System Elements 145
3.2.17 People Evaluation 146
3.2.18 People Evaluation Details 147
3.2.19 Evaluation of System Outcomes 147
3.2.20 Evaluation of System Outcomes – Information and Output 148
3.2.21 Evaluation of System Outcomes – User Friendliness 149
3.2.22 Evaluation of System Outcomes – Decision Support 149
3.2.23 Evaluation of System Outcomes – Benefits and Satisfaction 150
3.2.24 Overall Evaluation of Information System 150
3.3.1 Profile of Respondents 155
3.3.2 Reporting Relationships of Respondents 155
3.3.3 Perceived Role Clarity of Respondents 156
3.3.4 Dependence on Decision, Decision Making and Implementation 157
3.3.5 Perception about Information Received 158
3.3.6 Conference / Workshops Attended by the Respondents 160
3.3.7 Source of Information Used to Keep Updated 160
3.3.8 Use of Marketing Research in Decision Making 161

3.3.9 System Management Evaluation 161

3.3.10 System Management Evaluation - Leadership 162

3.3.11 System Management Evaluation - Plans 163

3.3.12 System Management Evaluation - Controls 164

3.3.13 System Management Evaluation - Security 165

3.3.14 System Management Evaluation - Change Management 166

3.3.15 Evaluation of Information System Management 167

3.3.16 Evaluation of Information System Management - System Elements 167

3.3.17 People Evaluation 168

3.3.18 People Evaluation Details 168

3.3.19 Evaluation of System Outcomes 169

3.3.20 Evaluation of System Outcomes - Information and Output 169

3.3.21 Evaluation of System Outcomes - User Friendliness 170

3.3.22 Evaluation of System Outcomes - Decision Support 171

3.3.23 Evaluation of System Outcomes - Benefits and Satisfaction 171

3.3.24 Overall Evaluation of Information System 172

4.1.1 Profile of Respondents 179

4.1.2 Reporting Relationships of Respondents 179

4.1.3 Perceived Role Clarity of Respondents 180

4.1.4 Dependence on Decision, Decision-Making and Implementation 181

4.1.5 Perception about Information Received 183

4.1.6 Conference / Workshops Attended by the Respondents 184

4.1.7 Source of Information Used to Keep Updated 184

4.1.8 Use of Marketing Research in Decision Making 185

4.1.9 System Management Evaluation 185

4.1.10 System Management Evaluation - Leadership 186

4.1.11 System Management Evaluation - Plans 187

4.1.12	System Management Evaluation – Controls	188
4.1.13	System Management Evaluation – Security	189
4.1.14	System Management Evaluation – Change Management	190
4.1.15	Evaluation of Information System Management	191
4.1.16	Evaluation of Information System Management – System Elements	191
4.1.17	People Evaluation	192
4.1.18	People Evaluation Details	192
4.1.19	Evaluation of System Outcomes	193
4.1.20	Evaluation of System Outcomes – Information and Output	193
4.1.21	Evaluation of System Outcomes – User Friendliness	194
4.1.22	Evaluation of System Outcomes – Decision Support	195
4.1.23	Evaluation of System Outcomes – Benefits and Satisfaction	195
4.1.24	Overall Evaluation of Information System	196
4.2.1	Profile of Respondents	199
4.2.2	Reporting Relationships of Respondents	200
4.2.3	Perceived Role Clarity of Respondents	200
4.2.4	Dependence on Decision, Decision Making and Implementation	201
4.2.5	Perception about Information Received	202
4.2.6	Conference / Workshops Attended by the Respondents	202
4.2.7	Source of Information Used to Keep Updated	203
4.2.8	Use of Marketing Research in Decision-Making	203
4.2.9	System Management Evaluation	204
4.2.10	System Management Evaluation – Leadership	205
4.2.11	System Management Evaluation – Plans	205
4.2.12	System Management Evaluation – Controls	207
4.2.13	System Management Evaluation – Security	208

4.2.14 System Management Evaluation – Change Management 209

4.2.15 Evaluation of Information System Management 210

4.2.16 Evaluation of Information System Management – System Elements 210

4.2.17 People Evaluation 211

4.2.18 People Evaluation Details 212

4.2.19 Evaluation of System Outcomes 212

4.2.20 Evaluation of System Outcomes – Information and Output 213

4.2.21 Evaluation of System Outcomes – User Friendliness 214

4.2.22 Evaluation of System Outcomes – Decision Support 214

4.2.23 Evaluation of System Outcomes – Benefits and Satisfaction 215

4.2.24 Overall Evaluation of Information System 215

4.3.1 Profile of Respondents 218

4.3.2 Reporting Relationships of Respondents 219

4.3.3 Perceived Role Clarity of Respondents 219

4.3.4 Dependence on Decision, Decision Making and Implementation 220

4.3.5 Perception about Information Received 220

4.3.6 Conference / Workshops Attended by the Respondents 222

4.3.7 Source of Information Used to Keep Updated 222

4.3.8 Use of Marketing Research in Decision-Making 223

4.3.9 System Management Evaluation 224

4.3.10 System Management Evaluation – Leadership 224

4.3.11 System Management Evaluation – Plans 225

4.3.12 System Management Evaluation – Controls 226

4.3.13 System Management Evaluation – Security 227

4.3.14 System Management Evaluation – Change Management 228

4.3.15 Evaluation of Information System Management 229
4.3.16 Evaluation of Information System Management - System Elements 229
4.3.17 People Evaluation 230
4.3.18 People Evaluation Details 231
4.3.19 Evaluation of System Outcomes 231
4.3.20 Evaluation of System Outcomes - Information and Output 232
4.3.21 Evaluation of System Outcomes - User Friendliness 233
4.3.22 Evaluation of System Outcomes - Decision Support 233
4.3.23 Evaluation of System Outcomes - Benefits and Satisfaction 234
4.3.24 Overall Evaluation of Information System 234
5.1.1 Profile of Respondents 242
5.1.2 Reporting Relationships of Respondents 243
5.1.3 Perceived Role Clarity of Respondents 244
5.1.4 Dependence on Decision, Decision Making and Implementation 244
5.1.5 Perception about Information Received 245
5.1.6 Conference / Workshops Attended by the Respondents 246
5.1.7 Source of Information Used to Keep Updated 247
5.1.8 Use of Marketing Research in Decision Making 247
5.1.9 System Management Evaluation 248
5.1.10 System Management Evaluation - Leadership 249
5.1.11 System Management Evaluation - Plans 249
5.1.12 System Management Evaluation - Controls 250
5.1.13 System Management Evaluation - Security 251
5.1.14 System Management Evaluation - Change Management 252
5.1.15 Evaluation of Information System Management 253
5.1.16 Evaluation of Information System Management - System Elements 253

5.1.17 People Evaluation 254
5.1.18 People Evaluation Details 255
5.1.19 Evaluation of System Outcomes 255
5.1.20 Evaluation of System Outcomes - Information and Output 256
5.1.21 Evaluation of System Outcomes - User Friendliness 257
5.1.22 Evaluation of System Outcomes - Decision Support 257
5.1.23 Evaluation of System Outcomes - Benefits and Satisfaction 258
5.1.24 Overall Evaluation of Information System 258
5.2.1 Profile of Respondents 261
5.2.2 Reporting Relationships of Respondents 262
5.2.3 Perceived Role Clarity of Respondents 262
5.2.4 Dependence on Decision, Decision Making and Implementation 263
5.2.5 Perception about Information Received 264
5.2.6 Conference / Workshops Attended by the Respondents 264
5.2.7 Source of Information Used to Keep Updated 265
5.2.8 Use of Marketing Research in Decision Making 265
5.2.9 System Management Evaluation 266
5.2.10 System Management Evaluation - Leadership 267
5.2.11 System Management Evaluation - Plans 267
5.2.12 System Management Evaluation - Controls 269
5.2.13 System Management Evaluation - Security 270
5.2.14 System Management Evaluation - Change Management 271
5.2.15 Evaluation of Information System Management 272
5.2.16 Evaluation of Information System Management - System Elements 272
5.2.17 People Evaluation 273
5.2.18 People Evaluation Details 273

5.2.19 Evaluation of System Outcomes 274
5.2.20 Evaluation of System Outcomes – Information and Output 274
5.2.21 Evaluation of System Outcomes – User Friendliness 275
5.2.22 Evaluation of System Outcomes – Decision Support 276
5.2.23 Evaluation of System Outcomes – Benefits and Satisfaction 276
5.2.24 Overall Evaluation of Information System 277

PREFACE

Today, organisations are witnessing an unprecedented change in the environment and facing formidable challenge to their survival and success. The change is caused by the information revolution that has ushered in the knowledge society. The challenge lies in the emergent need for knowing more and adapting quickly to the new environment.

Among the various functions of business organisations, marketing is more sensitive to and interactive with environment. That is why companies are becoming consumer centric and market driven. In this context, questions of interest are: Are they quick in facing the new problems and seeking IT opportunities? To what extent the organisations have taken IT advantage? What is the state of art of the information technology in these companies? Are they benefited by their IT initiatives?

This study focuses on marketing information systems in select companies in core, chemicals and service sectors. It is a modest attempt to highlight the marketing systems and evaluates effectiveness. I hope the study would be of benefit to students, professors and practising executives.

The study is divided into six chapters.

Chapter 1 presents a conceptual framework and growth of MKIS in India and identifies the research problem.

Chapter 2 makes a survey of literature and establishes objectives and methodology for the present study.

Chapter 3, 4 and **5** describe and evaluate MKIS in select organisations in the chemicals and services sectors respectively.

Chapter 6 summarises the findings and highlights the suggestions for improving MKIS.

Chandra Sekhar G.

Acknowledgements

A research work of this kind cannot be completed without the active cooperation and contribution by many.

At the outset I am indebted to the organisations that have took part in the study. My special thanks are due to the following executives for providing me the necessary data.

V. Chainnaiah, Chief Manager	CPCL, Chennai.
Dr. V. Phaneendrudu, Dy. Cheef Manager	VSP, Visakhapatnam
T.S. Ajith Kumar, Dy.Cheef Manager	VSP, Visakhapatnam
K. Ramesh Babu, Assistant Manager,	VSP, Visakhapatnam
Rajiv Kumar, Manager - Marketing	ACC, Bangalore
G.S.R.K. Bhaskar Sastry - Officer	ACC, Bangalore
Y. Sudheer, GM - Marketing	Neuland Laboratories Limited, Hyderabad
Dr. D. Rajagopala Reddy, Managing Director	Erythro Pharma, Hyderabad
Mr. D. Balachandra Reddy, Vice President	Erythro Pharma, Hyderabad
M.S. Balaji, Vice President-Intl. Marketing	Biological E. Limited, Hyderabad
Sri Avinash Kumar, Manager	Biological E. Limited, Hyderabad
K.R. Sridhar Murthy, Executive Director	Antrix Corporation Limited
R.L.N. Murthy, Business Development Manager	Antrix Corporation Limited
V. Siddiramulu, Manager	ISTRAC, Bangalore/ Sriharikota

Sri Jala Ramaiah, Group General Manager	ISTRAC, Bangalore.
K. Raghava Reddy, GM	Medinova Diagnostic Services Limited
Sri Kumara Swami, Marketing Manager	Medinova Diagnostic Services Limited
K. Daya Sekhar Babu - Business Manager	Medinova Diagnostic Services Limited

My deep sense of gratitude is to my research supervisor Prof. C.S.G. Krishnamacharyulu, Chairman, Board of Studies of School of Business Management, S.V. University, for his valuable guidance through out the work.

My sincere thanks are due to Prof. P. Murali, Vice Chancellor of S.V University, Prof. T. Siddaiah, Registrar of S.V University, Prof. S. Jayarama Reddy, Principal of S.V University, College of Arts and Science, S.V. University., Prof. S. Balarama Reddy, Head, School of Business Management of S.V University for their encouragement.

I am very much indebted to Prof. B.E.V.V.N. Murthy, Dr. P. Balaji Prasad, Dr. M. Srinivasa Reddy, and Sri. B. Suresh Rao, Dr. D.V. Ramana, Dr. S. Durga Rao, Sri. B. Sudheer, Sri. P. Raghunatha Reddy, Faculty members of School of Business Management, S.V. University for their concern.

My deep sense of gratitude is to Prof. M. Chandrasekhar, Founder Head and Principal (Retired), for his encouragement and support.

I owe my thanks to Dr. Lalitha Ramakrishnan, Academic Coordinator - Department of Business Management, Sri Padmavathi Mahila Viswa Vidyalayam and my co-scholars Miss. V. Santhi Latha, Mrs. N. Nawashad Begam, and K. Lavanya Latha for inspiring me from time to time.

I express my sincere gratitude to Mr. Venkatesh, CD work station, IIM, Bangalore for his support in collection of literature.

I owe my gratitude to the office staff K. Nagaraju, D. Vijaya Kumar, B. Vijaya Lakshmi for their support.

I wish to record my special thanks and reverence to my sisters Mrs. G. Krishnaveni and Miss. S.L. Jayanthi, brother - in - law Sri V. Rajagopal, and Brothers G. Koteswara Rao, and G. Jayaprakash for their encouragement, love and support through out my study.

With great affection I thank my friends D. Subramanyam, G. Uday Bhaskar, Dr. K. Raja Mohan Reddy, K. Sreedhar, N. Hariprasad Reddy, D.J. Sudheer Kumar and A. Chandramouli, P. Siva Kumar (Siva Graphics), A. Sujan, K. Ramana Reddy, Ch. Sujan for their inspiration in realising my goals.

Finally, I place on record my reverence to my loving parents, whose support is beyond description. I once again express my gratitude to all those who have made the research possible.

Chandra Sekhar G.

1

Marketing Information System : A Conceptual Frame Work

Introduction

Economic reforms together with have a thwarting effect on the marketing facet of the information technology changed the Indian business. Economic reforms have set into motion forces like liberalisation, privatisation and globalisation that have unleashed competition. In this context, many business organisations have started spending huge amounts on IT and developing marketing information systems. It will be of interest to know the state of the art of marketing information systems (MKIS) and their effectiveness.

Concept of MKIS

The definition of Marketing Information System (MKIS) by deifferent authors are galore, but opinions differ. However, content-wise and function-wise there is a common thread.

According to Kinnear and Bernhardt,

> *"MKIS is defined as a structured, interacting complex of persons, machines and procedures designed to generate an orderly flow of pertinent information, collected from both intra and extra firm's sources for use as the base for decision-making in specified responsibility areas for marketing management."*

Kotler maintained:

> *"A MKIS is a continuing and interacting structure of people, equipment and procedures to gather, sort, analyse, evaluate and distribute pertinent, timely and accurate information for use by marketing decision-makers to improve their marketing planning and control."*

Cox and Good observed:

> *"MKIS is a set of procedures and methods for regular, planned collection, analysis and presentation of information for use in making marketing decisions."*

Role of MKIS

From the above definitions, it can be said that the role of MKIS is to provide information support to marketing as well as functions in decision-making and implementation. In playing this role, it should perform the following six functions.

1. *Assembling* –searching for and gathering marketing data
2. *Processing*–editing, tabulating and summarising data
3. *Analysis*–computing percentages and ratios, combining sales and cost data and also other mathematical tasks
4. *Storage and retrieval*–indexing, filing and locating data
5. *Evaluation*–determining the quality (accuracy) of information
6. *Dissemination*–routing useful information to appropriate decision-makers

The information system specific to marketing, combines data in the company's data bases with outside data including economic, demographic, and industrial statistical data. These data serve as input into a variety of forecasts and competitive and pricing models to supply within minutes strategic information that will be impossible to be provided with manual systems. Moreover, new and improved information systems convert reams of numbers into charts, colourful graphs and maps that are easy for marketers to understand and digest. Telecommunications, word processors and electronic mail also enable reports, memos and product information to be transmitted simultaneously to a number of marketing personnels, sales people in the fields of and even customers for business.

MKIS Less Systematised

Marketing information system is less developed in many organisations for the following reasons:

- *Benefit intangible:* Improved information systems for marketing do not often receive priority because they cannot be justified on a cost saving basis and the benefits of the system may be extensively intangible and not readily observable.

- *Marketing is an art:* Marketers believe that marketing decision-making is primarily an art and cannot be systematised. Decisions like pricing and promotion rely more on tact than facts, more on intuition than on research.

The lack of systematisation of marketing information makes marketing a "seat-of-the-pants" activity in many companies.

Need for Systematisation

1. Marketing–the revenue generator

A well-developed MKIS can give competitive advantage by offering better services to customers and better information for market penetration efforts.

2. Critical linkages

Marketing information is not only important to marketing but also to its other functions.

3. Global marketing trends

With the globalisation of economies, even medium-sized domestic firms have the compulsion for thinking globally and acting locally. Consequently, information needs have grown exponentially demanding a system.

4. Info revolution

Blattberg, Glazer and Lazer (1994) traced the evolution of marketing information system to the "marketing information revolution", the fifth stage in evolution process characterised by "decentralised products in decentralised markets." Organisations succeeding in customer control are necessarily better producers and better system integrators. Bloom, Adler and Milne (1994) opined that marketing information systems using new information technologies serve in many ways. Specifically to improve :

- New market knowledge
- Response capabilities
- Persuasive communication, and
- Strategy making.

Stephan (1990) in his empirical analysis of successful

competitive strategies in the Austrian market of decoration fabrics noted the strategic role that IT plays in the context of development and transformation of the selected generic competitive strategies.

Structure of MKIS

The components of MKIS as perceived and described by different marketing specialists are briefly presented below.

Brien and Stafford Model

They made the first effort by presenting a diagram and a narrative. It showed how MKIS could support marketing managers in developing planned programmes for each of the four marketing mix ingredients. The model elements connected by both information and decision flows were as given below (Fig. 1.1) :

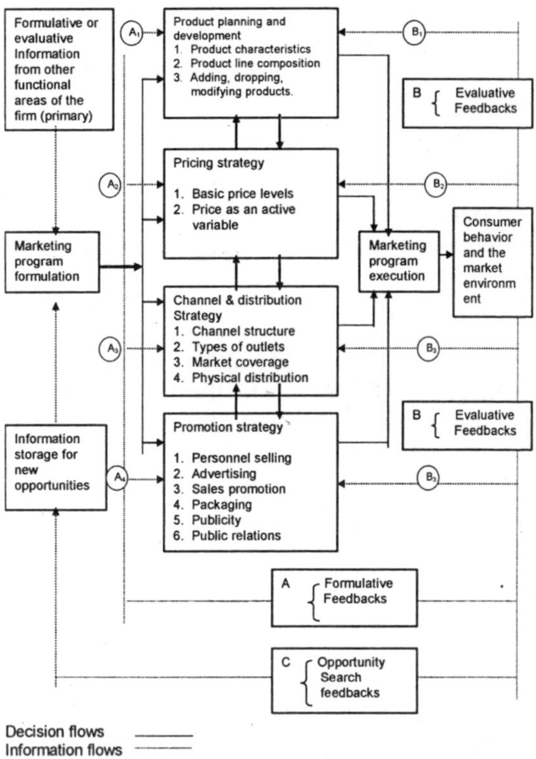

Fig. 1.1 : The Marketing Management Process and Information Flows

Kotler Model

According to Kotler, MKIS consists of four subsystems–internal accounting, marketing intelligence, marketing research and marketing management science. The subsystems take data from the environment and transform it into information for the marketing executives. The emphasis in marketing management science is on the use of sophisticated quantitative techniques, such as simulation. Kotler saw the marketing managers using the information output for planning, execution and control.

The output subsystems are the four marketing mix elements plus integrated–mix subsystem (Table 1.1). The fifth subsystem enables managers to develop strategies that consider the combined effects of the ingredients. For example, a manager might want the combined effects of high price, moderate quality product, high level promotion and selective distribution of packaged food products. In the recent versions, he dropped the fifth subsystem depicting interrelationship of four subsystems as shown in Fig. 1.2.

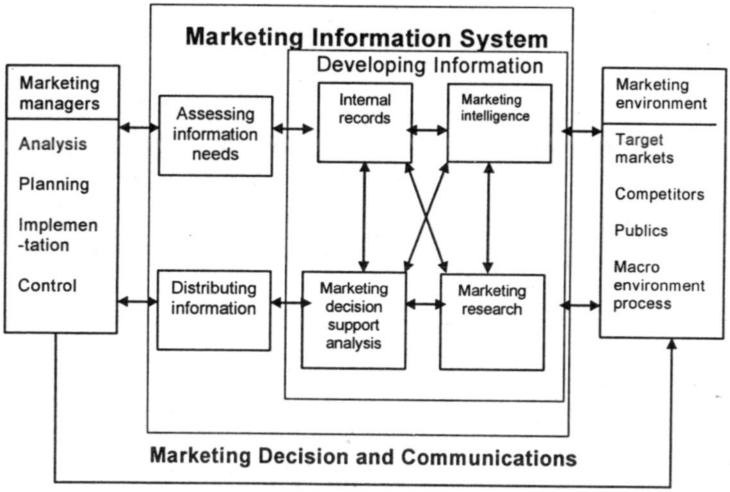

Fig. 1.2 : Marketing Information Systems

Cox and Good Model

MKIS is a step beyond logistics systems which handle inventory control, orders and so forth. MKIS can, therefore, be differentiated into two major components:

Table 1.1 : The Four Subsystems of Kotler

Type	Content
Marketing Intelligence System	Procedures and sources to obtain every day information - Undirected viewing, Conditioned viewing, informal search and Formal search.
Internal Report System	Regular, predetermined and formatted reports.
Marketing Research System	An occasional inquiry for new information on the specific areas for problem solving.
Analytical Marketing System	Statistical bank and model bank

1. Support Systems–They include those activities required to generate and manipulate data i.e. market research and other data gathering, programming and data processing.
2. Operating Systems–Those that use the data as an aid to planning and controlling marketing activities.

Wierenga and Bruggen Model

Wierenga and Bruggen integrated the decision-makers and decision support systems in marketing. They introduced the concept of marketing problem solving modes (MPSM)–the demand side perspective of marketing management support systems (MMSS), which refer to the set of tools and capabilities that assist in decision-making.

They identified four MPSMs by four problem solving modes–Optimising (0), Reasoning (R), Analoging (A) and Creating (C), under different decision-making situations as depicted in Fig. 1. 3.

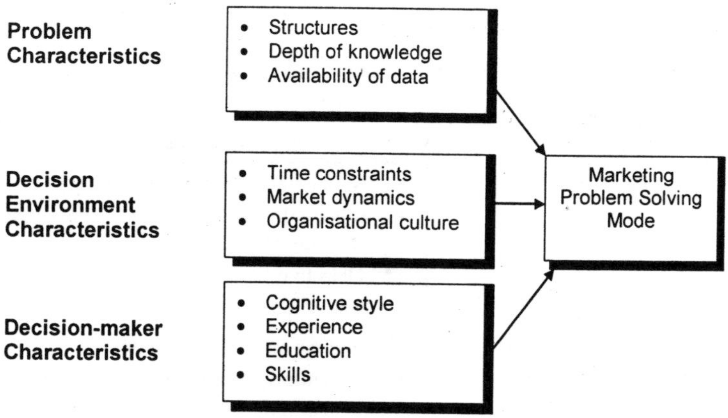

Fig. 1.3 : Antecedents of Marketing Problem Solving Modes

They examined the availability of MMSS's and the type of support they provide to decision-making as shown below in Fig. 1.4.

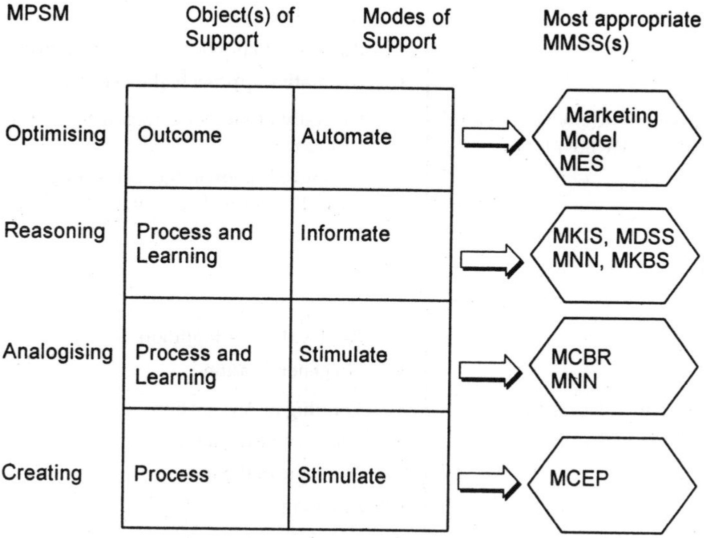

Fig. 1.4 : Matching MPSMs and MMSSs

The characteristics of different types of MMSS's are given in Table 1.2 as shown below :

Table 1.2 : Key Words Characterizing the Different Types of MMSSs

Date of origin	Main characteristics
Marketing Models 1960	▪ Mathematical representation ▪ Optional values for marketing instruments ▪ Objective ▪ Best solution
Marketing Information Systems (MKISs) 1965	▪ Storage and retrieval of data ▪ Quantitative information ▪ Registration of "What happens in the market" and "why" (analysis) ▪ Passive system
Marketing Decision Support Systems (MDSSs) 1980	▪ Flexible systems ▪ Recognition of managerial judgment ▪ Facilities to "what-if" questions
Marketing Expert Systems (MESSs) 1985	▪ Centres on marketing knowledge ▪ Human experts ▪ Rule-based knowledge representation ▪ Normative approach, the best solution
Marketing Knowledge Based Systems (MKBSs) 1990	▪ Diversity of methods, including hybrid approaches ▪ Structured knowledge representation, including frame based hierarchies ▪ Model based reasoning
Marketing Case Based Reasoning Systems (MCBRs) 1995	▪ Similarity with earlier cases ▪ Storage of cases in memory ▪ Retrieval and adaptation ▪ No generalisation
Marketing Neural Nets (MNNs) 1995	▪ Training of Associations ▪ Pattern recognition ▪ Not a priori theory ▪ Learning
Marketing Creativity Enhancement Programs (MCEPs) 2000	▪ Association through connections ▪ Idea generation ▪ Endorsement of creativity in problem solving

Murdick, Ross and Claggett Model

To overcome the shortcomings of month-end sales reporting system, Murdick, Ross and Claggett proposed a general marketing system depicted in Fig. 1.5. Characteristic of this type of system is an inquiry capability located in the field, branch, district and the head quarter offices.

These terminals are connected via teleprocessing facilities to a computer and the system can provide a broad inquiry coverage relating to sales activity updated on a daily basis. The four formats, Sales recap, Record summaries, Transactional analysis and Exceptional inquires would serve the three types of marketing systems-control system, planning system and market research system.

Sales Recap

It is an overall performance summary compared with previous budgets or other standards. This recap can be programmed to trigger successive levels of detailed reports, when the analysis indicates substandard performance. Major areas of performance analysis might include total sales by product sales expense, new accounts, replacement sales, cancellation rates and a variety of profitability analysis.

Record Summaries

Optimal level of details that permit in-depth analysis of deviations are spotted by sales recap. Ideally, this format should be programmed so that the user can structure his or her own reporting needs. These might include such items as sales by model, by sales plan, by industry, by customer type and sales to major and national accounts. Additionally, a variety of ratios such as sales units to travel expenses should be available if desired.

Transaction Analysis

This format might be called the significant transaction analysis because its purpose is to provide a "management by exception" approach to transactions that are so out of the ordinary that they require special treatment. Such transactions might be defined in terms of rupee volume, number of sales or other significant measures that exceed control limits.

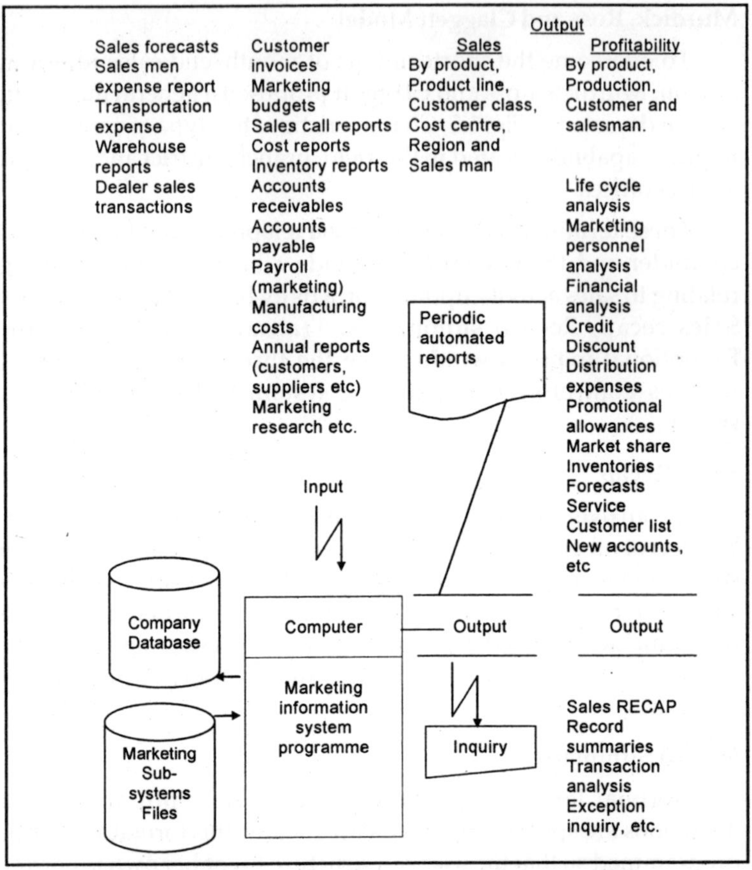

Fig. 1.5 : General Marketing Information System

Exceptional Inquires

This is the highest level of systems sophistication in that it gives a true inquiry capability to the user. This can be understood by such questions as, "Which sales offices have achieved a level of 50 per cent of their sales in the manufacturing industry but are less than 80 per cent sales quota in the retail industry?" This inquiry capability is a vital tool to any marketing / sales manager.

MKIS–An Overview

From the above presentation, it can be said that MKIS provides support to the marketing elements at the three hierarchical levels. Exhibit 1.1 and Exhibit 1.2 provide a summary view of MKIS

Exhibit 1.1 : Support of MKIS to Marketing Mix

Mix	Decision	Marketing Intelligence / Research	Internal Record	Decision Support
Product	Item (Brand) decision	♦ Sale of existing products ♦ Consumer preferences ♦ Market growth rates and market share trends ♦ Technological advancements ♦ Govt. policies	♦ Sale of company products ♦ Profitability level ♦ Production cost analysis ♦ Idle capacity ♦ Request for new products	♦ Demand forecasting ♦ Product design ♦ Concept testing ♦ Screening models ♦ Business analysis
Price	Price determination Price change	♦ Cost data ♦ Dealer preferences ♦ Discount structure	♦ Mark-up pricing ♦ B E Analysis ♦ Supply - demand graphs ♦ Price elasticity analysis ♦ Competitive bidding	♦ Price Structure ♦ Price changes
Place	Channel decision	♦ Competitor's practices ♦ Customer characteristics ♦ Environmental characteristics	♦ Product characteristics ♦ (standardisation,perishability, bulk, service requirements, unit price)	♦ Channel design ♦ Distribution strategies

[contd...]

[contd...]

Mix	Decision	Marketing Intelligence / Research	Internal Record	Decision Support
	Dealer appointment	♦ Intermediary characteristics ♦ Financial and marketing abilities ♦ Competitor's practices, location factors	♦ Market coverage needed ♦ Channel members:` ♦ Number and size ♦ Sales turnover	♦ Choice of dealers at different locations
Promoti on	Personal selling team	♦ Competitors practices ♦ Market growth rate ♦ Potential market size ♦ Geographical spread	♦ Current market coverage ♦ Target coverage ♦ Production levels ♦ Budget	♦ Manpower inventory and forecast ♦ Recruitment and selection techniques ♦ Territory allocation models
	Advertising	♦ Competitor's practices ♦ Consumer state(awareness, interest etc)	♦ Previous allocations ♦ Sales and ad expenditure data ♦ Sales force preferences	♦ AIDA model ♦ Promotion elasticity ♦ Ad budget models ♦ Effectiveness measures

Exhibit 1.2 : Support of MKIS to Marketing Decisions: Level-Wise

Level	Decision / Action	Description
Strategic	• Sales trend forecasting • Acquisition of a company • Addition of new product line • Entry into new market • New organization of company • Consideration of new markets and new marketing strategies	• Prepare 5- year sales forecasts • The evaluation of current capabilities, summarised in a special way for planning use. • Capabilities for new ventures based on current or expected developments. • Projections of resource requirements for the alternative strategy • Customer analyses, competitor analyses, consumer survey information, income projection, demographic projections, and technology projections
Management	• Market trend analysis • Pricing analysis • Sales region analysis • Selection of credit line institutions • Allocation of advertising • Comparisons of overall performance against a marketing plan	• Identify customers and markets using data on demographics, markets , consumer behaviour , and trends • Determine prices for products and services • Analyse performance of sales territories • Analyse distribution and dealer strengths • Reports of advertising budgets • Data on customers, competitors products and sales force requirements

[contd...]

[contd...]

Level	Decision / Action	Description
Operational	• Order processing • Point of sale system • Selection of vendor • Hiring of new supervisor • Sales orders • Hiring and training of the sales force	• Enter, process and track orders • Records sales data • Vendor information • Appointing new supervisor • Promotion ideas • The day-to-day scheduling of sales and promotion efforts and periodic analysis of sales volumes by region, product, customer, etc.

Benefits of MKIS

Cox and Good studied 15 major US corporations and observed the marketing information systems in operation and summarised some of the applications and probable benefits of each type of system. They are presented in Table 1.3.

Table 1.3 : Benefits of MKIS

Sl. No.	Typical Application	Benefits	Examples
	Control Systems		
1	Control of marketing costs.	More timely computerised reports.	Undesirable cost trends are spotted more quickly so that corrective action may be taken sooner.
2	Diagnosis of poor sales performance.	Flexible on-line retrieval of data.	Executives can ask supplementary questions of the computer to help pinpoint reasons for a sales decline and reach an action decision more quickly.
3	Management of fashion goods.	Automating spotting of problems and opportunities.	Fast-moving fashion items are reported daily for quick recorder and slow-moving items are also reported for fast price reductions.
4	Flexible promotion strategy	Cheaper, more detailed, and more frequent reports.	On-going evaluation of a promotional campaign permits reallocation of funds to areas behind target.

[contd...]

[contd...]

Sl. No.	Typical Application	Benefits	Examples
	Planning Systems		
1	Forecasting	Automatic translation of terms and classifications between departments.	Survey-based forecasts of demand for complex industrial goods can be automatically translated into parts, requirements and production schedules.
2	Promotional planning and corporate long-range planning.	Systematic testing of alternative promotional plans and compatibility testing of various divisional plans.	Complex simulation models both developed and operated with the help of data bank information can be used for promotional planning by product managers and for strategic planning by top management.
3	Credit management.	Programmed executive decision rules can operate on data bank information.	Credit decisions are automatically made as each order is processed.
4	Purchasing.	Detailed sales reporting permits automation of management decisions.	Computers automatically re-purchase standard items on the basis of correlation of sales data with programmed decision rules.

[contd...]

[contd...]

Sl. No.	Typical Application	Benefits	Examples
	Research System		
1	Advertising Strategy	Additional manipulation of data is possible when stored for computers in an un-aggregated file.	Sales analysis is possible by new market segment breakdowns.
2	Pricing Strategy.	Improved storage and retrieval capability allows new types of data to be collected and used.	Systematic recording of information about past R & D contract bidding situations allows improved bidding strategies.
3	Evaluation of advertising expenditures.	Well-designed data banks permit integration and comparison of different sets of data.	Advertising expenditures are compared to shipments by counts to provide information about advertising effectiveness.
4	Continuous experiments.	Comprehensive monitoring of input and performance variables yields information when changes are made.	Changes in promotional strategy by type of customer are matches against sales results on a continuous basis.

Features of MKIS

The important features of MKIS are:

1. Functionally complete

Sales information system (SIS) should be comprehensive closed loop SIS providing shared, up to date information about prospects, customers, products, service issues and competitors.

2. Querying the data (Data analysis)

Both predefined (standard) and custom (flexible) analysis are required in an SIS. Predefined analysis like customer, product, sales region and sales person analysis supported by graphs (time series, correlation etc), trend analysis, ABC analysis, classification, correlation etc., and custom analysis that tailors the data to suit individual needs are essential.

3. Reporting Features

Reporting features should have three levels of reporting—summary, detailed and exception.

4. Drilling and data slicing

With the help of drill down function user can see the detailed view of the data that is shown in the report, thereby, varying the degree of the information being shown.

Drill down can be characteristic drill down with regard to a characteristic for example, material, vendor, period etc.

Hierarchy drill down is with regards to hierarchy; for example, product group, customer hierarchy, material, material class etc.

5. Multidimensional database and analysis

In a multi-dimensional database, data is stored by dimension to enable fast access to information on various summarisation levels. For example, a sales analysis database may include the following dimension:

- Product group
- Geographical area
- Sales person
- Customer segment
- Department

6. Saving and sharing information (Library functions)

- Create and save analyses for later use
- Use saved selections to save repetitive queries
- Access and modify any related object at any time
- Create standard sets of analyses, measures and groupings that all users can access
- Distribute all analyses and selections that users create

6. Adhoc analysis

What if analysis and sensitivity analysis should be supported by SIS. For example, a sales manager should be able to do the following query: How will sales in a particular region increase the commission by one percent?

7. Exception reporting

The early warning system allows the user to search for exceptional situations and aids in early detection and correction of undesirable situations. An exception consists of specified characteristics or characteristic values (for example customer, material) and requirements. The following requirements can be defined:

- Threshold value (for example, materials / customers whose sales are greater than Rs. 10,000/-)
- Trend (for example, materials /customers with a negative trend in sales or lead times)
- Planned/actual comparison.

8. Support for multi-tiered distribution and service channels

Effective team selling and service requires collaboration across diverse channels and geographies. Mobile sales persons should be able to access all systems functionally from their local computers and synchronise their local database with server database quickly and efficiently.

9. Connectivity to enterprise applications

Fully scaleable server-based interfaces to share large volumes of information between the sales information system and other enterprise applications including their part systems should be there.

10. Defining sales organisation structure

In case of restructuring of the sales territories or hierarchy, the system should be able to quickly incorporate the change (updating of historical data, when organisational structures change). Moreover, the old structure should also be kept for comparative purposes. The feature of creating virtual selling teams should also be there.

11. Global enterprise support

Support sales and service professionals who transact business in multiple currencies and sales and service managers who require automatic conversion of quotas and forecasts into a common currency should be there.

12. Support personnel and virtual computing

Support personnel computing (includes synchronisation of mobile sales force data into the server data) and virtual computing (to support enterprise by uniting sales representatives, service representatives, resellers, partners and customers in a common information system) should be there.

13. Supporting opportunities and account management functions:

An opportunity management system (OMS) is a key component of any sales force automation system designed to attack the process side of selling. An OMS brings discipline to the sales process by requiring representatives to create a strategy (a set of steps) to close each sales opportunity in their pipeline. The system tracks the sales representative's progress against the plan providing important feedback to both the sales representative and his sales manager.

Contact management allows sales professional to effectively manage business and personal contacts by recording and tracking all contact information, creating lists of contacts, recording all contact activity and viewing all contacts related to a specific amount or opportunity.

Activity management enables the entire sales team to enter and track opportunity-specific account-specific contact-specific or personal activities including phone calls, meetings and marketing events.

Classification of Sale Information Systems

Sales information systems can be classified by the kind of technology (OLTP, OLAP etc.) they use and the features they support. The available sales information system packages can be classified into three categories (Appendix-I provides vendor's list):

- OLTP based SIS packages
- OLAP based SIS packages
- SFA oriented SIS packages

OLTP based SIS

- These kinds of SIS packages have limited features because they exploit only online transaction processing. These packages essentially have some predefined standard sales reports and a limited option for flexible and custom analysis and user-defined queries. Vendors like SBS, t-soft, CRC infosystems, JBA etc., have OLTP based sales information system packages. These packages provide analysis of current and past sales transactions. The predicted standard reports supported by these software packages include :

- Item sales report by customer
- Item sales report by territory
- Customer sales report by item
- Item sales report by salesperson
- Six month item sales summary
- Item by customer comparative
- Customer by item comparative
- Top 20 sales (YTD Sales)
- Top 20 items (YTD volume)
- Top 20 salespersons (YTD Volume)
- Top 20 customers (YTD profit)

On these summary reports limited drill down options are also available.

OLAP based SIS

But OLTP based SIS packages have limited use, because it is not possible to do flexible analysis on sales data with OLTP technology.

Sales executives and managers prefer an easy to use, highly visualised system providing access to the information, the need to perform their daily work. The end user interface should support:

- Multidimensional analysis
- Graphical and tabular presentation of data
- Drill down to underlying details
- Exception reporting
- Pre-defined reporting templates for easy to use graphs
- Shared text commenting
- What if analysis

- Slide show presentations of frequently used information
- Production of print-outs for presentation purposes.

The top level sales planners and analysts need additional functionality:

- Adhoc graph and report design
- Distribution of new graphs and reports to end users
- Retroactive updating of historical data, when organisational structures change.

All these are not possible with OLTP based sales information systems. Therefore, the SIS vendors have moved towards OLAP based packages, which supports multidimensional analysis on sales data. These SIS packages make use of multidimensional databases to rapidly manipulate and query large volumes of information quickly and easily.

The key characteristic features of OLAP based SIS are:

- Shared data
- Consolidated data
- Fast flexible access
- Analytical modelling and profitability calculations
- Multi user read / write access

Sales Force Automation Packages

The next level in the classification of sales information system is a higher end sales information system which is a part of sales force automation system. Transition of sales information system to a sales force automation systems requires the following additional features:

Opportunity management system

An opportunity management system (oms) is a key component of any sales system designed to attack the process side of selling. An OMS brings discipline to the sales process by requiring representatives to create a strategy (a set of steps) to close each sales opportunity in its pipeline. The system tracks sales representative's progress against the plan, providing important feedback to both the sales manager and the sales representative.

Sales configuration systems

These help companies put together accurate orders by

configuring products, pricing and financing in conjunction with each other.

Marketing encyclopedia systems

This system maintains repositories of all marketing information including product literature and pricing. Sales rentalives can even call for videos reference accounts to pitch products to potential customers. They provide, a repository of the organisation's sales-related information, including complete product information, competitive information deciding support and online literature.

Sales management (account/contact management) system

These provide traditional account management so that companies can keep track of data in a variety of ways.

Account management and profile feature enables service profession manage all service related information such as company names, designated service contacts, type of service level agreement, service calendar and product owned by the customer.

Contact Management **allows service professional to efficiently manage service events associated with given individuals, including historical lists of prior service requests associated with those contacts.**

Activity Management **allows multiple service professionals to work as a team by allowing users to create, assign and trace all activities against a service request.**

Team Sales solutions consist of telemarketing and filed sales integration tools, while low end sales configuration software supports rapid order entry.

SAP Sales Information System

The sales information system is a part of Logistic Information System (LIS) which exploits open information warehouse concept. On an application level, the LIS is a component of the SAP open information warehouse. Also belonging to this application level are the Finance Information System (FIS) and the Human Resources Information system (HRIS). The Executive Information System (EIS) is also included on a cross-application level.

The aim of the open information warehouse is to integrate the data of various information systems. The user can select various views and aggregation levels for the data. In the open information warehouse, important information is stored in separate databases parallel to the operative systems (purchasing, inventory controlling, shop floor sales, etc). Data from the operative system is thus converted into informative key figures that aid the decision-making process. In this way, the business process of the operative systems (for example, goods receipt, purchase order, billing document, notification) form the data basis for the open information warehouse.

Oracle Sales Analyser

Oracle sales analyser is a full range of tools for Online Analytical Processing (OLAP) of corporate data. The system combines a central, integrated information source with powerful analytics so that users can evaluate trends in diverse areas, including sales, manufacturing, distribution and marketing. Oracle sales analyser is a general purpose application for analysing sales, marketing or similar data. Sales trends, marketing campaigns, product or customer profitability, product life cycles, and promotional effectiveness can be evaluated with the product. When evaluations are complete, the system helps users to adjust their strategies through custom analysis :

- Analysing with marketing know-how
- Reporting to rank performance and find exceptions
- Drilling into details
- Querying data flexibly
- Querying data naturally
- Creating custom measures
- Analysing promotion response.

SAP Sales Force Automation Software (SAPSFA)

The SAPSFA solution uses several integral business components that help sales professional's move quickly and easily through the sales process during customer interaction and back in the office. It is a powerful collaborative tool that synchronises the communication and activities of sales representatives, managers and selling teams with other departmental functions within the enterprise. Listed below are the major business components planned to be integrated into SAP's sales force automation application:

- Customer / prospect management
- Contact management
- Activity management
- Calendar
- Opportunity management
- Order management
- Quotations
- Marketing encyclopedia
- Sales pricing engine
- Sales configuration engine
- Promotions / campaigns
- Customer agreement
- Inbox, outbox, email
- General functionality

Oracle Sales Force Automation Software

Oracle applications for sales force automation include:

- Oracle service
- Oracle Sales and Marketing
- Oracle sales compensation
- Oracle self-service applications
- Oracle financial analyser

II. Spending in India

Indian companies are computerising their information systems to gain competitive edge. Wayback in 1996, "Data Quest" reported that on an average, Indian companies had spent 0.75 % of their revenues on IT. Multinational corporations in the country spent as much as 2-3 percents of their net revenues on IT.

Table 1.4 shows the enterprise IT spends variations over the previous years.

Table 1.4 : Enterprise IT Spend (Growth Rates)

Sector	2000 – 01	2001 – 02
Auto Industry	1*	69
Manufacturing	12*	66
IT Companies	30*	14*
Finance	3*	42
Services	28	189
Insurance	73	161
Overall	23*	56

*Fall
Source: Data Quest, November 30, 2001, p. 68.

While the fiscal (2001) is on the downside with 23% fall in IT spending since last year, IT spending is expected to move up over 50% by the end of the next fiscal. Chief Information Officers (CIOs) across segments other than IT, are optimistic about their IT spending and are rolling out their projects and meeting IT requirements with their planned investments.

When we consider the ratios, Insurance companies lead the pack with 2.49% of its revenue going to IT spend. Next to them are IT companies with 1.60 per cent. IT spend per employee is the highest in IT companies being 0.29 lakhs with 1 PC per employee. Table 1.5 shows the details.

Table 1.5 : Using IT: Insurance Leads the Pack

Sector	**Employees Per PC**	**IT Spend Per Employee (Rs Lakh)**	**IT Spend (% of Revenues)**
Auto	9	0.10	0.50
Manufacturing	15	0.07	015
IT Companies	1	0.95	1.60
Finance	6	0.17	0.09
Services	6	0.16	0.24
Insurance	3	0.29	2.49
Others	40	0.03	0.03

Source: Data Quest, November 30, 2001, p. 73.

IT: State of the Art and Benefits

How have the Indian companies taken IT initiatives and benefited from them? Here are some examples that make the point clear.

Asian Paints is India's largest paint company today. It has a turnover of Rs. 1,490 crores and an enviable reputation in the Indian corporate world for professionalism, fast track growth, building shareholder equity and dealer networking. This market leader in the decorative and industrial paints segment has had a colourful tryst with Infotech. The company went on to deploy sophisticated supply chain management (SCM) solutions even before it implemented an ERP application. Driving out locked up cash in inventory was a strategy to achieve cost leadership and implementing an SCM was the only way to fulfill this goal. Asian paints went in for Rhythm–an i2 Technologies SCM solution, now called Trade Matrix. The entire capital expenditure and asset management system is available online, which helps budgeting and management control processes. The information subsystem also serves the other application areas that the company has put up–call centers, CRM, e-business and a collaborative initiatives based on technology include administration, office automation, knowledge management and online training.

Bharat Petroleum with a turnover exceeding $8 billion, Bharat Petroleum Corporation (BPCL) is the only Indian petroleum company to be listed in the *Forbes' International 800* **ranking**. BPCL has used information technology (IT) as an enabler to establish a leadership position in their industry. BPCL has 4,500 petrol pumps, 1000 kerosene dealers and 1,400 LPG distributors. The company also supplies fuel directly to hundreds of industries and several international and domestic airlines. BPCL uses the internet to reduce turnaround time besides expanding its customer base. Dr. Anand Teltumbde, GM-IS,BPCL, says, "Online Banks streamline the e-payment mechanism and over 90% of customer transactions could take place through the e-Business system."

Hero Honda: About three years ego, an information systems plan was drawn up even before the implementation of the new home grown systems to replace the legacy systems and an ERP package, the information technologists at Hero Honda made a conscious effort to improve the networking. They installed structured LAN systems and WAN links and introduced e-mail throughout the organisation. "Real–time communication was a long felt need and usage of e-mail spread like wild fire," says Hero Honda's Vice President (IT). This was followed up by the installation of an intranet and workflow applications. There was a surge in the demand for PCs and employees were eager to be a part of the network. The entire staff got used to the electronic form of communication and this change in work culture made using SAP easier.

Kirloskar Oil Engines Limited (KOEL): The contribution of IT to achieve business success is 15%, said Deshmukh. The company operated on a Burroughs mainframe earlier. Upgradations were a costly affair and therefore KOEL decided to switch on to an open platform. A serious IT initiative began in 1998 with the implementation of Oracle's Enterprise Solutions followed by the e-Business initiative in 1999. Today, about 70–80 % of business comes from dealers connected electronically. The company now has around 150 suppliers, 35 depots and 600 dealers.

The cost saving is not just in terms of money alone, but has ensured that the company is in a position to connect with dealers, suppliers and others in the chain. For instance, the order registration process, which would take 10 days earlier is now completed in minutes. There was laborious paper work involved. More than six documents had to be completed before the order could be registered. Now there are none. KOEL has eliminated its raw material store house and now works on the principle of just in time.

S Gopalakrishnan, Managing Partner of the Coimbatore–based Electro Controls is very happy with the IT implementation at KOEL. "Now we are able to get all the information on the web. We can register our orders straight on the web. Moreover, financial dealings are now transparent," he says. The firm has seen a 50% cut in telephone bills.

S Chandrashekeran, Managing Partner, Network Diesel, Madurai, agrees that the time-saving has been tremendous. Expenditure has been pruned by 35%. Meanwhile, all operations at KOEL are IT networked through Yantra, it is extranet for suppliers, dealers and product life-cycle management.

Maruti Udyog: Maruti's success can be attributed to its web–enabled supply chains. Using a combination of software from Oracle and Computer Associates, the company built a variety of applications that facilitated its business.

This homegrown system was extended to its sales and dealer network through an e-mail-based ordering system with about 250 outlets. For instance, if a dealer has to place an order, he generates it in his own machine with all the specifications (e.g. colour, model, etc.) and sends it through an e-mail to Maruti. The system there automatically checks it to the respective database. In order to standardise the data, the company has provided the software to all its dealers. Even the suppliers are being gradually brought online.

For a mass production player like Maruti, an e-enabled supply chain has been extremely instrumental in inventory management, both at the dealer level and in the company. Reduction in paper work has increased efficiency and the speed of processing orders and thereby improved working capital management.

SAMSUNG: Being a technology company, Samsung was in a better position to set up an online business for itself. Fortunately, its six main distributors are all large IT companies such as Ingram Micro, Redington and Tech Pacific, which are already web enabled. These distributors, which are in turn linked to several dealers, are also responsible for providing dealer information and updating the database regularly. This e- enabled environment has helped Samsung set-up an online B2B model. The internal ERP has been extended to the supply chain and all transactions are online. Without an online operation, it would have been impossible for 24 people to manage transactions with such a huge dealer network. Moreover, the company estimates a huge turnover of Rs. 1105 crore this year, from Rs. 740 crore recorded last year. A number of routine inquiries and transactions which do not need management decision can be tackled without any physical interaction. This not only allows efficient resource allocation with low manpower but also cuts down inventory costs.

Benefits

A survey of opinions of effect on IT spending by Data Quest (1996) indicates positive benefits in terms of speed of transactions, increase in velocity of business, improvements in factor productivity and efficiency, better access to information cost reduction, effective marketing and higher customer satisfaction (Table 1.6).

Table 1.6 : Effect of IT on Various Functions of Business Organisations

Sl. No.	Features	Figures in %
1.	Increasing the speed of transaction and velocity of Business.	23.50
2.	Increasing Factor productivity in all areas of business.	21.00
3.	Improving internal efficiency of business processes.	20.00
4.	Providing better access to information and thus helped individual performance.	13.00
5.	Making our customer happier.	9.50
6.	Reducing direct cost.	8.00
7.	Providing an advantage in marketing and sales.	5.00

Source : Data Quest, May 15, 1996.

Research Problem

In the light of above exposition, which explained the concept and components of MKIS, examined IT initiatives of the Indian companies with few case studies and enumerated the available benefits. Some pertinent questions can be:

- What is the state of the art of marketing information systems in the Indian organisations?
- How well are they performing?
- Do they need improvements? If yes, what kinds of measures are needed?

Plan of the book

Chapter 1 presents a conceptual framework and growth of MKIS in India and identifies the research problem.

Chapter 2 makes a survey of literature and establishes objectives and methodologies for present study.

Chapter 3, 4 and **5** describe and evaluate MKIS in select organisations in the Core, Chemicals and Service sectors respectively.

Chapter 6 summarises the findings and highlights the suggestions for improving MKIS.

References

Ambler Tim (1995), "Information Survival Kit", *the Financial Times guide to Marketing*. New York, Prentice Hall Inc. pp. 105-07.

Anand, Teltumbde, GM-IS, BPCL, "Oil the Gains", *Data Quest,* Vol. XX, No. 2, January 31, 2002, p. 171.

Balasubramanian S.R. VP, IT, Hero Honda, "Lighting an e-mail wildfire", *Data Quest,* Vol. XX, No. 2, January 31, 2002, pp. 173-74.

Balu S. (Executive Director, Ford Information Technology Services India), *Data Quest,* Vol. XIX, No 22, Nov 30, 2001, p. 57.

Berend, Wierenga and Gerrit H. Van Bruggen, "The Interpretation of problem solving models and marketing management systems", *Journal of Marketing,* Volume 61 (July 1997), pp. 21-37.

Blatterg, Rober C, Rashi Glazer and John D.C. Little, eds. (1994), *"The Marketing Information Revolution"* Boston, Harvard Business School Press.

Bloom, Paul N., Robert Adler and Mine, George R. (1994), "Identifying the legal and ethical risks and costs of using new information technologies to support marketing programmes", Blatbert and Glazer (eds) *Marketing Information Revolution,* Harvard Business School Press, pp. 289-305.

Brien and Stafford (1968), "Marketing Information Systems: A new dimension for marketing research" Journal of *Marketing,* Vol. 33, July 1968, pp. 192-93.

Cox, Donald F. and Good, Robert E. (1967), "How to build marketing information systems", *Harvard Business Review,* Vol. 45, No. 3 (May, June 1967), pp. 145-54.

Deshmukh S.R. Vice President, IT corporate Koel, S. Gopal Krishnan, Managing Director Electro Control, Coimbatore and S. Chandrasekaran, Managing Partner, Network Diesel, Mudarai, KOEL "Group Up with the technology", *Data Quest,* Vol. XX, No. 2 , January 31, 2002, p. 175.

Glazer, Rashi (1993), "Marketing into the information revolution", in *The marketing information revolution,* 1994, Boston, Harvard Business School Press, pp. 9-29.

Kinnear and Berharndt (1983), *"Principles of Marketing"*, Scott and Foresman and company, p. 204.

Kling (1980) in the thesis of Dickson, Warren Lee III (1980), "The Value of Information systems professionals on Investigation into Barriers preventing integration of IS with the organisation", Unpublished thesis, Houston University, Order No. AAC-9517495, *Proquest-Dissertation Abstracts.*

Kotler Philip (1996), *"Marketing management" analysis, planning, implementation and control*, Prentice Hall Inc., New York.

Manish Choksi, Vice president strategic planning and IT, Asian Paints Finishing Touches, *Data Quest*, Vol. XX, No. 2, January 31, 2002, p. 171.

Murdick, Rober C., Ross, Joel E. and Claggett, James R. (1985), *"Information systems for modern management"*, New Delhi, Prentice Hall of India.

Nolan (1979) in the thesis of Dickson, Warren Lee III (1980), "The Value of Information systems professionals on Investigation into Barriers preventing integration of IS with the organisation", Unpublished thesis, Houston University, Order No. AAC-9517495, *Proquest-Dissertation Abstracts.*

Prakash Vivek, National Sales Manager, Samsung "E-smart strategy", *Data Quest*, Vol. XX, No. 2, January 31, 2002, p. 177.

Rajesh Uppal, IT Head, Maruti Udyog "Web Savvy Augo Giant" *Data Quest*, Vol. XX, No. 2, January 31, 2002, pp. 176-79.

Srinivasan R. (Rane Group), *Data Quest*, Vol. XIX, No. 22, Nov. 30, 2001. p. 51.

Srnivasan S. (Sundaram Fastners), Data Quest Volume XIX No. 22, Nov. 30, 2001, p.53.

Suresh M. (Hyundai), *Data Quest* Vol. XIX, No. 22, Nov. 30, 2001, p. 53.

Thyagarajan V. (Ashok Leyland), *Data Quest*, Vol. XIX, No. 22, Nov. 30, 2001, p. 52.

2

Literature Survey, Objectives and Methodology

Introduction

In this chapter a brief survey of literature is made on the aspects related to the identified research problems. Also, the objectives and hypotheses of the study are stated and methodology is described.

Literature Survey

The survey covers the following four areas of importance:

- Concept and components of MKIS
- Importance of MKIS
- Development of MKIS
- Evaluation of MKIS

Concept and Components of MKIS

Studies in this area focussed on the need for systems approach, elements of marketing information and its applications and benefits.

Seymour Banks (1968) surveyed the practice of systems' concept in 125 top advertisers in the United States given in the Advertising Age. He reported that a minority of the largest firms were using the systems concept. Companies using the systems concept in marketing show a wide range in its implementation, the most users operating only sub-system applications.

Kenneth P. Uhl (1968) in his paper identified that the need for relevant marketing information had expanded rapidly, leading some firms to develop marketing information systems. Each system is likely to be different in order to fit with the unique circumstances of individual firms. Three general information sub-systems appear appropriate to all the firms :

(i) Selective Dissemination Sub-System (SDS)

(ii) Retrospective Research Sub-System (RSS)

(iii) Unsolicited Information Sub-Systems (UIS)

SDS maintains databank to provide current awareness. RSS provides indepth information on special problems or areas whereas UIS came through informal channels without being asked.

John M. Mc Cann (1986) reviewed the evolution of marketing information systems over the past few decades and explored its future developments. He proposed a new marketing discipline, "Marketing Informatics" which integrates traditional marketing information system with a range of new information technologies as well as information management procedures. He provided a framework for thinking about the development of expert systems in the marketing context. He illustrated the marketing information concept with some examples from the consumer packaged goods industry. Of particular interest is the use of graphics and audio / video information to help managers interpret data better. One notable idea is that of multimedia marketing plan, which harnesses the full power of computer technology to move beyond just number and text processing in order to help management make decisions based on more "realistic" modules of the market place.

Raymond R. Burke (1994) presented a perspective on the emerging use of expert systems for customer oriented marketing decision-making. He discussed the use of AI for both "everyday" and "strategic" decision-making and problem solving. Two important distinctions between the two are:

(1) The system requirements are different

(2) Current methodologies are better suited for the former than the later.

He identified a new technique that can further the development of AI systems for strategic decision. As a notable example of this he briefly described the ADCAD system, a procedure to assist advertising objectives, copy strategy, and the selection of communication techniques.

Hotaka Katahira and Shigeru Yagi (1994) described the state-of-the-art in "point of sale (POS) marketing system" in Japan. It is an instructive example because it illustrates how different market conditions across cultures lend to the use of essentially the same technology in somewhat different ways. This should be of value not only to those interested in how the information revolution is influencing marketing in Japan, but also to those concerned with the more general question of how alternative consumer behaviour patterns (whether in the same or different culture) may require different technology adoption patterns.

Timothy Peter Shea and Jane Fedoerowicz (1995) had attempted to measure the actual use of lateral and external information by the middle level manufacturing managers and to test the influence of three factors— (i) the lateral and external information demands of the department; (ii) the level of information distribution; and (iii) the use of IT.

They administered an executive questionnaire to gather departmental information and a middle manager questionnaire to gather information about these information acquisition activities. They canvassed the questionnaire in six large manufacturing firms representing various industries across the US Pharmaceuticals, Electronics, Office Systems, Surgical Products, Process Controls and Electronic Controls. They have applied regression, ANOVA, and t-test analysis. They found that the computer based information use is positively related to the use of both external and lateral information. The external information use is affected by the external information needs, computer expertise of the manager and the level of overall information distribution. The lateral information use is dependent on lateral information needs, satisfaction with corporate information systems and education level of managers.

Importance of MKIS

Use of IT depends on factors like size, investment capacity, competition and a host of factors. Organisations, in the process of their functioning, develop a large amount of data. It is essential to create appropriate databases, discover their potential in building relationships with customers and fortifying competitive advantage. The studies cited here, point out various benefits of MKIS.

Bonnie K. Buckland and James C. Brancheau (1995) found the following from their research on the use of IT in small business :

(1) The use of IT decreases as business size decreases.

(2) When IT is used in small businesses, successful implementation depends in large part on the level of computer knowledge of the small business owner / manager.

(3) Differences in their members' overall level of computer education and training.

They developed alternative research models based on classical and enhanced versions of diffusion theory. It addresses IT utilisation with the following variations:

- Perceived contribution of IT to the firm.
- Number of sources from which computer education and training were received.
- Firms size.
- User involvement.
- Years of inhouse Information Systems ISO experience.
- Computer knowledge in the firm and perceived availability of technical support.

David Ing and Angdew A. Mitchell (1993) described different sources of electronic POS (Point of Sale) data. They discussed many of the uses of data while providing a typology of decisions for which electronic POS data are best suited. They sum up with a discussion on designing the strategy for accessing and utilising data and transforming it into information.

John Deighton, Don Peppers, and Martha Pogers (1994) reviewed the power and potential of customer databases with a focus on the use of these databases as a new marketing medium. They suggested 'interactive' marketing in the place of 'broadcast' marketing. This disseminates messages widely but not precisely. In interactive marketing, programs can now be directly addressable. They go to only those customers or prospects whose past behaviour suggests that they are receptive.

They opined that information technology may be used not only to improve decision-making or logistics, but also to help manage customer relationships. There is a necessity to marry "high-powered analytical tools" with specialised interactive marketing communications techniques.

George Day and Rashi Glazer (1994) opined that, the developments in information systems that unleashed the data deluge have also enhanced the ability of organisations to learn about their markets. The feasible organisation changes that can overcome impediments and ensure competitive advantage can be realised from investment in information systems.

Van Engelen and Johannes Marie Lucien (1989) identified that the drastic developments in information technology have the potential of bringing forth the new strategic (marketing) opportunities. A marketing system, for instance, will serve as a diagnostic tool for analysing a full array of marketing problems. An empirical study was conducted. It proved that the hypothesised relation between marketing strategy and the information system exists with the product market contribution.

Richard B. Rosecky (1986) identified delayed sales information at the producer level can cause inappropriate sales estimates; mistimely promotion efforts, inadequate channel inventory levels and other marketing dysfunctions.

Jiro Kokuryo (1992) described how information technology triggers the reorganisation of logistics systems and specifically, the EDI based Quick Response (QR) systems being implemented.

Gaillynn Cook (1990) addressed the research problem, "Does an integrated computer based information system facilitate coordination"? A laboratory experiment was conducted to test the effects of sharing of marketing data, decision models and feedback with production managers. All combinations of providing and not providing these three independent variables were included in the experiment.

Students assumed the roles of the production manager in a manufacturing organisation. The task required the student to decide the quantity to produce from each of the three sub-assemblies, schedule six machines, schedule labour and order raw materials. Decisions were evaluated on cumulative profit, ending cash balance and weighed average Return on Investment (ROI) for five decision periods. Statistical analysis included ANOVA, comparisons and a post hoc Dunnett's test. The results indicated that sharing marketing feedback, feedback and decision models or data and decision models increased coordinated decision-making above the control level.

Edvard Philip Bovich (1987), through an experimental inquiry, explored the effects of usage of computerised decision support system on marketing management decision-making process and decision quality. Experienced and specially trained marketing planners participated in a comprehensive, realistic computerised product management simulation. Half of the subjects were provided access to simulated market research and company performance information through a sophisticated computerised decision support system. The other half were given access to the same information in traditional paper report form. All subjects were required to develop comprehensive strategic and tactical plans for their simulated corporation. Subjects were asked to record their activities as they developed their plans. In addition they completed a questionnaire, which captured their activities and attitudes towards the process. Their tactical plans were entered into the computerised simulation to derive short-term corporate performance results. The experiment showed that the subjects with computer support fared well.

Development of MKIS

The development considerations include top management support, staff knowledge and skills, outsourcing and end-user computing.

Donald F. Cox and Robert E Good (1967) presented a brief review of some of the characteristics and advantages of sophisticated MIS and the current "State of thought." They identified some of the key decisions, which must be made by top management in the MIS development process.

Gernot Bernhand Langle (1988) conducted a study which focussed on knowledge which relates to a specific functional area of business (such as accounting, manufacturing or marketing) and the presence or absence of some firm's specific domain knowledge in IS development.

His specific study was an empirical investigation involving eight experienced business system analysts. Each subject was asked to analyse and design two information systems. One in a familiar area of business, the other in an unfamiliar area of business. Subjects were instructed to think about during the tasks and their verbalisations were tape recorded and transcribed for analysis. The results indicated that the presence of function specific domain knowledge affected the construction of representation as well as modeling, discovery and validation process. Subjects with function specific domain knowledge were found to (1) build representations considering a large number of facts and concepts relating to the information system application domains, (2) discover and validate the representations requesting additional domain specific information more frequently; and (3) model the information system utilising analogical reasoning more often than the subjects without function specific domain knowledge.

Interpretation of results suggests that when experienced system analyst possesses function specific domain knowledge, they are more likely to construct accurate and complete system representation and exhibit focused and efficient information gathering behaviour.

Robert C. Blattberg, and Byong-Do Kim and Jiangming Ye (1990, 1992) presented a framework for "Mass Produced." Mass produced models are statistical analyses of large databases where literally thousands of models are created for a single data set with little or no human intervention. They described a typical application of MDSS development of a price simulator for setting retail prices across many items in a product category. Next, they discussed the requirements necessary for models to be mass-produced.

Somendra Pant and HSU. Cheng (1997) reviewed the business use of internet technology and identified that there is a lack of stable models and frameworks to plan for incorporating it into business. He proposed a push model for internet strategy planning. In actualising this "Push" model into a concrete planning framework, through internet based information system, they made use of a reference model. This framework is empirically tested in two industrial situations. In the Korea Long term Bank (KLB) case, the reference model is used to generate internet goals for the bank and, subsequently, to redesign their processes. Based on the initial plan generated for the bank, they have embarked on establishing an internet based online bank and are a test-bed for the rest of the planning framework. Second case was that of the study of a Conglomerate Heavy Machinery and Shipbuilder, Samsung Heavy Industries Company Limited (SHL) of Korea. Additional cases were taken from literature and usefulness of reference model and planning frame work were established.

Myungoong Cheon and Varun Grover and James Tegn (1992) developed a contingency model of outsourcing from the literature. Two hypotheses were tested.

- Organisational attributes influence the change in the extent of an organisation's outsourcing of 'IS' functions.
- Success of outsourcing is dependent upon both the change in degree of 'IS' outsourcing and the quality of outsourcing implementation.

From the mail survey of 188 top 'IS' executives, they found support to the hypotheses to a large extent :

(1) The change in the degree of IS outsourcing is determined by gaps in information quality, IS supporting quality, IS cost effectiveness and financial performance.

(2) The quality of outsourcing service providers and the nature of partnerships with them are implementation factors determining the degree of outsourcing success.

(3) The change in the degree of IS outsourcing differs between outsourcing and non-outsourcing firms with respect to the following:

  (i) Gaps in information quality, IS support quality, and IS cost of effectiveness

  (ii) The condition of these gaps (high deprivation versus equilibrium or moderate deprivation)

(4) The change in the degree of outsourcing

(5) The degree of outsourcing success is related to the change in the degree of outsourcing of specific types of IS functions. For example, outsourcing success is highly related to changes in the degree of outsourcing of both systems operations and telecommunication management and maintenance.

Jeanne Wenzel Ross and Kate M. Kaiser (1987) focussed on End-User Computing (EUC), which consumes a significant proportion of many organisational computing budgets. The need to contain EUC costs as well as ensure effectiveness has led many authors to recommend that top managements of organisations device EUC strategies. The goal of this study was to identify the factors related to EUC control and note variances by industry.

Data were collected through telephone interviews with a marketing manager and an ISD manager in 87 organisations in four industries. Analysis of the data showed that IS control is positively related to four factors:

(a) its ability to cope with EUC uncertainties,

(b) its non-substitutability,

(c) the pervasiveness of the department's data needs and

(d) the importance of EUC to the department coping with uncertainty.

The last factor has the greatest predictive power of the four variables. Data pervasiveness proves insignificant in multiple regression equations. They proposed a model by which ISD can gain EUC control.

Chang Liu (1997) conducted a study to identify consumer reactions to a well-designed website. Four functions that are critical to the design of electronic markets were identified; they are (1) information and service quality (2) system use (3) playfulness and (4) system design quality. He identified that a well-designed website will increase the level of customer recall and recognition. Also, the kind of website will lend customers to have a favorable attitude toward the site and also toward the products / services that are presented through the site.

Ray Joseph Blankenship and Barnes, James H. Jr. and John D. Johnson (1994) opined that MIS has a responsibility to evaluate different methodologies (or) information technologies as they are developed and become available for use to ensure that the MIS function is meeting its responsibility. They compared the performance of Multi Layered Feed Forward Artificial Neural Network (MLFFNN) that use a Genetic Adoptive Neural Network Training (GANNT) algorithm against the back propagation training algorithm for MLFFNN, the inductive dichotomise 3 (ID3) algorithms, and a multi-nominal logic model. These algorithms represent several prevalent methods of machine learning. They explored modeling of consumer choices. They found that the GANNT algorithm is able to significantly predict better than the back propagation algorithm and the predicted multi-nominal legit model.

Evaluation of MKIS

Researchers have explored the factors and models which help evaluate information systems. Also they offered suggestions to make "IS" effective.

1. Nature of Function

Ackoff (1967) in his paper analysed the weakness of management information systems and recommended a program for overcoming their weaknesses. Ackoff notes: "Contrary to the impression produced by the growing literature, few computerised management information systems have been put into operation. Of those that I have seen.... most have not matched expectations and some have been outright failures." Ackoff indicated some reasons why systems development has not been successful:

- First, marketing decision is increasing in complexity at an accelerating pace.
- Second, marketing decision, as a class is more difficult to model than other business decisions.
- Third, many of the methods that have been developed for modelling the marketing decisions are inadequate when checked with real world results.

2. I S and User Conflict

Richard H. Brien (1968) observed that too many firms, mistaking computers for information systems, acquired a large machine capability before management is really systems-oriented. The result is a gap between the managers and the information systems. Problem of time, pride, language, and premature computer acquisition resulted in failure of MIS. There is a clear need for a very special kind of intermediary between systems 'users' and system 'technicians'. He found in one company two new positions "information systems manager" and "operations research manager" were created before acquisition of a larger, more sophisticated computer system and it was successful.

Warren Lee Dickson and Leon R. Price (1994) identified a variety of problems that prevent IS professionals and non-IS professionals form joint realisation of the ideal. Individual differences, social differences and interaction (communication) problems relating to difficulties in integration have been explored. They made an attempt to identify difference in values between information system professionals and non-information system professionals that may be blocking integration efforts.

3. IS People and Technology

Lind, Marry Louise Robinson (1988) examined whether effective communication between information systems personnel and non-information systems personnel would result in greater information technology innovativeness. Two means were proposed for achieving more effective information systems / organisation communication. (1) More frequent communications; and (2) the use of richer communication channels. In the research model, two proposals were made. The level of communication frequency and communication richness determines the level of convergence: (convergence is the degree of mutual understanding between IS and the non-IS personnel about the business activities performed in the firm's departments) and the importance of IT in supporting these business activities. More the conveyance, higher the level of IT innovativeness.

Five periods of data collection were used in testing this research model, using longitudinal causal research techniques. The following research results were obtained:

1. Convergence between information systems personnel and non-information systems personnel on the importance of the firm's business activities and IT to support them was found to be an important predictor of convergence.
2. Communication richness is an important predictor of convergence.
3. Communication frequency is not only an important predictor of convergence but also an important predictor of communication richness as well.

Malcolm A. Mc. Nevin (1968) reviewing Ackoff's paper identified reasons for the failure of information systems in marketing: (i) the tremendous gap between expectations of information systems people and (ii) the state of the art in business today. He described how Coca-Cola Company was bridging the gap by setting the management information system department at corporate level and carrying out developmental research (to build new models) and continuing research (solving predictable marketing problems).

Claire Maureen Forrest (1984) described the design and implementation of a Decision Support System (DSS) for marketing planning and control in a small, but complex company and examined the nature of the difficulties encountered. An intermediary with functional, rather than technical expertise is used in a strategy for overcoming the problems.

The findings of the research showed how the main focus of the intermediary's role needs to be adopted over the systems development cycle. From co-ordination in design stages to system champion during the first part of the implementation stage, and finally to a catalyst to ensure that the DSS is integrated into decision-making process.

Two practical marketing exercises were undertaken to illustrate the nature of the gap between the provision of information and its use. The lack of a formal approach to planning and control is shown to have a significant effect on the means the DSS is used and the role of the intermediary is extended successfully to accommodate this factor. The conclusion was for the DSS to perform effective role so that small firms may introduce more structure into their marketing planning and that the role of the intermediary, or information coordinator, should include responsibility for introducing new techniques and ideas.

Charles D. Schewe and James L. Wiek (1977) suggested a marketing approach to the successful design and implementation of management information systems. They have drawn parallels between MIS Development function and marketing function utilising Taylor's framework of marketing: marketing delineation, purchase motivation, product adjustment, physical distribution communications, transactions and post transactions.

Donald R. Lehman (1970) attempted to sketch the elements of marketing information system by starting with a "model of individual choice" and then developing a system for evaluating marketing decision based on the model. Thus the key element in the system becomes the individual choice model. They included evaluation of new products and effective advertising.

4. Models for Evaluation

Kamna Malik and D.P. Goyal (2000) attempted to understand the concept of effectiveness and the application of different models for evaluating the information systems. An analysis of existing models, being used for measuring the effectiveness of IS has also been made. An integrated model has been suggested that comprehends the effectiveness of organisational IS with respect to product, process and environment effectiveness. The findings in this paper would provide a basic material for furthering the research in this area and while providing also the right directions for the corporates to carry out the evaluation process of their information systems.

W.H. Delone and Mc Lean (1992) identified the possibility of two types of measures in IS evaluation, viz. qualitative and quantitative. They developed a quantitative IT utility index to quantify measures of effectiveness.

Eldon Y. Li (1997) summarised IS success factors into eight categories and further sub-categories as given bellow:

(i) **System Quality:** Response time, conveyance of access programming, language features used, security, realisation of user needs, documentation, flexibility, and integration of systems.

(ii) **Information quality:** Accuracy, timeliness, precision, reliability, currency, completeness, format, clarity and instructiveness.

(iii) **Information use:** Volume of output.

(iv) **User satisfaction:** Top management involvement, charge back method of payments for service, user's participation, user's confidence and support of productivity tools.

(v) **Individual Impact:** User's expectation of IS support, job effect of IS support, perceived utility.

(vi) **Service Quality:** Technical competence, attitude of staff, scheduling of CBIS products and services, time required for system development, processing of change requests, maintenance support, means of I/O, user's understanding of systems and training of users.

(vii) **Conflict resolution:** Competition between CBIS and non-CBIS units, allocation priorities for CBIS resources users and CBIS staff relations and communication, personal control over CBIS, organisational position of CBIS unit and user's attitude towards CBIS.

(viii) **Organisational Impact:** Productivity improved by CBIS, efficiency of systems and effectiveness of the systems.

Timo Saarimen (1996) recommended four measurement scales for IS success model as stated below :

- Development process (Cost and Efficiency use)
- Use process (User Satisfaction)
- IS product quality (Performance Efficiency)
- Impact of IS on organisation (Benefits)

The emphasis is both on process and product evaluations.

P.G. Kulkarni (1997) suggested the use of IT utility index to measure the effectiveness of IT in banking. The measures are as follows:

- Technology costs as a percentage of the total operating cost.
- Transaction processing costs.
- Technology led exposures and risks.
- System availability indicators.
- Technology awareness of the knowledge works.
- Customer friendliness, flexibility and innovativeness of the system.

He suggested that similar index parameters can be developed for other industries also.

Erik Brynjolfson (1996) suggested three approaches to IT value estimation :

- Output and productivity estimation.
- Business performance. Various business metrics are profits, sales, market share, growth, stock price appreciation etc.
- Consumer surplus from derived demand.

James W. Cortada (1995) identified three major questions that companies keep on asking and try to answer as:

- Are we selecting and funding the right IT project?
- Are we getting our money's worth?
- Do our measurements tell us how well are we achieving the goal?

The answer to these can be found in the effectiveness of IS. IS is said to be effective if its product is effective. The product of IS can be termed as effective if they –

- Provide quality information as per the user's perception.
- Improve management function.
- Improve resource utilisation.

Jemes W. Cordata (1998) recommended the use of Balnidge criteria for getting the snapshot of IS effectiveness. Balnidge criteria have seven categories defined for any quality assessment. They are :leadership, information and analysis, strategic planning, HRD and HRM, process management, business results and customer satisfaction.

Glenn Edward Maples (1997) examined service quality as a component of overall information systems quality. He tested three related studies of SERVQUAL. He found that SERVPERF' outperformed SERVQUAL in all three studies.

Miller, Marc Donald and Rainer, R. Kelly Jr. (1994) extensively examined the success or failure of IS. Success variables such as user satisfaction were proposed. They attempted to examine the perceived ease of use and usefulness of the IS as a means to predict its use. The Technology Acceptance Model (TAM) assumes complete volition control over the IS or technology in question. Volitional control, therefore ,the TAM may not be able to predict use in these situations. They had proposed and tested the Extended Technology Acceptance Model (ETAM). This model was designed to predict usage behaviours where volitional control over using the technology was absent. They concluded that ETAM model significantly explains more variance in IT usage behaviours than the TAM, and also indicates that the active participation change strategy gives the user optional control over the technology, while the persuasive communication change strategy does not.

Karahanna, Elena and Detmar W Straub Normal L. Chervany, (1993) identified that though organisations adopt information technology to support knowledge workers, many users were unwilling to use available systems, and thus, the full benefits of IT are often not realised. Guided by a theoretical model derived by combining innovation diffusion theory with the theory of reasoned action to contribute to a better theoretical understanding of the antecedents of user acceptance and user resistance to the adoption of information technology, they carried out their study and found that:

(a) Potential adopters base their adoption decisions on a sparser set of innovation characteristics than suggested by the innovation diffusion literature;

(b) Users and potential adopters differ on their determinants of behaviour intention and attitude, and

(c) There are significant differences between low and high innovativeness and users in the determinants of subjective norm and behavioural interim.

James Edward Turner and Julian W Riehl (1993) proposed a model to analyse the influence of factors related to use and satisfaction with information systems. The more satisfied firms follow a plan for system development, have top management interest in IS, provide periodic technology updates for management and users, and use prototypes to speed development. Firms with more experience with scanning were more satisfied with IS support while firms with more computer experience rated IS support lower. Advanced communication technologies were used by the more successful firms including central processing of sales data and Electronic Data Interchange (EDI).

Bernadettee Agatha Szajna (1990) suggested that user's attitude towards a proposed information system would provide system developers with some knowledge of the potential success or failure of that information system.

Ginzberg (1981) and Desantis (1983) suggested the importance of investigating user's expectations of information systems particularly the effects of realistic expectations. Their research investigated user expectation system and the consequences of realistic versus unrealistic expectations. These treatment groups consisting of subjects with user expectations made up the independent variable. After using an information system to make decisions, the dependant variables of user satisfaction, perceived decision performance and system usage were measured to detect the effects of differing levels of expectations on system effectiveness.

Their finding in this experiment suggests that pre-implementation expectations have an effect on user satisfaction and perceived decision performance. No effect was found for either decision performance or IS usage. The results are consistent with the predictions of cognitive dissonance theory–those users with unrealistically high expectations and perceptions of the information system that were higher than those with moderate expectations and those users with unrealistically low expectation had significantly lower perceptions. Even after repeated uses of the information system, significant differences were found among the three expectation groups although the trend indicated a moderating of the high and low expectations groups both in their perceptions and post implementation expectations.

Allan Fletcher Gillman (1995) tried to develop a comprehensive examination of the influence of Electronic Data Interchange (EDI) on marketing channels of distribution. He derived some propositions that are loosely organised for structural outcomes, efficiency outcomes, or strategic outcomes. He examined three different industry groups such as telecommunications, information systems and food retailing. He found no support for the structural outcomes, partial support for the efficiency outcomes, and strong support for the strategic outcomes. He found that the role of EDI in promoting electronic commerce in marketing channels of distribution is a complex and interesting one. As a new medium for information transfer it simultaneously expands and adds value to inter organisational communications. What it does is shift the emphasis in channel theory from a structural to a more strategic orientation.

Vijaya Sarathy, Leo Ramesh, and Daniel Robey (1994) examined the consequences of Electronic Data Interchange (EDI) use on Inter-organisational Relations (IR) in the retail industry. EDI is a type of Inter-organisational Information System that facilitates the exchange of business documents in structure, machine processable form. The model links EDI use and three IR dimensions– structural, behavioural and outcome. They proposed 14 hypotheses and tested them by using multiple regression analysis. The analysis supports the following hypothesis :

(a) EDI use is positively related to information intensity and formalisation.
(b) Formalisation is positively related to cooperation.
(c) Information intensity is positively related to cooperation.
(d) Conflict is negatively related to performance and satisfaction.
(e) Cooperation is positively related to performance; and
(f) Performance is positively related to satisfaction.

A Bird's Eye View

A brief presentation of the review of literature is depicted in Tables 2.1 to 2.4.

Table 2.1: Concept and Components of MKIS

Sl. No.	Researcher	Year	Sample	Method	Findings
1.	Seymour Banks	1968	125 Top advertisers	Survey questionnaire	System concept was being used by a minority of even the largest firms. Companies using the system concept in marketing show a wide range in its implementation, the most users operating only sub-system applications.
2.	Kenneth P. UHL	1968	–	–	Marketing information system components: (i) Selective Dissemination Sub-System (SDS) (ii) Retrospective Research Sub-System (RSS) Unsolicited Information Sub-Systems (UIS)
3.	John M. Mc Cann	1986	–	–	A new marketing discipline "marketing informatics" was proposed. The term was designed to describe the integration of traditional marketing information systems with a range of new information technologies as well as information management procedures gave frame work for marketing expert system.

[contd...]

[contd...]

Sl. No.	Researcher	Year	Sample	Method	Findings
4.	Raymond R. Bruke	1994	–	–	Identified new technologies that can further the development of artificial intelligence (AI) systems for everyday and strategic decisions. He briefly described ADCAD system.
5.	Hotaka Katahira and Shigeru Yagi	1994			Described the state-of-the-art Point of Sale Marketing Systems in Japan. Illustrated how different market conditions across cultures lend to the use of essentially the same technology in somewhat different ways.
6.	Shea, Timothy Peter and Jane Fedoerowicz	1995	Six large manu-facturing firms	Survey questionnaire	Computer based information use is positively related to the use of both external and lateral information. The external information needs of the department affect the external use of information, along with computer expertise of the manager and the level of overall information distribution. The lateral information needs of the department, satisfaction with corporate information systems, and education level also influence lateral information use.

Table 2.2 : Importance of MKIS

No	Researcher	Year	Sample	Method	Findings
1.	Bannie K. Buckland James C. Bancheau	1995	Small firms (employing fewer than 100 people)	Mail survey (Telephonic interview)	To explain IT use developed a different theory. Variables are perceived contribution of IT to the firm, number of sources from which computer education and training were received, firm size, user involvement, years of in-house information systems (IS) experience, computer knowledge in the firm, and perceived availability of technical support.
2.	David Ing and Andrew A. MitchelL	1993	–	–	Described different sources of electronic POS (Point of Sale) data, and discussed a typology of decisions for which electronic POS data are best suited.
3.	John Deighton, Don Peppers, and Maritha Poggers	1994	–	–	Reviewed the power and potential of customer databases. Suggested 'interactive' marketing in the place of 'broadcast' marketing. There is a necessity to marry "high-powered analytical tools" with specialized interactive marketing communication techniques.

[contd...]

[contd...]

No	Researcher	Year	Sample	Method	Findings
4.	George Day and Rashi Glazer	1994	–	–	Opined that, the feasible organisation changes that can overcome impediments and ensure competitive advantage can be realised from investment in information systems.
5.	Van Engelen, and Johannes Marrie Lucien	1989		Empirical study	Compared the usual dyadic models. An empirical study conducted and proved that the hypothesized relation between a marketing strategy and the information system with regard to success of the product market combination.
6.	Richard B. Rosecky	1986	–	Survey and empirical test	This research shows that an existing information gathering system, i.e. registration cards, can be used to reduce information delays experienced by producers and hence reduce the affects of some marketing dysfunctions.
7.	Jiro Kokuryo	1992	8 firms (67 responses)	Case studies	Describes how information technology triggers the reorganisation of logistics systems specifically, explains EDI based Quick Response (QR) systems being implemented.

[contd...]

[contd...]

No	Researcher	Year	Sample	Method	Findings
8.	Gaillynn Cook	1990		Laboratory experiment	The results indicated that sharing marketing feedback, feedback and decision models, or data and decision models increased coordinated decision making above the control level.
9.	Edvard Philip Bovich	1987	Experienced and specially trained marketing planners	Experimental inquiry (questionnaire)	Examined the relationship between marketing management, decision-making process and decision quality and usage of computerised decision support system. Results suggest that usage of the decision support system have its most direct benefits.

Table 2.3 : Development of MKIS

1.	Donald F. Cox and Robert E. Good	1967	–	–	Presented current "State of thought" and identified some of the key decisions which must be made by top management in the MIS development process.
2	Gernot Bernhand Langle	1988	8 experienced business systems analysts	Empirical investigation	Found that presence of function specific domain knowledge affected the construction of representation as well as modeling, discovery and validation process.
3	Robert c. Blatiberg and Byong-do kim and Jiangming Ye	1990	–	–	Evolved frameworks for "Mass produced". They described a typical application of MDSS development of a price simulator for setting retail prices across many items in a product category.
4.	Somendra Pant and HSU. Cheng	1997	Two companies of two industries	Case method and empirical test	Reviewed the business use of internet technology and identified the lack of stable models. He proposed a 'push' model for internet strategy planning. Additional case studies were taken from literature and usefulness of reference model and planning frame work were established.

[contd...]

[contd...]

5.	Cheon, Myunjoong and Grover, Varun;Tegn, James	1992	188 top 'IS' executives	Mail survey questionnaire	A contingency model of out-sourcing was developed from the literature. Two hypotheses were developed ➢ Organisational attributes influence the change in the extent of an organisation's outsourcing of 'IS' functions. Success of outsourcing is dependent upon both the change in degree of 'IS' outsourcing and the quality of outsourcing implementation.
6.	Ross, Jeanne Wenzel Ross and Kate M. Kaiser	1987	87 Organisations in 4 Industries (marketing managers & ISD managers	Theoretical framework & telephonic interviews	Conducted a study with the goal of identifying the factors related to EUC control and noted variables in the industry.

[contd...]

[contd...]

7.	Change Liu	1997	1000 Web masters	E-mail questionnaires, experimental visits	Four functions that are critical to the design of electronic markets were identified; they are (1) information and service quality (2) system use (3) playfulness, and (4) system design quality. He identified that a well-designed website will increase the level of customer recall and recognition.
8.	Ray Joseph Blankenship James H. Barnes Jr. and John D. Johnson	1994	Different machine algorithms	Empirical	They explored modeling of consumer choice. They found that the GANNT algorithm is able to significantly predict better than the back propagation algorithm and the predicted multi-nominal legit model.

Table 2.4 : Evaluation of MKIS

No.	Researcher	Year	Sample	Method	Findings
1.	**Nature of Function**				
1.	Ackoff	1967			According to Ackoff systems development has not been successful because: first, marketing decision is increasing in complexity at an accelerating pace. Second, marketing decisions, as a class are more difficult to model than other business decisions. Third, many of the methods that have been developed for modeling these decisions are inadequate when checked with real world results.
2. I S and User Conflict (Interpretation)					
1.	Richard H. Brien	1968	One 'X' company	Case study	There is a clear need for a very special kind of intermediary between systems 'users' and system technicians. He found in one company two new positions. Information systems manager and operations research manager were created before the acquisition of a larger, more sophisticated computer system and it was successful.
2.	Dickson Warren lee and Leon R. Price	1994	Marketing departments in telecom firms	Explorat-ory (Questio nnaire)	Identified a variety of problems that prevent IS professionals and Non-IS professionals from joint realisation of the system. Individual differences, social differences and interaction (communication) problems relating to difficulties in integration have been explored.

[contd...]

No.	Researcher	Year	Sample	Method	Findings
3. I S people & Technology					
1.	Linkd, Mary Louise Robinson	1988	One organisation	Longitudin -al casual research	Convergence between information systems personnel and non-information systems personnel on the importance of the firm business activities and IT to support them was found to be an important predictor of IT innovativeness. Communication richness is an important predictor of convergence. Communication frequency is not only an important predictor of convergence but is an important predictor of communication richness as well.
2.	Malcolm A. Mc. Nevin	1968	One organisation	Study	A reason for the failure of information systems in marketing is tremendous gap between expectations of information systems people and the state of the art in business today. He described how Coco-Cola company is bridging the gap by setting the management information system.
3.	Claire Maureen, Forrest	1984	A Small company	Case study Action research approach	DSS to play effective role, small firms may need to introduce more structure into their marketing planning and that the role of the intermediary as such include responsibility for introducing new techniques and ideas.

[contd...]

[contd...]

No.	Researcher	Year	Sample	Method	Findings
4.	Charles D. Schewe and James I. WieK	1977	-	-	They have drawn parallels between MIS development function and marketing function utilising Taylor's framework of marketing delineation, purchase motivation, product adjustment, physical distribution communications, transactions and post transactions.
5.	Donald R. Lehman	1970	1203 adults 20 television shows 6 attributes 8 soft drinks	Empirical cross sectional study	Sketched the elements of marketing information system by starting with a model of individual choice and then developing a system for evaluating marketing decision based on the model. The several applications of this system seem feasible. They include evaluation of new products, advertising effectiveness and product aging.
4. Models of Evaluation					
1.	Kamna Malik and DP. Goyal	2000		Survey of research & analysis	An analysis of existing models, being used for measuring the effectiveness of IS has also been made. An integrated model has been suggested that comprehend the effectiveness of organisational IS with respect to product process and environment effectiveness.

[contd...]

[contd...]

No.	Researcher	Year	Sample	Method	Findings
2.	W.H. Delone and Mc. Lean	1992	-	-	Identified the possibility of two types of measures in IS evaluation, viz. qualitative and quantitative development.
3.	Eldon Y. LI	1997	-	-	Summarizes IS success factors into eight categories and further sub categories as: (i) System gravity; (ii) Information gravity; (iii) Information use; (iv) User satisfaction; (v) Individual impact, (vi) Service quality; (vii) Conflict resolution; (viii) Organisational impact.
4.	Timo Saarimen	1996	-	-	Recommends four measurement scales for IS success model, as stated: ➢ Development process (Cost and efficiency use) ➢ Use process (User satisfaction) ➢ IS product quality (Performance efficiency) ➢ Impact of IS on organisation (Benefits) The emphasis is on process and product evaluations.

[contd...]

[contd...]

No.	Researcher	Year	Sample	Method	Findings
5.	P.G. Kulkarni	1997	-	-	Suggested the use of IT utility index to measure the effectiveness of IT in banking. They are as follows: ➢ Technology costs as a percentage of the total operating cost. ➢ Transaction processing costs. ➢ Technology led exposures and risks. ➢ System availability indicators. ➢ Technology awareness of the knowledge works. ➢ Customer friendliness, flexibility and innovativeness of the system. Similar index parameters can be developed for other industries also.
6.	Erick Brynjolison	1996	-	-	Suggests three approaches to IT value estimation : ➢ Output and productivity estimation. Output = 1 (computers, labour, capital etc.) ➢ Business performance metrics = 1 (Computers, environment, strategy etc.) ➢ Various business metrics - profits, sales, market share, growth, stock price appreciation etc. ➢ Consumer surplus from derived demand.

[contd...]

[contd...]

No.	Researcher	Year	Sample	Method	Findings
7.	James W. Cortada	1995	-	-	Information system is said to be effective if its product is effective. The product of IS can be termed as effective if they: ➢ Provide quality information as per the user's perception. ➢ Improve management function. ➢ Improve resource utilisation.
8.	James W. Cortada	1998	-	-	Recommended the use of Balnidge Award criteria for getting the snapshot of IS effectiveness. Balnidge criteria have seven categories defined for any quality assessment. They are leadership, information and analysis, strategic planning, HRD and HRM, process management, business results and customer satisfaction.
9.	Glenn Edward Maples	1997	Three studies	Empirical test	Service component of information systems yields better results than SERVQUAL and SERVPERF instruments.
10.	Miller, Marc Donald and Kelley R. Rainer jr.	1994	177 UG students	Laboratory experiment	Proposed user satisfaction as a success variable. They found that the Technology Acceptance Model (TAM) may not be able to predict use in these situations. They had proposed and tested the Extended Technology Acceptance Model (ETAM).

[contd...]

[contd...]

No.	Researcher	Year	Sample	Method	Findings
11.	Karahanna, Elena and Detmar W,.Straub and Chervany, Norman L	1993	161 users and 107 potential adopters.	Questionnaire	Identified that the organisations adopt information technology to support knowledge workers. Yet many users are unwilling to use available systems, and thus, the full benefits, of IT are often not realised. Guided by a theoretical model derived by combining innovation diffusion theory with the theory of reasoned action to contribute to a better theoretical understanding of the antecedents of user acceptance and user resistance to the adoption of information technology, they carried out their study and formed that (a) potential adopters base their adoption decisions on a sparser set of innovation characteristics than suggested by the innovation diffusion literature; (b) users and potential adopters differ on their determinations of behaviour intention and attitude and (c) there are significant differences between low and high innovativeness and users in the determinants of subjective norm and behavioral interim.

[contd...]

[contd...]

No.	Researcher	Year	Sample	Method	Findings
12.	James Edward Turner and Julian W. Riehl	1993	143 Super market Executives	Mail survey	Proposed a model to analyse the influence of factors related to use and satisfaction with information systems. The more satisfied firms follow a plan for system development, has top management interest in IS, provide periodic technology updates for management and users and use prototypes to speed development. Firms with more experience with scanning are more satisfied with IS support while firms with more computer experience rate IS support lower.
13	Bernadettee Agatha Szajna	1990	Three treatment groups	Laboratory Experiment	Suggested that user's attitude towards a proposed information system would provide system developers with some knowledge of potential success or failure of information system

[contd...]

[contd...]

No.	Researcher	Year	Sample	Method	Findings
14.	Ginzberg & Desantis	1981 & 1983	Three treatment groups	Laboratory experiment	Pre-implementation expectations have an effect on user satisfaction and perceived decision performance. No effect was found on either decision performance or IS usage. The results are consistent with the predictions and perceptions of the information system that were higher than these with moderate expectations and those users with unrealistically low expectation had significantly lower perceptions. Even after repeated use of the information significant difference was found among the three expectation groups although the trend indicated a moderating of the high and low expectations groups both in their perceptions and post implementation expectations.
15.	Allan Fletcher Gillman	1995	Three Industry groups Telecomm-unications, Information systems and Food retailing	Case study	The role of Electronic Data Interchange (EDI) in promoting electronic commerce marketing channels of distribution is a complex and an interesting one. As a new medium for information transfer, it simultaneously expands and adds value to inter organisational communications. What it does, it shifts the emphasis in channel theory from a structural to emphasize more strategic orientations.

[contd...]

[contd...]

No.	Researcher	Year	Sample	Method	Findings
16.	Vijaya Sarathy, Leo Ramesh and Daniel Robey	1994	97 Retail companies	Empirical Investigation with questionnaires.	The analysis supports the following hypotheses : ➢ EDI use is positively related to information intensity and formalisation. ➢ Formalisation is positively related to cooperation. ➢ Information intensity is positively related to co-operation. ➢ Conflict is negatively related to performance and satisfaction. ➢ Cooperation is positively related to performance; and ➢ Performance is positively related to satisfaction.

Need for the Study

In India, many organisations have set up marketing information systems (MKIS) for various reasons. However, due to lack of publicity and research, the status of the MKIS, its configuration, its applications and its effectiveness are less known to the management world of practitioners, researchers, teachers and students.

Earlier studies on marketing information systems reviewed in the previous section indicate that research was mostly carried out in developed countries like USA and UK. The studies focused on concept and components [*Banks 1968, Uhl 1968, McCann 1986, Burke 1994, Shigeru Yagi 1994 and Jane 1995*], importance [*Buckland and Brancheau 1998, Ing and Mitchell 1993, Deighton and Others 1994*], development [Cox and Good 1967, langle 1988, Somenda 1997] and evaluation [Ackoff 1967, *Brien 1968, Li 1997, Cortada 1995, and Malik and Goyal 2000*]. In India, research on information systems is still at a nascent stage. Few researchers like [*Sharma 1990, Goyal 2001 and Vittal 1999*] studied information systems in Indian organisations. The studies examined the general information systems and accounting information systems.

A comprehensive research on marketing information systems is yet to take place. The available literature comprises mostly conceptual explorations and journalistic descriptions of existing marketing information systems. As such, there is a need to undertake a systematic study on the status, working and effectiveness of the marketing information systems.

Research Problem

In view of the above, the study is undertaken to find answers to the questions below :

- What is the state of the art of marketing information systems in the Indian organisations?
- How well are they performing?
- Do they need improvements? If yes, what kinds of measures are needed?

Objectives of the study

Following are the objectives of the study :

- To describe marketing information systems in select organisations

- To evaluate the effectiveness of the systems based on
  (i) Comparative study of information systems in similar organisation(s)
  (ii) User's opinions
- To identify measures to improve the effectiveness of the systems.

Research Model

An analytical model representing system effectiveness variables under study is shown in the following Fig. 2.1.

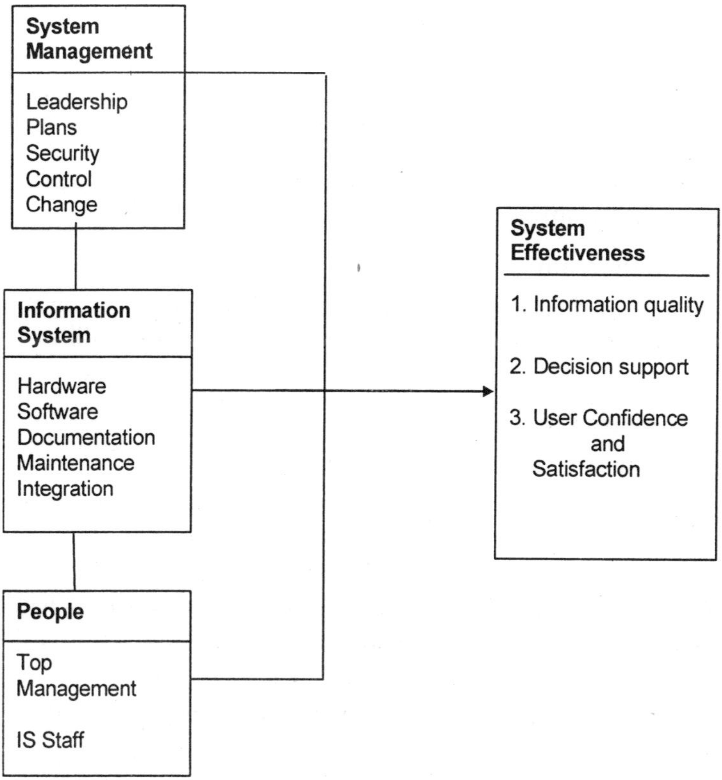

Fig. 2.1: An Analytical Model of Information System Effectiveness

Propositions

The study examines the following propositions:

- Design / Technological effectiveness

The information systems represent the current state of the art

- Functional effectiveness

The information systems are effective in serving the functional needs of marketing.

- Change effectiveness

The information systems are change oriented.

- Use effectiveness

The information systems are user friendly

- Cost effectiveness

The information systems are cost effective.

- System management effectiveness

The information systems have effective leadership, plans, security and controls.

Scope of the study

The study focuses on marketing information system and on how functional needs and user needs of an enterprise are fulfilled by MKIS.

Significance of the study

The study is beneficial in many respects:

1. **Academicians:** There is a dearth of research literature on marketing information systems. It bridges the gap, stimulates interest for further research in this area.
2. **Executives:** An audit of the information systems helps executives identify the inadequacies, if any, and improve the system.
3. **Organisations:** The organisations will have an opportunity to improve system effectiveness.

Research Methodology

The procedure adopted for the study is briefly stated here.

Research Design

The study is descriptive as well as analytical. It employs "Case Method" as it provides an opportunity to understand the phenomena as it appears and evolves. This method will be helpful particularly when respondent organisations are busy and can not respond to mailed questionnaires.

Data Sources

Data required for the study are primary as well as secondary. The secondary data include the company brochures and reports. The primary data comprises the view points of employees using the information systems and information system personnel.

Research Site

In all 8 organisations are studied representing three important sectors of industry-core, chemicals and services. The inclusion of the organisations is influenced by their acceptance. However, care is taken to select organisations:

- Which have minimum of 10 years of existence
- Which are progressive and facing competitors and
- Which are classified as large organisations by Indian standards

The selected organisations are as follows :

Sector	Organisation	Year of Establishment
Core	➢ Chennai Petroleum Corporation Limited ➢ Viskhapatnam Steel Plant ➢ ACC Cement	1969 1982 1936
Chemical	➢ Neuland Laboratories Limited ➢ Erythro Pharma Limited ➢ Biological E Limited	1984 1991 1953
Services	➢ Antrix Corporation Limited ➢ Medinova Diagnostic Services Limited	1972 1987

Data are also collected from all the managers in the marketing department of the participant organisations. The managers have designations like Vice-president, General Manager, Deputy General Manager, Assistant General Manager, Senior Manger, Manager and Officers. The number of marketing managers varied from 6 to 14 in the corporate or regional offices of select organisations.

Data Collection

Data are collected with the help of two questionnaires, one for organisations (Appendix–II) and another for users (Appendix–III). Besides the questionnaires, unstructured interviews are used as a major data collection method.

The questionnaire for organisations consist of :

Part- A	Organisational Profile
Part- B	Marketing Organisation
Part- C	Marketing Information Systems
Part- D	System Development
Part- E	System Functions
Part- F	Evaluation

The questionnaire for users consist of :

Part- A	Personal Profile
Part- B	Data Analysis Methods
Part- C	Information Flows
Part- D	Transactions and Reporting
Part- E	Intelligence
Part- F	Marketing Research
Part- G	Systems Management
Part-H	Evaluation of Information Systems.

Data Analysis

Data are presented in the form of tables. Simple statistical tools like ratios, percentages, means and standard deviations are used.

Limitations

The limitations to the study are:

(1) Unwillingness of organisations to take part in the research: Several organisations have declined the request of researcher to undertake study on this topic, in the name of confidentiality. Those organisations, which have permitted the study, have also not supported it whole heartedly. As a result, getting desired information has become a difficult task.

(2) Financial Problems: The researcher had to spend more time and money, waiting for the consideration of managers and obtaining relevant data from them. Lack of financial support for the study and longer stays with each of the organisations, has posed financial difficulties. Due to this, the researcher has to wind up the study in some organisations requesting them to mail the information. Though the organisations have responded positively, the information dispatched was not up to expectations.

Despite these limitations, the researcher has collected the relevant information tapping various communication media—telephone, e-mail, postal and courier and also by influencing participating managers through friends.

Plan of the book

Chapter 1 presents a conceptual framework and growth of MKIS in India and identifies the research problem.

Chapter 2 makes a survey of literature and establishes objectives and methodology for the present study.

Chapter 3, 4 and **5** describe and evaluate MKIS in select organisations in the core, chemicals and services sector respectively.

Chapter 6 summarises the findings and highlights the suggestions for improving MKIS.

References

Ackoff (1967). "Management Misinformation Systems - Management Service" December 1967.

Blankenship, Ray Joseph, Barnes, James H. Jr. Johnson, John D (1994). "Modeling Consumer choice an export mental comparison of concept learning system, logic and artificial neural network models", The university of Mississippi, AAC 9522467, *Proquest–Dissertation Abstracts.*

Blattberg, Robert C. and Byong-Do Kim and Jiangming Ye (1990-1992). "The New Marketing Challenge", Blattberg, Robert C., Glazer Rashi and Little, John D.C. (eds) *The Marketing Information Revolution,* HBS Publishing, pp. 173-203.

Bovich, Edvard Philip (1987) "Marketing management decision-making and the role of decision support systems" The university of Michigan, AAC 8712075, *Proquest–Dissertation Abstracts.*

Brien, Richard H. (1968). "Marketing information systems in practice: The user's view", *AMA 1968 Fall Conference proceedings,* series No. 28, pp. 172-75.

Buckland, Bonnie K. Brancheau, James C (1995). "Testing the role of knowledge barriers in the diffusion of information technology within and among small business", University of Colorado at Boulder, AAC, Proquest–Dissertation Abstracts.

Burke, Raymond R. (1994). "Artificial Intelligence for Designing Marketing Decision making Tools" Blattberg, Robert C., Glazer Rashi and Little, John D.C. (eds) *Marketing Information Revolution,* HBS Publishing.

Cheon, Myungoong, Grover, Varun, Tegn, James (1992). "Outsourcing of Information systems functions: A contingency model", University of South Carolina, AAC 9307921, *Proquest–Dissertation Abstracts.*

Cook, Gaillynn (1990). "A systematic study of coordinated decision-making across functional areas (accounting information systems (AIS)). University of AAC 9114008, *Proquest–Dissertation Abstracts.*

Cordata, James W. (1998) *Best practices in information technology.* Prentice Hall Inc. NJ.

Cortada, James W. (1996). "*TQM for Information system management*" McGra Hill Inc.

Cox, Donald F. and Good, Robert E. (1967). "How to build marketing information systems?", *Harvard Business Review,* Vol. 45 No. 3, May–June 1967, pp. 145-54.

David Ing and Andrew A. Mitchell (1993). "Point of Sale Data in Consumer Goods Marketing: Transforming the art to Marketing into The Science of Marketing", Blattberg, Robert C., Glazer Rashi and Little, John D.C. (eds) *Marketing Information Revolution* , HBS Publishing, pp. 30-57.

Delone W.H and Mc Lean (1992). "Information success: Quest for the dependent variable", *Information systems research,* Vol. 3, No. 1, March, pp. 60-95.

Dockson, Warren Lee, Leon, Price R. (1994). "The values of information systems professionals: An investigation into barriers preventing integration of IS with the organisation", the University of Oklahoma, AAC 9517495, *Proquest-Dissertation Abstracts.*

Eldon Y. Li (1997). "Perceived importance of Information system success factors: A Meta analysis of group difference: *Information and Management,* 32 (1). February, pp. 15-28.

Erik Brynjolison (1996). "The contribution of IT to consumer welfare." *Information systems research,* 7(3), pp. 281-300.

Forrest, Claire Maureen (1984). "A methodology for implementing a decision support system—a small company case study", Aston University (UK), AAC D 80390, *Proquest-Dissertation Abstracts.*

George Day and Rashi Glazer (1994). "Harnessing the Marketing Information Revolution: Towards the Market Driven Learning Organisation", Blattberg, Robert C., Glazer Rashi and Little, John D.C. (eds) *Marketing Information Revolution,* HBS Publishing. pp. 270-88.

Gillman, Allan Fletcher (1995). "Electronic Commerce: A role for electronic data interchange in marketing channels", Queen's University at Kindston (Canada), AAC NN04814, *Proquest-Dissertation Abstracts.*

Goyal D.P. (2001). "Information Resource management practices: An Empirical study of two Automobile organisations in India", *Indian Management Studies Journal* 5 (2001), pp. 57-76.

Hotaka Katahira and Shigeru Yagi (1994). "Marketing Information Technologies in Japan", Blattberg, Robert C., Glazer Rashi and Little, John D.C. (eds) *Marketing Information Revolution,* HBS Publishing, pp. *306-27.*

John Deighton, Don Peppers, and Martha Pogers (1994). "Consumer Data bases: Present status and prospects", Blattberg, Robert C., Glazer Rashi and Little, John D.C. (eds) *Marketing Information Revolution,* HBS Publishing, pp. 58-79.

Kamna Malik and Goyal D.P.(2000). "Effectiveness of Information Systems-A survey and analysis", *Indian Management Studies,* Journal 4 (2000), pp. 105-20.

Karahanna, Elena and Straub, Detmar W and Chervany, Normal L (1993). "Evaluative criteria and user acceptance of end-user information technology: A study of end-user cognitive and normative pre-adoption beliefs (innovation diffusion)", University of Minnesota, AAC 9331916, *Proquest-Dissertation Abstracts.*

Kokuryo, Jiro (1992). "The impact of the retailing industry's EDI based quick response systems on vendor logistics operations (Logistics)", Harvard University, AAC 9237163, *Proquest–Dissertation Abstracts.*

Kulkarni P.G. (1997). "Trends and effectiveness of IT in banking sector", Shivraj Kanongo, *Information Technology at Work,* Hindustan Publishing Corporation, New Delhi.

Langle, Gernot Bernhand (1988). "An investigation of the effect of specific knowledge in functional areas of business of specific knowledge in functional areas of business on information systems analysis and design", University of Minnisota, AAC 8811084, *Proquest–Dissertation Abstracts.*

Lehman, Donald R. (1970). "A basic for marketing information", *AMA 1970 Fall Conference proceedings,* p. 39.

Lind, Marry Louise Robinson (1988). "The influence of rich communication channel usage on IT innovativeness-the communication channel usage on IT innovativeness", The university of North Carolina at Chapel Hill, AAC 8905663, *Proquest–Dissertation Abstracts.*

Liu, Change (1997). "Critical success factors for designing an electronic market on the World Wide Web: An exploratory study (Website design)", Mississippi State University, AAC 9818691, *Proquest–Dissertation Abstracts.*

Maples, Glenn Edward (1997). "Information systems quality : An examination of service-based models and alternatives (SERVQUAL, Service Quality)", University of North Texas, AAC 9801393, *Proquest–Dissertation Abstracts.*

Mc. Cann, John M. (1986). "Generating, Managing and Communicating Insights", Blattberg, Robert C., Glazer Rashi and Little, John D.C. (eds) *Marketing Information Revolution,* HBS Publishing, pp. 120-49.

Mc. Nevin (1968). "Marketing research and marketing information system", AMA *1968 Fall Conference proceedings,* Series No. 28, pp. 169-71.

Miller, Marc Donald and Rainer, R. Kelly Jr. (1994), "The extended technology acceptance model: theory and empirical test", Aubern University, AAC 9512653, *Proquest–Dissertation Abstracts.*

Pant, Somendra (1997). "An information strategy for Internet enterprises (World Wide Web), strategic information systems planning", Renseller polytechnic institute, AAC 9823684, *Proquest–Dissertation Abstracts.*

Rosecky, Richard B. (1986). "A model for facilitating information flow in a channel of distribution: The consumer response to registration cards (Retail sales)", University of Maryland College Park, AAC 8625724, *Proquest–Dissertation Abstracts.*

Ross, Jeanne Wenzel and Kaiser, Kate M. (1987). "Management information systems department control over end-user computing in marketing departments". The university of Wisconsin-Milwaukee, AAC 8811107, *Proquest-Dissertation Abstracts.*

Schewe Carles D. and James L. Wied (1977). "Guide to misuser satisfaction", *Journal of systems management,* June 1977, pp. 6-10.

Seymour Banks (1968). "A non-systematic look at systems: A triumph of optimism over experience", *AMA 1968 Fall Conference Proceedings,* Series 28, pp. 24-28.

Shea, Timothy Peter and Foderowicz, Jane (1994). "The information acquisition activities of manufacturing middle managers-determinations of lateral and external information use", BOSTON University, AAC 9507144, *Proquest-Dissertation Abstracts.*

Szajna, Bernadettee Agatha (1990). "An experimental investigation of the effects of Information system user expectations on their perceptions and performance", University of Houston, AAC 9034556, *Proquest-Dissertation Abstracts*

Timo Saarimen (1996). "An expanding instrument for evaluation IS success". *Information and management,* November, pp. 103-18.

Turner, James Edward and Riehl, Julian W (1993). "AD empirical study of factors that determine the effectiveness of computer based information systems on food retail decision-making", Virginia Common Wealth University, AAC 9417623, *Proquest-Dissertation Abstracts.*

Uhl, Kenneth P. (1968). "Marketing Information Systems and Sub-systems", *AMA 1968 Conference Proceedings,* Series No. 128, pp. 163-68.

Van Engelen and Johannes Marie Lucien (1989). "*The tuning of information systems to marketing strategies: A systematic Approach*", Vitgevery Keikes Grote Straat 187478, AC Diepenkeim, The Netherlands.

Vijaya Sarathy, Leo Ramesh and Robey, Daniel (1994). "Consequences of inter-organisational information systems: an empirical investigation of the effects of EDI use on inter-organisational relationships in the retail industry", Florida International University, AAC 9511268, *Proquest-Dissertation Abstracts.*

3

Marketing Information System in Core Sectors

3.1 MARKETING INFORMATION SYSTEM IN CHENNAI PETROLEUM CORPORATION LIMITED

Introduction

Chennai Petroleum Corporation Limited (CPCL) was established in 1969 by the Government of India. CPCL has collaborated with NIOC (National Iranian Oil Corporation), IIP and EIL (Engineers India Limited).

CPCL–Facing Deregulation with Improved Strategies

In liberalised business scenario, CPCL has been placed in a relatively unpredictable open market situation from April 2002, subsequent to complete dismantling of administrated pricing mechanism. Factors which have influenced this transition are:

(a) Market forces which exert more pressure on refineries to manage all factors that would ultimately result in increased productivity and profitability.

(b) Quality of products, which influence the market share of companies in the petroleum sector.

(c) Changes in the environmental standards, which call for quick adjustments from the organisation.

CPCL's approach and strategies in the years to come will focus on three pivotal issues:

➢ The need to be globally competitive regarding productivity, product quality, price and supply.

- The need to adapt quickly to changes in external environment, and
- The need to augment to a great extent human resource management capability.

CPCL derives strength from its impressive performance record, periodic expansion programs undertaken, keeping abreast of technology developments, pioneering efforts in areas like energy conservation, health, safety and environment management. CPCL is gearing to meet the competitive challenges through multi-pronged strategies. From the systems point of view, CPCL decided to to start an Integrated Refinery Information System at its Manali Refinery.

Products

CPCL has been producing the following petroleum products:

- LPG
- Motor Spirit
- Naphtha
- ATF (Aviation Turbine Fuel)
- SKO (Superior Kerosene Oil)
- 0.25% Sulpher HSD (High Sulpher Diesel)
- Asphalt
- Fuel Oil
- Wax
- LOBS (Lube Oil Base Stock)
- Bitumen (CRMB) (Crumb Rubber Modified Bitumen)

IT and Business Applications

The information technology has undergone dramatic changes in the global scenario. CPCL is equally in tune with the latest technology by upgrading the existing systems. As a result of the effective in-house initiatives to handle possible Y2K roll-over issues, the roll-over of the information system was very smooth into the new millennium.

CPCL has teamed up with Computer Maintenance Corporation (CMC), a leading IT company, for its IT solutions. The major hardware requirements and their service are taken care of by CMC. CPCL is presently proceeding on an ambitious IT strategy for achieving an Integrated Refinery Information System (IRIS). The first step towards this plan is to have an integrated business system through Enterprise Resource Planning (ERP) software. CPCL has teamed up with CMC to achieve this goal. CMC conducted a detailed scooping study of the business requirements of CPCL to get the best ERP software. CPCL has now teamed up with Ramco Systems, a leading software solution provider, who is presently implementing the ERP software. With this implementation, CPCL will achieve the objective of data availability, data integrity and information flows between various modules of business systems.

CPCL has also teamed up with leading global software giants like Microsoft, Oracle and IBM for its software requirements like Operating System (OS), Relational Data Base Management System (RDBMS) and Information exchange like E-mail. CPCL has teamed with Videsh Sanchar Nigam Ltd. (VSNL), a government organisation and a premier Internet Service Provider (ISP), which has provided Internet through a terrestrial microwave link.

CPCL has also teamed up with CMC to meet the networking requirements. A fiber optic Local Area Network (LAN) and a Very Small Aperture Terminal (VSAT) Wide Area Network (WAN) has been designed and implemented by CMC for reliable transmission of data and voice. CPCL has now teamed up with National Informatics Centre (NIC), a government organisation for video conferencing, which was successfully implemented recently.

Marketing

Sustained and concerted efforts were made to increase the sale of products directly marketed by the company. The turnover on account of direct marking, in terms of quantity, accounted for 5,37,813 MTs during the year as compared to 5,21,977 M.T.s during the previous year.

A significant step in the diversification of marketing was the introduction of new grade of Bitumen known as 'Crumb Rubber Modified Bitumen' to meet the demand for better quality modified Bitumen. The company took a lead role among the refineries in India to manufacture this type of Bitumen. The product, approved by Ministry of Surface Transport, has been successfully launched and accepted by the industry. The company has also launched direct sale of Furnace Oil and Rubber Process Oil to various end-users.

With effect from 2001–2002, Indian Oil Corporation has been entrusted with the rights of marketing. This new arrangement continues to ensure profit sharing and other privileges, which the company was assured of under the earlier marketing arrangement.

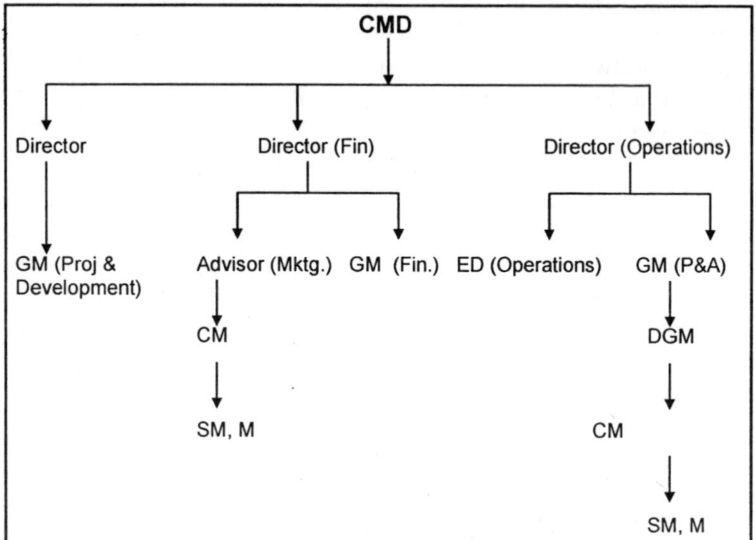

ED : Executive Director
CM : Chief Manager
GM : General Manager
DGM : Deputy General Manager
SM : Senior Manager
M : Manager

Fig. 3.1.1 : Organisation Chart of CPCL

Marketing Organisation

The marketing organisation (Fig. 3.1) is headed by Director (finance). Advisor (marketing) who is hierarchically at the level of executive director coordinates the marketing activity. He supervises–chief manager, senior managers and managers. The chief manager assists advisor in coordinating marketing activity. Senior managers and managers are concerned with product-wise marketing. One senior manager is entrusted with the coordination work at the refinery.

Marketing Information System

Marketing information system was computerised in the year 1995. The reasons for setting up of computerised marketing information system are:

- To make complex decisions easy
- As competitors have set up MIS
- It is an extension to computerisation in other departments
- On the request of marketing managers.

Objectives Served

The identified principal benefits of marketing information system are :

1. Helps improve decision-making
2. Helps in better coordination
3. Helps in generating a variety of reports.

The other benefits are :

1. Maintains a general database
2. Makes planning and controlling effective
3. Increases profits.

The company is implementing ERP. The system helps in integrating marketing department with production, technical services and quality control. It provides region-wise market potential data and helps develop suitable marketing plan. Also it furnishes sales data and analysis and facilitates credit control.

About the System

There are more than 200 computers with suitable configuration for implementing ERP. The marketing information system wing has about 10 employees. Advices from consultants are sought as and when necessary. Users are trained to provide skills for using windows and ERP.

Reports

The reports generated for decision-making include:

- Sales reports
- Customer feed-back
- Quality control laboratory reports
- Industry performance reports
- ICIS - LOR (London oil reports for lubes)
- Internet sites
- Petroleum Bazaar
- Analysis by specialists / experts in the field.

Evaluation

The following inadequacies are identified :

1. The hardware is inadequate to the users
2. Development requirements are not considered actively
3. The response to management requests for modifications is rigid and hence slow.

Future Plans

The company is planning to complete the implementation of ERP by 2002.

Profile of Respondents

Table 3.1.1 describes the profile of the respondents from the organisation. The respondents include Chief Manager, Senior Manager, two Managers and seven Officers. Experience-wise the respondent group consists of about 63.6% decision-makers with more than 10 years of experience. Level-wise about 63.6% of them are at the senior management level. Thus the respondent group is dominated by senior managers with more than 10 years experience.

Table 3.1.2 shows the reporting relationships. Chief Manager Marketing reports to Advisor Marketing; the Senior Manager to Chief Manager and the Officers report to Senior Managers. All the respondents have subordinates as shown in Table 3.1.2.

Table 3.1.1 : Profile of Respondents
(N = 11)

S.No.	Elements	F	%
1.	**Designation :**		
	Chief Manager	1	9.1
	Senior Manager	1	9.1
	Manager	2	18.2
	Officer	3	27.3
	Assistants	4	36.4
2.	**Experience (years) :**		
	Less than 10	4	36.4
	10 & Above	7	63.6
3.	**Level in hierarchy :**		
	Senior	7	63.6
	Junior	4	36.4

Table 3.1.2 : Reporting Relationships of Respondents
(N = 11)

Reporting to	F	%
Advisor (Marketing)	1	9.1
Chief Manager	3	27.3
Senior Manager	3	27.3
Officer/Manager	4	36.4
Subordinate positions under Respondents :		
Chief Manager	10	90.9
Senior Manager	9	81.8
Manager	7	63.6
Marketing Officer	4	36.4

The respondents did not provide job descriptions but informed the researcher that they are concerned with:

- Marketing of refinery products
- Marketing coordination
- Product management and any other function related to marketing

Role Clarity

Respondents were asked to identify their levels of clarity about the roles they play in the organisation. The role clarity is measured on a 5 point scale–5 representing very much and 1 indicating very less. The responses indicate that they have reasonably good role clarity (4.0). They have clear view about their relationships (3.8), authority (3.7) and responsibility (3.7). Dimension-wise analysis considers, role Clarity, role conflicts, clear authority, clear responsibility and clear knowledge of their contribution. Table 3.1.3 shows the details. They do not have role conflicts (3.6). The measurement of role clarity on the four dimensions also establishes an average score of 3.7 which is near to the overall score of 4.0

Table 3.1.3 : Perceived Role Clarity of Respondents

(N = 11)

Perceptions	Mean	SD
My role is clear to me	4.0	2.5
I do not have conflicts in playing my role (No over- lapping)	3.6	2.3
My authority is clear to me	3.7	2.4
My relations with others are well defined	3.8	2.6
I was told clearly about my responsibility	3.7	2.4
(What I have to contribute)		
Overall	3.7	2.4

Decision Making

On whom the decision-makers depend in arriving at solutions to problems? Table 3.1.4, shows that they are mostly depending upon their seniors (4.4), and very less on subordinates (1.4) and peers (1.9). The responses are measured on a 5 point scale of very much to very less.

Table 3.1.4 : Dependence in Decision Making and Implementation (N = 11)

Positions	Mean	SD
On superiors	4.4	2.3
On subordinates	1.4	1.0
On peers	1.9	1.6

What methods do the decision-makers employ in data analysis? The respondents have observed that they make use of mostly quantitative analysis techniques for key decisions as well as routine decisions. They have emphasised that qualitative analysis is also necessary as a supportive mechanism to the quantitative approach.

Information Flow

The information flows to the different persons in the hierarchy of marketing is as follows:

- The Chief Manager receives policy information from 'Advisor Marketing' on a continuous basis. He receives demand and supply information daily from Senior Manager and Manager.
- The Senior Manager receives from their superiors, information inputs on current marketing strategy as and when required. From their subordinates they receive information on day to day sales requirements, sales reports, and progress reports from their peers. They obtain production status reports.
- The officers receive from their superiors information about demand, customer information and Inventory details. From their subordinates they receive customer payment details.

The Chief Manager sends monthly sales performance reports to the Executive Director and Director (Finance). He sends customer reports, feed back and complaints to Senior Managers and Managers as and when necessary. He sends demand and supply details and customer requirements to manufacturing department once in a month. He disseminates new product development information to manufacturing and technical section.

The Senior Manager reports daily sales and other highlights to the Chief Manager. He informs his officers daily, about production programme and constraints therein.

The officers report frequently, the information about market developments and submit daily sales reports.

Perception about Information

An inquiry about the availability of information in terms of sufficiency or overload or shortage has revealed that all the respondents with the exception of one Manager have sufficient information for their effective functioning. Only one manager felt that there is information shortage. The shortage according to him relates to the external information i.e., about market developments.

Table 3.1.5 : Perception about information received

(N = 11)

Perceptions	F	%
Information over-load	0	0
Information sufficiency	10	90.9
Information shortage	1	9.1

Processing

Evidently, the information related functions of the managers are:

Chief Manager

- He forwards with remarks the information on sales credits and discounts.
- He circulates performance reports
- He approves the customers and vendors
- He collects information to provide status reports to the superiors.
- He receives sales reports from marketing section and he sends monthly sales reports to the superiors.
- He receives global production demand status reports, region / country-wise, from the government and research agencies.

Senior Manager

The Senior Manager receives the following reports :

- From OMI section–tank dip statement
- From Maintenance and P&D section–statements of packed asphalt 1 wax.

Manager

- A manager receives daily sales reports and monthly sales reports and sends monthly sales report and quarterly sales report to their superiors.

Officer

- Officers receive reports on product demand, collection and payments and customer feedback.

When asked about the necessity of the existing reports, the respondents felt that all of them are necessary. When inquired about the need for any new reports, they said as of now the existing reports are adequate to meet their present and future requirements.

Marketing Intelligence

Table 3.1.6 shows that participation of respondent managers in the conferences and workshops are very less.

Table 3.1.6 : Conferences / Workshops Attended by the respondents. (N = 11)

Year	Conference	Workshop	Seminar	Others	F	%
1998	---	1	1	---	2	18
1999	---	---	1	---	1	9
2000	1	---	---	---	1	9
2001	1	---	---	1	2	18

Table 3.1.7 shows the different sources of information used by the managers to keep them update. They are newspapers, journals, Internet, discussion with company personnel and persons belonging to other companies. The other sources are conferences and workshop/ seminars (36.4%) and T.V. news and programs (27.3%).

Table 3.1.7 : Sources of Information Used To Keep Updated

(N = 11)

Source	F	%
Discussion with company personnel	10	90.9
Discussion with other company personnel	10	90.9
T. V. news and programs	3	27.3
Conference / Workshops / Seminars	4	36.4
News papers/ Journals	11	100
Internet	10	90.9

Marketing Research

The importances of marketing research as well as its frequency are inquired using a 5 point scale. It is considered fairly important for effective decision-making by the respondents. It is conducted frequently for the purpose of decision-making. Table 3.1.8 shows the details.

Analysis of the individual responses shows that chief manager considers marketing research important and uses it frequently. The senior manager also considers it important but prefers to use it less frequently than the chief manager. The managers have opined that marketing research is moderately important and they use it moderately. Thus differences in perception regarding importance of marketing research are evident.

Table 3.1.8 : Use of Marketing Research in Decision-Making

(N = 11)

Factors	Mean	SD
Importance	3.6	2.8
Frequency	3.5	2.7

System Evaluation

The system effectiveness is evaluated based on the views of respondent managers as follows:

- System management evaluation

- Information system evaluation
- People evaluation
- Outcomes evaluation
- Overall evaluation

System Management Evaluation

The system management is analysed with reference to 5 factors:

- Leadership
- Plans
- Controls
- Security and
- Change

Table 3.1.9 shows the responses signifying system management factors. According to it, about 90% of the respondents are of the view that system is flexible and adaptive. Plans are effective and leadership is good. About 86% of the respondents have opined that security of the system is good. Controls are effective according to 74% of the respondents.

Table 3.1.9 : Systems Management Evaluation

(N = 11)

S.No	Factor	Average Score (%)	
		F	%
1	Leadership	9.2	90.9
2	Plans	10.2	92.7
3	Controls	6.5	74.0
4	Security	9.5	86.3
5	Change	9.5	93.1

Leadership

The marketing information system in the organisation is under the direction of qualified manager. The management is ably motivating its personnel to provide effectively information service. There are training programs for employees and they consider them necessary. However, some of the officers are of the view that the availability of such programs is limited. About 91% of the respondents have felt that management is not effective in motivating them.

Table 3.1.10: Systems Management Evaluation–Leadership (N = 11)

No.		Factors	F	%
1.		Is the MKIS under the direction of qualified manager (specify)?	11	100
2.		Does management motivate its personnels to effectively provide a desired information service?	10	90.9
3.		Is there a formal training program where deemed necessary?		
	(i)	New employees?	9	81.8
	(ii)	Transferred employees?	8	72.7
	(iii)	Regular employees?	8	72.7

Plans

According to 90% respondents, the master plan of marketing information system is well defined and integrated with departmental long range plans and organisational objectives. Also the marketing information system plan is well integrated with procedures and standards. Top management, the management steering committee and information system management, periodically review the MIS plan. Table 3.1.11 shows the details :

Table 3.1.11 : Systems Management Evaluation – Plans

(N = 11)

No.		Factors	F	%
1.		Does the management have a well-defined master-plan for MKIS?	10	90.9
2.		Is the master-plan integrated		
	(i)	Objectives?	10	90.9

[contd...]

[contd...]

No.	Factors	F	%
(ii)	Strategies?	10	90.9
(iii)	Projects?	10	90.9
(iv)	Policies?	10	90.9
(v)	Procedures?	10	90.9
(vi)	Standards?	10	90.9
3	Are the department long range plans related to organisational objectives?	10	90.9
4.	Is the master plan subjected to periodic review?		
(i)	Top management?	11	100
(ii)	Management steering committee?	11	100
(iii)	Information systems management?	11	100

Controls

The following IS control measures are considered effective (Table 3.1.12) by the respondents. According to them:

Table 3.1.12 : Systems Management Evaluation–Control
(N = 11)

No.	Factors	F	%
1.	Does management exercise the necessary control over its operations so that fraud, theft, and irregularities of IS methods and procedures can be detected?	11	100
2.	Does management segregate the functions of the department in order to minimize fraud, theft, and irregularities?	11	100
3.	Are there provisions for back-up personnel in key information system positions?	11	100

[contd...]

[contd...]

No.		Factors	F	%
4.		Does internal auditing periodically check on the operations of the information systems department?	11	100
5.		Is the information system audited periodically by an independent third party (out-side auditor or consultant)?	10	90.9
6.		Is there a surprise audit of the information systems department for detecting?		
	(i)	Fraud?	2	18
	(ii)	Theft?	2	18
	(iii)	Collusion?	2	18
	(vi)	Embezzlement?	2	18
	(v)	Sabotage?	2	18
	(vi)	Irregularities?	2	18
	(vii)	Does the computer system have adequately powered air condition?	11	100
7.		Are systems and procedure manuals kept current?	8	72.7

- Management has segregated the functions of the department in order to minimise fraud, theft and irregularities.
- Provision for back-up personnel in key information systems positions has been created.
- Internal auditing periodically checks operations of IS department.
- There are surprise audits (internal) to check irregularities.

However, the senior management has pointed out the following:

- There is no external, independent auditing of the system.
- The system procedures and documents are not kept current.

Security

Table 3.1.13 shows the evaluation of security aspects. All the respondents have felt that security controls are required by IS management. The security measures are well-designed and implemented in the organisation. There are sufficient security controls to ensure that all input data and corrections are processed properly and accurately. However, some of the respondents are of the view that :

- Security controls are not fully understood and implemented
- Manuals of security procedures are not available.

Table 3.13 : Systems Management Evaluation–Security
(N = 11)

No.	Factors	F	%
1	Are security controls required by information systems management?	11	100
2	Are security controls fully understood and implemented by systems and programming personnels?	9	81.8
3.	Are security controls sufficient to ensure that all input data and corrections to data have been processed properly and accurately?	10	90.9
4.	Are security controls written and contained in appropriate systems and procedure manuals for ready reference, when necessary?	8	72.7

Change Management

According to Table 3.1.14, the system is perceived by respondents as change-oriented. A control mechanism with well-designed procedures is set up in the organisation. It functions by seeking approvals of top management. The change plans are well documented including the reasons for changes. The users are involved in the change process. Written memoranda are issued to appropriate personnels concerning changes. Auditors are also appraised of important changes. During the change process effective control systems to prevent unauthorised changes in the master files and transaction files are also established. On the whole, the marketing information system is dynamic and adaptative.

Table 3.1.14 : Systems Management Evaluation–Change (N = 11)

No.		Factors	F	%
1.		Is there a control mechanism for making appropriate information system change?	9	81
2.		Does this control mechanism include a provision for approval?	6	54
3.		Are procedures established for making?		
	(i)	System changes?	11	100
	(ii)	Program changes?	11	100
	(iii)	Library (Program and file) changes?	11	100
	(iv)	Computer operator charges?	11	100
4.		Are all system and program changes immediately documented, including the reason for the change?	8	72
5.		Are written memoranda issued to the appropriate personnel concerning changes?	8	72
6.		Is the user involved in making changes where necessary?	8	72
7.		Are the internal and external auditors apprised of important changes?	11	100
8.		Are master files and transaction files controlled to prevent unauthorised changes during conversion?	11	100

Information System Evaluation

Table 3.1.15 shows system related appraisal. The respondents have given positive scores for system, software, maintenance and integration of the system with other systems. However, the documentation is rated poor. Element-wise evaluation of the system is provided in Table 3.1.16 :

Table 3.1.15 : System Evaluation–System Elements
(N=11)

Elements :	**Mean**	**SD**
Hardware	3.4	2.6
Software	3.4	2.3
Documentation	3.4	2.4
Maintenance	3.3	2.8
Integration	3.5	2.6

Table 3.1.16 : Information System Evaluation–System Details
(N = 11)

No.	**Factors**	**Mean**	**SD**
	Hard ware :		
1.	The response of the system is fast	3.6	2.1
2.	Accessing information is easy	3.7	2.4
4.	System security is very good	3.4	2.6
5.	In realisation of user needs, the system is the best	3.3	2.8
6.	The system has good flexibility	3.6	1.6
7.	Information processing is efficient	3.3	2.8
8.	Computer systems are adequate	3.0	2.2
	Total Average :	3.4	2.6
	Software :		
1.	Features used in programming languages are excellent	3.5	2.6
2.	Data analysis programs are updated.	3.1	2
	Total Average :	3.4	2.3
	Documentation :		
1.	Documentation if the system is completed.	3.4	2.4
	Maintenance :		
2.	The system is well maintained.	3.3	2.8
	Integrated :		
1.	The system is integrated with other systems.		
2.	There is coordination between MKIS and other systems.	3.5	2.6
	Average Total :	2.5	2.6

People Evaluation

Table 3.1.17 shows people element of system evaluation, the respondents have rated good aspects like top management support, IT staff competence and support and user involvement and utilisation of the system. Element-wise evaluation of the people is provided in table 3.1.18

Table 3.1.17 : People Evaluation
(N=11)

Element	Mean	SD
Top management	3.6	1.6
IS staff	3.6	2.2

Table 3.1.18: People Evaluation Details
(N=11)

No.	Factors	Mean	SD
	Top Management :		
1.	Top management is involved in the development of the system.	3.6	1.6
	IS Staff :		
1.	The staff in the organisation like to use the system.	3.4	2.5
2.	IS staff are competent.	3.8	1.9
	Total Average :	3.6	2.2

Outcomes Evaluation

The different outcomes of a system like information quality, output, user friendliness, decision support, benefits and satisfaction are evaluated by the respondents. The results are shown in table 3.1.19. According to it, the system is good in all respects particularly, the benefits.

Table: 3.1.19 : Evaluation of System Outcomes

(N=11)

Aspect	Mean	SD
Information	3.5	2.1
Output	3.3	2.1
User friendliness	3.5	3.3
Decision Support	3.5	2.1
Benefits	3.7	2.8
Satisfaction	3.5	2.7

Information and Output

Table 3.1.20 shows that information available from the system is good (information quality, relevance, accuracy, timeliness etc). However, the respondents are less happy about the output in respect of the volume, though they are happy that the reports and other information products are well scheduled.

Table 3.1.20 : Evaluation of System Outcomes – Information and Output

(N=11)

No.	Factors	Mean	SD
	Information :		
1.	Computer systems are capable.	3.3	2.8
2.	Information is relevant.	3.3	2.8
3.	Information is kept confidential when required.	3.3	2.2
4.	Information Provided by the system is accurate.	3.9	2.4
5.	System provides timely information.	3.6	2.8
6.	System furnishes exact information.	3.2	2.7
7.	The information provided is reliable.	3.7	2.4

[contd...]

[contd...]

No.	Factors	Mean	SD
8.	Current information is provided by the system.	3.8	3.4
9.	The information is complete in all aspects.	3.4	2.6
10.	It provides well designed formats.	4.1	2
11.	Information furnished has clarity.	4.1	2
	Total average :	3.5	2.1
	Output		
1.	The reports and other information products are well-scheduled.	3.5	2.7
2.	Adequate volume of output is generated by the system.	3.0	1.7
	Total Average :	3.3	2.2

User Friendliness

Table 3.2.21 shows the user friendliness of the system. The aspects include training and user involvement in system development and implementation, and user confidence of the system.

Table 3.1.21 : Evaluation of System Outcomes – User friendliness (N=11)

No.	Factors	Mean	SD
1.	Users are well-trained to use the system.	3.4	2.7
2.	The system is used by all concerned employees.	3.4	2.5
3.	There is participation of users in the system development and instrumentation.	3.9	1.8
4.	Users have confidence in the system.	3.4	2.7
	Total average :	2.5	3.3

Decision Support

According to the respondents the system is fairly helpful on an average to the managers in making decisions relating to product and price. It is also helpful in the market analysis and forecasting, place and promotion decisions. Table 3.1.22 shows the details :

Table 3.1.22 : Evaluation of System outcomes–Decision Support (N=11)

Factors	Mean	SD
Market analysis and forecasting	3.2	2.1
Product decisions	3.6	2.3
Price decisions	3.5	1.3
Place decisions	3.3	1.8
Promotion decisions	3.1	2.6
Average Total :	3.5	2.1

Benefits and Satisfaction

Table 3.1.23 shows that the respondents are pleased with the benefits of the system. They have considered it beneficial (3.7). They have agreed with the statement–"The system has tools to improve productivity of operations." They have also accepted that their jobs have become easy and efficient. The respondents have expressed satisfaction with the system (3.5).

Table 3.1.23 : Evaluation of System Outcomes–Benefits and Satisfaction

(N=11)

No.	Factors	Mean	SD
1.	The system has tools to improve productivity of operations.	4.0	2.2
2.	My job has become easy with the support of the system.	3.6	2.9
3.	MKIS has improved the results of the organisation.	3.8	3.4

[contd...]

[contd...]

No.	Factors	Mean	SD
4.	MKIS is making the activities more efficient.	3.8	3.4
5.	MKIS has boosted the profits of organisation.	3.7	3.1
6.	My expectations of benefits of system are realised.	3.4	2.4
	Total average	3.7	2.8
	Satisfaction :		
1.	The system is satisfactory to me.	3.5	2.7

Overall Evaluation

The respondents are asked to evaluate the present marketing information system in the organisation on a 5-point scale representing exceptional and poor at the polar points. The system is considered good by majority of the respondents. Table 3.1.24 shows the details:

Table 3.1.24 : Overall Evaluation Information System

(N=11)

Factor	Mean	SD
Present marketing information system	3.6	2.8

3.2 MARKETING INFORMATION SYSTEM IN VISAKHAPATNAM STEEL PLANT

Introduction

Visakhapatnam Steel Plant (VSP) of Rashtriya Ispat Nigam Limited (RINL) was established in 1982. It is a major integrated steel plant in the public sector, located on the shores of Bay-of- Bengal in Andhra Pradesh. The plant has capacity to produce 3 million tones of liquid steel and 2.56 million tones of saleable steel. With the state-of the-art and latest technology to make steel of world-class quality, Visakhapatnam Steel Plant is the most modern steel complex of its kind in the country.

Products of the Company

1. Wire rods: a) medium / low carbon b) high carbon
2. Hot Rolled Rebars
3. Other sections:

   Equal angles, Beams, Channels, Billets, Rounds, Pig Iron
4. By-Products

   Ammonium Sulphate, Benzene, Tolvene, Light Solvent Naphtha, Sol-110 (Non Aromatic), Crude Coal Tar, Phenol Fractions, Hot Pressed Naphthalene, Coal Tar Wash Oil, Anthracene Oil, Drained Naphthalene Oil, Coal tar Fuel / Pitch Creosote Mixture, Medium Hard Pitch, Coke Fractions, Blended Cement Raw Material : Blast Granulated Slag, Coarse Aggregate / Ballast : SMS / LD Slag.
5. Miscellaneous Products

   Calcined Lime Fines, Fly Ash, Liquid Argon, Liquid Oxygen, Liquid Nitrogen, Boiler Coal Dust and JPP Mill Ejects.

Mission

To be a continuously growing company by producing steel at international standards as well as through strategic diversification of products and services with concern for customers.

Organisation

The organisation chart of Fig. 3.2.1 depicts the key positions.

Marketing

VSP has an efficient marketing network fully backed by a competent and dynamic technical services group which helps in updating the customers on the products of VSP and recommending their best use for the customer applications.

VSP has branch offices and stockyards at all major consuming centers in India, manned by experienced marketing professionals. The field personnels undertake extensive customer contact programmes including frequent visits to customers' premises for discussing and assessing their immediate and future requirements. The branch managers regularly organise customer meets at branch offices and these meets are attended at least once in three months by regional managers and senior executives from head quarters. The

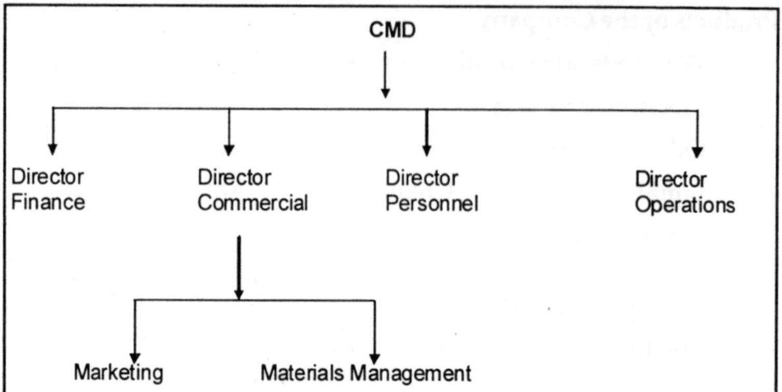

Branches of VSP

East	West	North	South	Andhra
Bhubaneswar	Mumbai	Agra	Bangalore	Hyderabad
Kolkatta	Indore	Chandigarh	Chennai	Vizag
Patna	Ahmedabad	Delhi	Coimbatore	
	Nagpur	Faridabad	Kochi	
	Pune	Ghaziabad		
		Jaipur		
		Ludhiana		

Fig. 3.2.1 : Organisation Chart of VSP

branches, through this exercise, send regular feedback to HQ regarding the current and emerging requirements and demand patterns in their respective areas. Quarterly and monthly production and dispatch plans are made based on these projections as well as export orders.

VSP continuously interacts with structural designers / fabricators and consultants all over the country and projects and construction authorities of central and state governments for broad banding customer base as well as to assess the market for construction steel in the country. An inter-disciplinary group has been constituted for the development of special steel grades to meet the specific requirements of selected customers.

Thus, VSP funnels information on customer requirements into the business systems and culture of the organisation. Lastly, with a view to ascertain the effectiveness of VSP's various initiatives, customer's opinion survey is carried out every year through an external reputed agency. These surveys bring awareness about the strength and weaknesses of VSP with regard to key areas determining customer satisfaction level. Concerted efforts are taken to improve on the required areas. Besides, this, VSP also keeps track of competitors' efforts towards customer satisfaction.

Computerisation

Computers are being utilised in the steel industry since 1960 for process automation and production controls. VSP has sizable amount of computerisation in-built into its design, while in line with the latest trends in technology. The main objective of computerisation in VSP is to assist the operations in controlling repetitive jobs, to optimise utilisation of scarce resources by real time process control and to assist in operation and production management.

The computerisation and automation in VSP is envisaged at three levels for effective integration between the planning processes. The highest level assists the management decision-making by collection, analysis and providing the production and management information on a real time basis and the lowest level assists the actual process operators by reducing their tedium in the form of automation. Thus the structure is designed for assisting all levels of operation and management of the plant.

Profitable Performance

Despite the rising input prices, overlapping interest burden and sluggish market, VSP could still achieve cash profits in 2001-02 to the tune of Rs. 262 crores. The sales for the year were Rs. 4077 crores.

Marketing Organisation

The marketing organisation is headed by the Director (Commercial). He coordinates the marketing activity. He is assisted by General Manager (Marketing) who is responsible for all the activities of marketing. He supervises Deputy General Manager, Additional Chief Manager and Assistant General Manager.

Marketing Information System

Marketing information system was computerised in the year 1998. The prime reason for setting up of computerised marketing information system is:

- To make complex decisions easy

Objectives Served

The important purposes that the marketing information system is supposed to serve are:

1. Help improve decision-making.
2. Help in better coordination.
3. Help in generating a variety of reports.
4. Keep a general database.
5. Make planning and controlling effective and increase profits.

The company is using the latest technology of "Network" and "Oracle" software. The system helps in integrating marketing department with all other departments. It provides information about region-wise market potential and helps develop suitable marketing plan. Also it furnishes sales data and sales analysis and facilitates credit control.

About the System

The company is laying sufficient Hardware with suitable configuration for using the system. The marketing MIS wing has about 6 employees. Users are trained to provide skill for using Windows, Oracle etc.

Reports

Various reports are generated by the system. The key reports are:

- Gross Sales Realisation
- Net Sales Realisation
- Stock
- Price movement

Evaluation

The following inadequacies are identified :

1. The hardware is inadequate to the users.
2. Development requirements are not considered actively.

Future Plans

The company is planning to complete implementation of SAP.

Profile of Respondents

Table 3.2.1 describes the profile of the respondents from the organisation. The respondents include General Manager, Deputy General Manager, Assistant General Manager, Additional Chief Manager, four Deputy Chief Managers and Deputy Manager and two Assistant Managers. Experience-wise the respondent group consists of about 81.8% decision-makers with more than 10 years of experience. Level-wise can be observed that about 81.8% of them are at the senior management level.

Table 3.2.1 : Profile of Respondents

(N = 11)

S.No.	Elements	F	%
1.	**Designation:**		
	General Manager (GM)	1	9
	Deputy General Manager (DGM)	1	9
	Assistant General Manager (AGM)	1	9
	Additional Chief Manager (ACM)	4	36
	Deputy Chief Managers (DCM)	1	9
	Deputy Managers (DM)	1	9
	Assistant Managers (AM)	2	18
2.	**Experience (years) :**		
	Less than 10	2	18.1
	10 & Above	9	81.8
3.	**Level in hierarchy:**		
	Senior	9	81.8
	Junior	2	18.2

Thus the respondent group is dominated by senior managers with more than 10 years experience. Table 3.2.2 shows the reporting relationships of Manager.

Table 3.2.2 : Reporting Relationships of Respondents (N = 11)

Respondents	Reporting to
GM	Director Commercial
DGM	GM
AGM	DGM, GM
ACM	DGM
DCM (Marketing)	GM
DCM (Marketing)	AGM
DCM (MMIS)	ACM
DCM (MMIS)	ACM
Dy.M	ACM
AM	ACM
AM	ACM
Subordinate positions under Respondents	**Subordinate positions**
GM	DGM, AGM, ACM, DCM, Dy.M, AM
DGM	AGM, ACM
AGM	DCM, Dy.M., AM
ACM	Manager (Mktg), Asst. Manager, Jr. Staff officers
DCM (Marketing)	Dy.M, AM
DCM (Marketing)	Dy.M, AM
DCM (MMIS)	Dy.M, AM
DCM (MMIS)	Dy.M, AM
Dy.M	AM
AM	Jr. Executives
AM	Jr. Executives

The respondents did not provide complete job descriptions but informed their major concerns as follows:

- GM, DGM, AGM, ACM: All the activities of marketing.
- DCM (Marketing): Assisting General Manager.
- Dy. Manager: Marketing information system.
- DCM (MKMIS): Marketing research and analysis.
- ACM Marketing : Product planning and dispatch.
- DCM (Mktg.): Marketing value added products.
- DCM (MMIS): Marketing information system.
- AM: Planning and dispatch of steel.

Role Clarity

Respondents were asked to identify their levels of clarity about the roles they play in the organisation. The responses indicate that they have reasonably good role clarity (4.6). They have clear view about their relationships (4.0), authority (4.5) and responsibility (4.2). They don't have role conflicts (3.8). Table 3.2.3 shows the details:

Table 3.2.3 : Perceived Role Clarity of Respondents (N = 11)

Perceptions	Mean	SD
My role is clear to me	4.6	2.9
I do not have conflicts in playing my role (No over- lapping)	3.8	2.6
My authority is clear to me	4.5	3.1
My relations with others are well defined	4.0	1.9
I was told clearly about my responsibility	4.2	2.0
(What I have to contribute)		
Overall	4.2	2.5

Decision-Making

The dependence of decision-makers in arriving at solutions to problems can be seen in Table 3.2.4. It shows that they are mostly depending upon their seniors (4.3) :

Table 3.2.4 : Dependence on Decision-Making and Implementation (N = 11)		
Positions	**Mean**	**SD**
On superiors	4.3	2.3
On subordinates	3.3	1.3
On peers	3.9	1.6

What methods do the decision-makers employ in data analysis? The respondents have observed that they make use of mostly standard methods for key decisions as well as routine decisions.

Information Flow

The information flows to different persons in the hierarchy of marketing is as follows:

- The General Manager receives policy information from the Director (Commercial) on a daily basis. He receives details regarding dispatches and planning from Additional Chief Manager (Marketing) on daily basis. He also receives demand and supply information from the Deputy General Manager. He also receives prices and customer requirements from DCM (marketing) on monthly basis and from DCM (Mktg) marketing feed-back periodically on regular basis.
- Deputy General Manager receives information regarding daily activities from GM on daily basis.
- Assistant General Manager receives activity implementation plans from Deputy General Manager.
- Additional Chief Manager receives advices from the Director (Commercial) on daily basis.
- Deputy Chief Manager receives policy requirements from GM as and when necessary. He also receives information on competitor's prices and price operated by VSP from his peers on monthly basis. DCM receives advices and instructions from AGM / DGM on daily basis.
- Assistant Managers receive requirement account from ACM on weekly and monthly basis. They also receive Inventory

information at various branches from Junior Executives on weekly basis.

Out Flow

- GM sends policy related plans and instructions to his subordinates.
- DGM sends demand and supply information to GM.
- AGM sends performance related information to DGM.
- ACM sends details regarding dispatches and planning to Director (Commercial) and GM on monthly basis.
- DCM (Marketing) sends market prices and customer requirements to GM on monthly basis.
- DCM (Marketing) sends feedback information to his superior periodically, instructions to his subordinates regularly and views to his colleagues.
- DCM (MMIS) sends daily sales information to RMS / BMS on daily basis. He sends monthly sales to MD monthly basis. He also sends annual performance reports to RMS / BMS on yearly basis.
- Deputy Manager (MKIS) sends daily, weekly and monthly information to RMS/ BMS on daily, weekly and monthly basis.
- Assistant Manager sends status of dispatches and availability of information to ACM on daily basis.

Perception about Information

An inquiry about the availability of information in terms of sufficiency or overload or shortage has revealed that all the respondents with exception of one manager have sufficient information for their effective functioning. Only one manager felt that there is information shortage. The shortage according to him relates to the external information about market developments.

Table 3.2.5 : Perception about Information Received

(N = 11)

Perceptions	*F*	%
Information over load	1	9
Information sufficiency	8	72
Information shortage	2	18

Processing

Evidently, the information related functions of the managers are: File, forward with remarks, decide report and circulate.

General Manager

- He forwards with remarks – Information on sales credits and discounts.
- He circulates performance reports.
- He approves the customers and vendors.
- He collects information to provide status reports to the superiors.
- He receives sales reports from marketing section and he sends monthly sales reports to the superiors.
- He receives global production demand status reports region-/ country-wise from the government and research agencies.

Deputy General Manager

- He reports to General Manager regarding sales credits and discounts.
- He circulates sales information.
- He maintains research information up to date.

Assistant General Manager

- He receives directions from General Manger and Deputy General Manager.
- He receives daily activity reports.
- He sends daily sales report summaries to his superiors.
- He sends report preparation requirements to his subordinates.

Additional Chief Manager

- He supervises the team of marketing managers.
- He receives report summaries from his subordinates.
- He sends summary report to his superiors.
- He sends exceptional reports to his superiors.

Deputy Chief Manager (Marketing)

- He receives materials management reports from transportation.

- He receives production report from PPM (production planning and maintenance).
- He receives sales reports from Branch / regions.
- He sends monthly reports to his superiors.
- He sends requirements dispatch plan to his peers.

Deputy Chief Manager (two) (MMIS):

- He receives mill stock report from mills.
- He receives sales report from regions.
- He receives production report from PPM.
- He receives BSY stock report from BCSY.
- He receives sales report from head quarters.
- He sends daily reports to 14 addresses (Regional managers and Branch managers).
- He sends monthly reports to 10 addresses (Regional managers and Branch managers).
- He sends DCIS (Development Commission for Iran and Steel) report to JPC (joint plant committee), Calcutta.

Deputy Manager

- He receives mill stock report from mills.
- He receives sales report from regions, production report from PPM.
- He receives BSY stock report from BCSY.
- He receives sales report from head quarters.
- He sends daily reports to 14 addresses.
- He sends monthly reports to 10 addresses.
- He sends JPC reports to JPC
- He sends DCIS report to JPC (joint plant committee), Calcutta.
- He sends ministerial report to steel ministry.

Assistant Manger

- He receives sales reports from MIS.
- He receives production report from plant.
- He receives inventory reports.
- He sends dispatch and dispatch planning report to peers and superiors.

When asked about the necessity of the existing reports, the respondents felt that all of them are necessary. When inquired about the need for any new reports, they said the existing reports are adequate to meet their present and future requirements.

Marketing Intelligence

Marketing intelligence requires exposure to mass media and attendance at seminars and conferences and workshops. Such an exposure is very low. Table 3.2.6 shows particulars :

Table 3.2.6 : Conferences / Workshops Attended by the Respondents (N = 11)

Year	Conference	Workshop	Seminar	Others	F	%
1998		1	-	-	1	9
1999		1	-	-	1	9
2000	1	-	-	-	1	9
2001	1	-	-	-	1	9

Table 3.2.7 shows the different sources of information used by the managers to keep them update. They are newspapers, journals, internet, discussion with company personnel and persons belonging to other companies. The other sources are T.V. news and programs (90.9%), conferences and workshops / seminars.

Table 3.2.7 : Sources of Information Used To Keep Updated **(N = 11)**

Source	F	%
Discussion with company personnel	10	90.9
Discussion with other company personnel	9	81.8
T. V. news and programs	10	90.9
Conference / Workshops / Seminars	8	72.7
News papers/ Journals	11	100
Internet	7	63.6

Marketing Research

Marketing research is considered fairly important for effective decision-making by the respondents. It is conducted frequently for the purpose of decision-making. Table 3.2.8 shows the details :

Table 3.2.8 : Use of Marketing Research in Decision-Making
(N = 11)

Factors	Mean	SD
Importance	2.2	2.1
Frequency	2.2	2.1

SYSTEM EVALUATION

The system effectiveness is evaluated based on the views of respondent managers as follows:

- System management evaluation
- Information system evaluation
- People evaluation
- Outcomes evaluation
- Overall evaluation

System Management Evaluation

The system management is analysed with reference to the following factors:

- Leadership
- Plans
- Controls
- Security and
- Change

Table 3.2.9 shows the responses signifying system management factors. According to it, the 85.5% of the respondents are of the view that, system is flexible and adaptive; leadership is good (81.8%), plans are effective (81.8%). About 93% of the respondents opined that security of the system is very good. Controls are effective according to 74% of the respondents. System has change characteristics according to 89.2% of the respondents.

Table 3.2.9 : Systems Management Evaluation

(N = 11)

S.No	Factor	Average Score	
		Frequency	%
1	Leadership	9.0	81.8
2	Plans	9.8	89.2
3	Controls	8.1	74.1
4	Security	10.2	93.1
5	Change	9.8	89.2

Leadership

The marketing information system in the organisation is under the direction of a qualified manager. The management is ably motivating its personnel to effectively provide information service. There are training programs for employees which they considered necessary. About 81.8% of the respondents felt that the management is not effective in motivating them. Table 3.2.10 shows the details.

Table 3.2.10 : Systems Management evaluation–Leadership

(N = 11)

No.	Factors	F	%
1.	Is the MKIS is under the direction of qualified manager (specify)?	10	90.9
2.	Does management motivate its personnels to effectively provide Desired information service?	10	90.9
3.	Is there a formal training program where it is deemed necessary?		
(i)	New employees?	9	81.8
(ii)	Transferred employees?	7	63.6
(iii)	Regular employees?	9	91.8

Plans

According to 90% of the respondents, the master plan of marketing information system is well defined and integrated with departmental long range plans and organisational objectives. Also the marketing information system plan is well integrated with procedures and standards. Top management, the management steering committee and information system management periodically review the master plan. Table 3.2.11 shows the details.

Table 3.2.11 : Systems management Evaluation – Plans

(N = 11)

No.		Factors	F	%
1.		Does the management have a well defined master plan for MKIS?	8	72.7
2.		Is the master plan an integrated one?		
	(i)	Objectives	10	90.9
	(ii)	Strategies	9	81.8
	(iii)	Projects	10	90.9
	(iv)	Policies	10	90.9
	(v)	Procedures	10	90.9
	(vi)	Standards	10	90.9
3		Are department long range plans related to organisational objectives?	11	100
4.		Is the master plan subjected to periodic review?		
	(i)	Top management?	11	100
	(ii)	Management steering committee?	8	72.7
	(iii)	Information systems management	11	100

Controls

The following IS control measures are considered effective by all the respondents. According to them:

- Management exercises the necessary controls over its operations.

- Management has segregated the functions of the department in order to minimise fraud, theft and irregularities.
- Provision for back-up personnel in key information systems positions is created.
- Internal auditing periodically checks operations of IS department.
- System has powerful air conditioning environment which is adequate.
- There are limited audits (internal) to check irregularities.

However, the senior management has pointed out the following:

- There is no external, independent auditing of the system.
- The system procedures and documents are not kept current.

Table 3.2.12 : Systems Management Evaluation – Control

(N = 11)

No.	Factors	F	%
1.	Does management exercise the necessary control over its operations so that fraud, theft, and irregularities of IS methods and procedures can be detected?	9	81.8
2.	Does management segregate the functions of the department in order to minimise fraud, theft, and irregularities?	9	81.8
3.	Are there provisions for back up personnel in key information systems positions?	9	81.8
4.	Does internal auditing periodically check on the operations of the information system department?	9	81.8
5.	Is the information system audited periodically by an independent third party (outside auditors or consultants)?	9	81.8
6.	Is there a surprise audit of the information systems department for detecting?		

[contd...]

No.	Factors	F	%
(i)	Fraud?	6	54.5
(ii)	Theft?	6	54.5
(iii)	Collusion?	6	54.5
(iv)	Embezzlement?	6	54.5
(v)	Sabotage?	6	54.5
(vi)	Irregularities?	8	72.7
(vii)	Does the computer system have adequately powered air condition?	11	100
7.	Are systems and procedure manuals kept current?	4	36.3

Security

All the respondents felt that security controls are required by IS management. The security measures are well-designed and implemented in the organisation. There are sufficient security controls to ensure that all input data and corrections to them are processed properly and accurately. However, some of the respondents are of the view that security manuals are not available. Table 3.2.13 furnishes the information :

Table 3.2.13 : Systems Management Evaluation–Security
(N = 11)

No.	Factors	F	%
1	Are security controls required by information systems management?	11	100
2	Are security controls fully understood and implemented by systems and programming personnel?	11	100
3.	Are security controls sufficient to ensure that all input data and corrections to data have been processed properly and accurately?	10	90.9
4.	Are security controls written and contained in appropriate system and procedure manuals for ready reference when necessary?	9	81.8

Change Management

According to Table 3.2.14 the system is perceived by respondents as change oriented. A control mechanism with well-designed procedures is set up in the organisation. It functions by seeking approvals of top management. The change plans are well documented including the reasons for changes. The users are involved in the change process. Written memoranda are issued to the appropriate personnel concerned. Auditors are also apprised of the important changes. During the change process, effective control systems to prevent unauthorised changes in the master files and transaction files are also established. On the whole, the marketing information system is dynamic and adaptative.

Table 3.2.14 : System Management Evaluation–Change Management
(N = 11)

No.	Factors	F	%
1.	Is there a control mechanism for making appropriate information systems changes?	11	100
2.	Does this control mechanism include a provision for approval?	10	90.9
3.	Are procedures established for making?		
(i)	System changes	9	81.8
(ii)	Program changes	11	100
(iii)	Library (Program & file) changes	11	100
(iv)	Computer operator charges	9	81.8
4.	Are all system and program changes immediately documented, including the reason for the changes?	11	100
5.	Are written memoranda issued to the appropriate personnel concerning changes?	11	100
6.	Is the user involved in making changes where necessary?	11	100
7.	Are the internal and external auditors apprised of important changes?	6	54.5
8.	Are master files and transaction files controlled to prevent unauthorised changes during conversion?	8	72.7

Information System Evaluation

Table 3.2.15 shows system related appraisal. The respondents have given positive scores for system, software, documentation, maintenance and integration.

Table 3.2.15 : Evaluation of Information System

(N=11)

Elements	Mean	SD
Hardware	3.7	2.0
Software	3.8	1.9
Documentation	3.8	2.6
Maintenance	4.5	3.0
Integration	3.9	1.7
Total Average	3.9	2.2

Element-wise evaluation of the system is provided in table 3.2.16.

Table 3.2.16 : Evaluation of Information System–System Elements

(N = 11)

No.	Factors	Mean	SD
	Hardware :		
1.	The response of the system is fast	3.6	2.1
2.	Accessing information is easy	3.7	2.4
4.	System security is very good	3.4	2.6
5.	In realisation of user needs, the system is the best	3.3	2.8
6.	The system has good flexibility	3.6	1.6
7.	Information processing is efficient	3.3	2.8
8.	Computer systems are adequate	3.0	2.2
	Total Average :	3.4	2.6

[contd...]

[contd...]

No.	Factors	Mean	SD
	Software :		
1.	Features used in programming languages are excellent.	3.5	2.6
2.	Data analysis programs are updated.	3.1	2
	Total Average	3.4	2.3
	Documentation :		
1.	Documentation if the system is completed.	3.4	2.4
	Maintenance :		
1.	The system is well maintained.	3.3	2.8
	Integrated :		
1.	The system is integrated with other systems.		
2.	There is coordination between MKIS and other systems.	3.5	2.6
Total Average		2.5	2.6

People Evaluation

Table 3.2.17 shows people element of system evaluation. The respondents have rated good aspects like top management support, I.T. staff competence and support and user involvement and utilisation of the system. Element-wise evaluation of the system is provided in table 3.2.18.

Table 3.2.17 : People Evaluation

(N=11)

Element	Mean	SD
Top management	4.0	2.4
IS staff	4.0	2.4
Total average	4.0	2.4

Table 3.2.18 : People evaluation Details
(N=11)

No.	Factors	Mean	SD
	Top Management :		
1.	Top management is involved in the development of the system.	4.0	2.5
	IS Staff :		
1.	The staff in the organisation like to use the system.	4.1	2.6
2.	IS staff are competent.	3.9	2.2
	Total Average :	4.0	2.4

Outcomes Evaluation

The different outcomes of a system like information quality, output, user friendliness, decision support, benefits and satisfaction are evaluated by the respondents. The results are shown in table 3.2.19. According to it, the system is good in all respects, particularly, the benefits.

Table 3.2.19 : System Evaluation–Outcomes
(N=11)

Aspect	Mean	SD
Information	3.5	2.1
Output	3.3	2.1
User friendliness	4.0	1.7
Decision Support	3.5	2.1
Benefits	3.7	2.8
Satisfaction	3.5	2.7

Information and Output

Table 3.2.20 shows that information available from the system is good in content, relevance, accuracy and timeliness. However, the respondents are less happy about the output in respect of the volume.

But they are happy that the reports and other information products are well scheduled.

Table 3.2.20 : Evaluation of System Outcomes–Information and Output

(N=11)

No.	Factors	Mean	SD
	Information :		
1.	Computer systems are capable	3.3	2.8
2.	Information is relevant	3.3	2.8
3.	Information is kept confidential when required	3.3	2.2
4.	Information provided by the system is accurate	3.9	2.4
5.	System provides timely information	3.6	2.8
6.	System furnishes exact information	3.2	2.7
7.	The information provided is reliable	3.7	2.4
8.	Current information is provided by the system	3.8	3.4
9.	The information is complete in all aspects	3.4	2.6
10.	It provides well-designed formats	4.1	2.0
11.	Information furnished has clarity	4.1	2.0
	Total average	3.5	2.1
	Output :		
1.	The reports and other information products are well-scheduled	3.5	2.7
2.	Adequate volume of output is generated by the system	3.0	1.7
	Total Average :	3.3	2.2

User Friendliness

Table 5.2.21 shows the user friendliness of the system. The aspects like training, and user involvement in system development and implementation, and user confidence of the system are rated good.

Table 3.21 : Evaluation of System Outcomes–User friendliness (N=11)

No.	Factors	Mean	SD
1.	User are well trained to use the system	3.9	1.8
2.	The system is used by all concerned employees	3.8	1.4
3.	There is participation of users in the system development and instrumentation	3.9	1.8
4.	Users have confidence in the system	4.5	1.9
	Total average :	4.0	1.7

Decision Support

According to the respondents, the system is fairly helpful on an average to the managers in making decisions relating to product and price. It is also helpful in the market analysis and forecasting, place and promotion decisions. Table 3.2.22 shows the details:

Table 3.2.22 : Evaluation of System Outcomes–Decision Support (N=11)

Factors	Mean	SD
Market analysis and forecasting	3.4	1.9
Product decisions	3.7	2.4
Price decisions	3.7	2.4
Place decisions	4.0	1.9
Promotion decisions	3.8	2.0

Benefits and Satisfaction

Table 3.2.23 shows that the respondents are pleased with the benefits of the system. They considered it beneficial (3.9). They agreed with the statement : "The system has tools to improve productivity of operations." They have also accepted that their jobs have become easy and efficient. The respondents have expressed satisfaction with the system (3.8).

Table 3.2.23 : Evaluation of System Outcomes–Benefits and Satisfaction

(N=11)

No.	Factors	Mean	SD
	Benefits :		
1.	The system has tools to improve productivity of operations.	3.9	2.2
2.	My job has become easy with the support of the system.	3.6	2.2
3.	MKIS has improved the results of the organisation.	4.0	1.8
4.	MKIS is making the activities more efficient.	4.0	2.1
5.	MKIS has boosted the profits of organisation.	3.9	1.7
6.	My expectations of benefits of system are realised.	4.0	2.1
	Total average :	3.9	2.0
	Satisfaction :		
1.	The system is satisfactory to me.	3.7	1.4

Overall Evaluation

The respondents are asked to evaluate the present marketing information system in the organisation on a 5-point scale representing exceptional and poor at the polar points. The system is considered good by majority of the respondents. Table 3.2.24 shows the details:

Table 3.2.24 : Overall Evaluation of Information System

(N=11)

Factor	Mean	SD
Present marketing information system	3.7	2.0

3.3 MARKETING INFORMATION SYSTEM IN ASSOCIATED CEMENT COMPANIES LIMITED (ACC)

Introduction

Associated Cement Companies Limited was established in 1936. The company has always sought to produce market premium quality products to fulfill the diverse needs of various consumers including individuals, corporates and institutions. Towards this end, it has developed a remarkable range of cements and cementation products fully confirming to the highest standards of quality. With a view to gaining a competitive edge, it is leveraging its brand equity and has recently promoted certain premium products like 'ACC SURAKHSA', 'ACC SUPER' and 'ACC SAMRAT'. Besides, most of the company's manufacturing units have been awarded ISO 9000 certificates with regard to quality accreditation.

The company takes great pains to ensure that the customer gets the cement when and where he wants it. In addition to a network of over 10,000 dealers and sub-dealers, the company has established customer service cells at all its sales outlets. These cells are not just a re-assurance to the customer in terms of after sales service or trouble shooting, but also offer advice in selection of the type of cement to be used for a particular application, the correct concrete mix design and other aspects that help to achieve quality constructions. These services underscore ACC's priority commitment to the customer, in the belief that a satisfied customer returns to the source of his satisfaction.

Information Technology and Communication

The company's refractory division was one of the first in the country to introduce state of the art SAP R3 Enterprise Resource Planning (ERP) systems with all functional modules going on line. The company is also one the of first to have the largest Microsoft Exchange site in India, in terms of the vast number of 31 locations covering its VSAT network ensuring effective voice and data communication.

ACC is continually endeavoring to improve upon its operating parameters and to institute the best corporate practices. It is aiming to focus on the needs of its customers and how best to continually provide and add value to this relationship and evolve an appropriate total organisation strategy that will carry it successfully to the next millennium and the challenges thereafter.

Future Plans–Cement Business

In line with the growth of cement market, ACC will be adding capacity in strategic markets to maintain its leadership in the company's core business. Continuing emphasis on better supply chain management and streamlining of distribution logistics is expected to yield substantial gains due to the freight intensive nature of the business. Effective management and promotion of the company's strong brands are expected to continue to yield a premium for its products in each of the markets where it operates.

Internal Control Systems

The company has a management audit team comprising finance/engineering professionals commensurate with the size of the company who visit all the units and carry out extensive audit of the units and ensure that laid down systems and procedures are followed and who assist the management in review of operation.

The company has a sound budgetary control system in force. There is monthly comparison of actual and budgeted costs and performance measurement and any variations are being scrutinised with a view to taking concrete action and to improve performance. The company also has separate budgets for all revenue expenditure heads for each unit as well as for the corporate office and these are reviewed by the management every month.

The company conducts systems audit from external agencies from time to time to validate their adequacy and security. This exercise was last done after the company achieved complete Y2K compliance in all its systems, hardware and software. It was recommended that these systems be revised to take full advantage of latest technological developments. A complete and detailed systems of upgradation plan is currently under implementation.

Business Locations

Corporate Office: Cement House, Mumbai, Maharashtra.

Regional Offices: Ahmedabad, Bangalore, Bhopal, Kolkata, Chandigarh, Coimbatore, Kanpur, Mumbai, New Delhi, Patna and Secunderabad.

Marketing Organisation

The marketing organisation is headed by the Vice-President. He coordinates the marketing activity. He is assisted by Regional

Manager who in turn supervises a team consisting of Area Managers, Branch Managers, Deputy Managers, Managers, Assistant Managers and Officers.

Marketing Information System

Marketing information system was computerised in the year 1998. The reasons for setting up of computerised marketing information system :

- Early adaptation of new technology
- To make complex decision easy
- To monitor the global business

Objectives Served

The identified principal benefits of marketing information system :

1. Helps improve decision-making by furnishing quality information.
2. Helps in better coordination by integrating various departments.
3. Helps in generating a variety of reports.

Other benefits are:

1. Keeps a general database for accessing around when required.
2. Makes planning and controlling effective through analysis and reports.
3. Increases profits by improving performance.

The company is working on the software state of the art technology SAP R3 ENTERPRISE RESOURCE PLANNING (ERP) system with all functional modules going on line. The company is also one of the first to have the largest Microsoft Exchange site in India in terms of the vast number of 31 locations covering its VSAT Network ensuring effective voice and data communication.

About the System

There are adequate number of computers one per each with suitable configuration for implementing SAP R2 ERP System. The marketing wing has about 30 to 40 employees at regional level. Need based consultancy is sought from the local consulting firms. Users are trained to provide skill in using "Windows", E-mail, voice mail, data communication and SAP R3 Modules etc.

Reports

The main reports generated for decision-making include:

- Daily activity report
- Sales reports
- Competition report
- Daily collections report
- Price trend analysis report
- Daily retailers report
- Daily site report
- Previous day sales reports
- Previous day stock report
- Previous day outstanding report
- Area-wise and region-wise sales reports
- Agent-wise sales
- Purchase and procurement report
- Market research report
- Distribution report
- Financial report

Evaluation

The present system is considered good as it meets even future requirements.

Profile of Respondents

Table 3.3.1 describes the profile of the respondents from the organisation. The respondents include Regional Manager, Deputy Manager, Manager, Branch Manager, and Assistant Managers. Experience-wise, 85% of the respondent group has less than 10 years experience. Level-wise it can be observed that about 57% of them are at middle management, 14% at senior management and 28% at junior management level.

Table 3.3.1 : Profile of Respondents
(N = 14)

S.No.	Elements	F	%
1.	**Designation :**		
	Regional Manager (marketing)	1	7.1
	Branch Manager (Marketing)	1	7.1
	Deputy Manager (Marketing)	1	7.1
	Assistant Manager	1	7.1
2.	**Experience (years) :**		
	Below 10 years	12	85.7
	10 years and above	2	14.2
3.	**Level in hierarchy :**		
	Senior	2	14.2
	Middle	8	57.1
	Junior	4	28.5

Table 3.3.2 shows the reporting relationships. Regional Manager reports to Vice President (Marketing). The Branch Manager to Regional Manager and Deputy Manager and Assistant Managers report to Managers. All the respondents have subordinate positions as shown in Table 3.3.2 :

Table 3.3.2 : Reporting Relationships of Respondents
(N = 14)

Reporting to :	F	%
Director (Marketing)	1	7.1
Regional Manager (Marketing)	1	7.1
Branch Manager	13	92.8
Deputy manager	12	85.7
Assistant Manager	-	-

[contd...]

[contd...]

Reporting to :	F	%
Subordinate positions under Respondents		
Regional Manager (Marketing) : Branch Manager, Regional Manager, Deputy Manager	3	21.4
Regional Manager : Deputy Manager, Assistant Managers, Officers	13	92.8
Deputy Manager : Assistant Managers, Officers & Senior Officers	12	85.7
Assistant Managers : Officers and Senior Officers	-	-

The respondents did not provide job descriptions but informed the researcher that they are concerned with all functions of marketing which include:

Advertising, Marketing Research, Brand Management, Brand Promotion, Dealer Management, Collections, Warehouse Activities, Sales, Receivables, Channel Management and Supply Chain management.

Role Clarity

Respondents were asked to identify their levels of clarity about the roles they play in the organisation. The role clarity is measured on a 5-point scale–5 representing very much and 1 indicating very less. The responses indicate that they are very much clear about their roles. A mean score of 3.9 to 4.7 overall and item-wise statements are shown in Table 3.3.3 :

Table 3.3.3 : Perceived Role Clarity of Respondents (N = 14)

Perceptions	Mean	SD
My role is clear to me	4.7	4.2
I do not have conflicts in my playing my role (No over-lapping)	3.9	2.4
My authority is clear to me	4.3	3.4
My relations with others are well-defined	4.5	3.4
I was told clearly about my responsibility (What I have to contribute)	4.5	3.4
Overall	4.0	3.3

Decision-Making

Table 3.3.4 shows that they are mostly dependent upon their superiors (3.5) and less on subordinates (2.3) and peers (2.2). The respondents have observed that they make use of most of standard techniques for key decisions as well as routine decisions.

Table 3.3.4 : Dependence in Decision-Making and Implementation

(N = 14)

Positions	**Mean**	**SD**
On superiors	3.5	3.4
On subordinates	2.3	3.6
On peers	2.2	2.4

Information Flow

The information flows to the different persons in the hierarchy of marketing is as follows:

- Regional Manager receives information pertaining to future plans from the Vice-President (Marketing) on a daily basis. He receives sales and competitors' information daily from Branch Managers and Deputy Managers and Managers.
- Branch Manager receives information regarding daily activities from Regional Managers.
- Deputy Manager receives information on price, CMA from Manager (Marketing) and sales and collections from Assistant Manager on daily basis. He also receives marketing information from Officer / Junior / Senior Officers for every 2 days and market information from Assistant Managers thrice a week.
- Assistant Manager receives plans and feed back information from Deputy Manager on daily basis. They receive market information from Application Engineer on hourly basis. They also receive market information from colleagues on daily basis. Assistant managers receive information on price and price changes from Deputy Manager weekly / fortnightly. They receive price / payments and market information from officers daily.

Reports

- Regional Manager receives sales reports, competition reports, customer report, dealers and distributor's reports, collection and payments, and market research reports from his subordinates, branch managers, deputy managers, and managers. He considers all the reports are necessary for his effective functioning in the organisation.
- Deputy Manager receives sales report from warehouse, and competition report and market information from Assistant Manager / Officer. He observes that the reports are necessary to effective discharge of his job in the organisation.
- Deputy Manager sends sales reports, collection reports, competition report and market information to Vice-President (Marketing) / Regional Manager.
- Assistant Manager receives daily reports, price and trend analysis, daily retailers report and daily site report from application engineer / officer. He also receives daily collection, past sales, stocks and outstanding reports from warehouse.
- Assistant Managers send daily report to Deputy Manager and sales, collection and price trends to Deputy Manager. They also send weekly reports to Regional Manager and monthly reports to Manager (marketing). According to them all the reports are necessary.

Perception about Information

An inquiry about the availability of information in terms of sufficiency or overload or shortage has revealed that all the respondents with the exception of three Managers have sufficient information for their effective functioning. Only three managers felt that there is information shortage. The shortage according to them relates to the external information about market developments.

Table 3.3.5 : Perception about Information Received
(N = 14)

Perceptions	F	%
Information over load	0	0
Information sufficiency	11	78.5
Information shortage	3	21.4

Processing

Evidently the information related major functions of the managers are:

Regional Manager

- He forwards with remarks, reports on sales, credits and discounts.
- He decides and approves list of dealers.
- He collects information to provide status reports and monthly sales reports to the Vice President (Marketing).
- He circulates performance reports and global production demand status reports etc.

Deputy Manager

- He forwards with remarks reports to his superiors as well as subordinates as and when necessary.
- He decides and approves the list of reports prepared by subordinates.
- He reports to the superiors on sales, collection, payments, etc.
- He circulates performance and status reports.

Branch Manager

- He forwards with remarks area-wise sales.
- He decides the list of dealer to get approved by his superiors.
- He reports to the superiors as regards sales, collections, stock position, Market information etc.
- He circulates status and performance reports.

Assistant Managers

- They file whatever information they got and forward information with remarks.
- They decide to whom information need to be sent.
- They report to the concerned managers.
- They circulate reports as and when necessary.

Marketing Intelligence

What are the sources of marketing intelligence? Table 3.3.6 shows the participation details of respondents in conferences and workshops. From the table, it can be observed that their participation is very less:

Table 3.3.6 : Conferences / Workshops Attended by the Respondents (N = 14)						
Year	Conference	Workshop	Seminar	Others	F	%
1998	1	-	-	-	1	7.1
1999	1	-	-	-	1	7.1
2000	1	-	-	-	1	7.1
2001	1	-	-	-	1	7.1

Table 3.3.7 shows the respondents use different sources of information. They include newspapers, journals, internet and discussion with company personnels and also with peers belonging to other companies. The other sources are T.V. news and programs. However, two of them said that they use internet less and attend conferences and workshops rarely. The two less users belong to lower management level.

Table 3.3.7 : Source of Information Used To Keep Updated (N = 14)

Source	F	%
Discussion with company personnel	14	100
Discussion with other company personnel	14	100
T. V. news and programs	14	100
Conference / Workshops / Seminars	8	57.1
News papers/ Journals	14	100
Internet	4	28.5

Marketing Research

Marketing research is considered very important for effective decision-making by the respondents. According to the respondents, it is conducted frequently for the purpose of decision-making. Table 3.3.8 shows the details:

Table 3.3.8 : Use of Marketing Research in Decision-Making (N = 14)		
Factors	**Mean**	**SD**
Importance	3.6	2.92
Frequency	3.2	2.92

System Evaluation

The system effectiveness is evaluated based on the views of respondent managers as follows:

1. System management evaluation
2. Information system evaluation
3. People evaluation
4. Outcomes evaluation
5. Overall evaluation

System Management Evaluation

The system management is analysed with reference to five factors:

- Leadership
- Plans
- Controls
- Security and
- Change

Table 3.3.9 : Systems Management Evaluation (N = 14)			
S.No	**Factor**	**Average Score**	
		Frequency	**%**
1	Leadership	9.80	69.94
2	Plans	10.00	62.96
3	Controls	10.70	76.37
4	Security	9.75	69.8
5	Change	11.36	82.63
	Average	10.32	72.14

Table 3.3.9 shows the responses signifying system management factors. According to it, 72% of the respondents are of the view that system is flexible and adaptive. Leadership is good and plans are effective. About 69.8% of the respondents opined that security provisions of the system are good. Controls are effective according to 76.3% of the respondents.

Leadership

The marketing information system is supervised by a qualified manager. The management is motivating competently its personnel to provide effective information service. Training programs are conducted for employees to enhance usage.

Table 3.3.10 : Systems Management Evaluation–Leadership

(N = 14)

No.	Factors	F	%
	Leadership		
1.	Is the MKIS under the direction of qualified manager? (specify)	14	100
2.	Does management motivate its personnels to effectively provide the Desired information service?	11	78.5
3.	Is there a formal training program where deemed necessary?		
(i)	New employees?	11	78.5
(ii)	Transferred employees?	2	14.2
(iii)	Regular employees?	11	78.5

Plans

About 62.9% of the respondents have opined that master plan of marketing information system is well defined. Also it is integrated properly with departmental long range plans and organisational objectives. According to them the marketing information system plan is well established with defined procedures and standards. Top management, the management steering committee and information system management review the master plan periodically. Table 3.3.11 shows the details :

Table 3.3.11 : Systems management details–Plans
(N = 14)

No.	Factors	F	%
1.	Does the management have a well defined master plan for MKIS?	12	85.7
2.	Is the master plan integrated with the following ?		
(i)	Objectives	10	7.1.4
(ii)	Strategies	9	64.2
(iii)	Projects	5	35.7
(iv)	Policies	7	50
(v)	Procedures	13	92.8
(vi)	Standards	13	92.8
3	Are departments long range plans related to organisational objectives?	13	92.8
4.	Is the master plan subjected to periodic review?		
(i)	Top management	14	100
(ii)	Management steering committee	7	50
(iii)	Information systems management	7	50

Controls

The following IS control measures are considered effective by all the respondents:

- Management exercises the necessary control over Its operations so that fraud, theft, and irregularities of IS methods and procedures can be detected.
- Management has segregated the functions of the department in order to minimise fraud, theft and irregularities.
- Provision for back-up personnel in key information systems positions is created.
- There are surprise audits (internal) to check irregularities.
- The systems and procedure manuals are not kept current.

However, the senior management has pointed out the following:

1. There is no external, independent auditing of the system.
2. System needs powerful air-conditioning unit.

Table 3.3.12 : Systems Management Details–Control (N = 14)

No.		Factors	F	%
1.		Does management exercise the necessary control over its operations so that fraud, theft, and irregularities of IS methods and procedures can be detected?	10	71.4
2.		Does management segregate the functions of the department in order to minimise fraud, theft, and irregularities?	11	78.4
3.		Is there a provision for backup personnel in key information systems positions?	6	42.8
4.		Does internal auditing periodically check on the operations of the information systems department?	14	100
5.		Is the information system audited periodically by an independent third party (outside auditors or consultants)	11	100
6.		Is there a surprise audit of the information systems department for detecting?		
	(i)	Fraud?	14	100
	(ii)	Theft?	12	85.7
	(iii)	Collusion?	13	92.8
	(iv)	Embezzlement?	12	85.7
	(v)	Sabotage?	9	64.2
	(vi)	Irregularities?	11	78.5
	(vi)	Does the computer system have adequately powered aircondition?	6	42.8
7.		Are systems and procedure manuals kept current?	11	78.5

Security

Majority of the respondents felt that security controls are required by IS management. The security measures are well-designed and implemented in the organisation. The security controls are sufficient to ensure that all input data and corrections to them are processed properly and accurately. Table 3.3.13 furnishes the details:

Table 3.3.13 : Systems Management–Security

(N = 14)

No.	Factors	F	%
1	Are security controls required by information systems management?	12	85.7
2	Are security controls fully understood and implemented by systems and programming personnel?	11	78.5
3.	Are security controls sufficient to ensure that all input data and corrections to data have been processed properly and accurately?	8	57.5
4.	Are security controls written and contained in appropriate systems and procedure manuals for ready reference when necessary?	8	57.5

Change Management

According to the respondents the system is flexible and sensitive to change. According to them :

- There is a control mechanism for making appropriate information system changes.
- The control mechanism includes a provision for approval from top management.
- The procedures are established for making system changes, program changes, library (program and file) changes and computer operator changes.
- The changes are documented including reasons for changing.
- A written memorandum is issued to the appropriate personnel concerning changes.

- The users are involved in making changes where necessary.
- Master files and transaction files are controlled to prevent unauthorised changes during conversion.

Table 3.3.14 : System Management Evaluation–Change Management

(N = 14)

No.		Factors	F	%
1..		Is there a control mechanism for making appropriate information systems changes?	14	100
2.		Does this control mechanism include a provision for approval?	13	92.8
3.		Are procedures established for making?	10	71.4
	(i)	System changes?		
	(ii)	Program changes?	9	64.2
	(iii)	Library (Program & file) changes?	14	100
	(iv)	Computer operator changes?	11	78.5
4.		Are all system and program changes immediately documented, including the reason for the changes?	12	85.7
5.		Are written memoranda issued to the appropriate personnel concerning changes?	12	85.7
6.		Is the user involved in making changes where necessary?	11	78.5
7.		Are the internal and external auditors apprised of important changes?	8	57.5
8.		Are master files and transaction files controlled to prevent unauthorised changes during conversion?	11	78.5

Information System Evaluation

Table 3.3.15 shows system related appraisal. The respondents have given positive scores for hardware, software, documentation, maintenance and integration of the other systems. The mean scores are in the range of 3.0 to 3.6. Element-wise evaluation of the system is provided in table 3.1.16.

Table 3.3.15 : Evaluation of Information System
(N=14)

Elements	Mean	SD
Hardware	3.08	3.76
Software	3.35	4.26
Documentation	3.14	3.48
Maintenance	3.35	2.92
Integration	3.67	3.59
Total average :	3.31	3.60

Table 3.3.16 : Evaluation of Information System–System Elements (N = 14)

No.	Factors	Mean	SD
	Hardware :		
1.	The response of the system is fast	4.0	5.6
2.	Accessing information is easy	3.7	4.2
3.	System security is very good	3.7	2.9
4.	In realisation of user needs, the system is the best	3.1	2.4
5.	The system has good flexibility	3.3	4.2
6.	Information processing is efficient	3.3	2.9
7.	Computer systems are adequate	4.2	3.9
	Total Average :	3.0	3.7
	Software :		
1.	Features used in programming languages are excellent	2.7	2.9
2.	Data analysis programs are updated	3.3	4.2
	Total Average :	3.0	3.5

[contd...]

[contd...]

No.	Factors	Mean	SD
	Documentation :		
1.	Documentation if the system is completed	3.1	3.4
	Maintenance :		
1.	The system is well-maintained	3.3	2.9
	Integrated :		
1.	The system is integrated with other systems.	4.0	2.9
2.	There is coordination between MKIS and other systems	3.3	4.2
	Average Total :	3.6	3.5

People Evaluation

Table 3.3.17 show the evaluation of people elements of system. The respondents have given an overall rating of 3.7. The aspects like top management support, IT staff competence and support and user involvement, training and utilisation of the system are rated good. Element-wise evaluation of the system is provided in table 3.1.18.

Table 3.3.17 : People Evaluation

(N=14)

Element	Mean	SD
Top management	4.1	2.9
IS staff	3.6	2.7
Total average	3.8	2.8

Table 3.3.18 : People Evaluation Details

(N=14)

No.	Factors	Mean	SD
	Top management :		
1.	Top management is involved in the development of the system	4.1	2.9
	IS Staff :		
2.	The staff in the organisation like to use the system	3.7	2.9
3.	IS staff are competent	3.6	2.7
	Total Average :	3.6	2.7

Outcomes Evaluation

The different outcomes of a system like Information quality, output, user friendliness, decision support, benefits and satisfaction are evaluated by the respondents. The results are shown in table 3.3.19. According to it, the system is good in all the respects particularly, the benefits.

Table: 3.3.19 : Evaluation of System Outcomes

(N=14)

Aspect	Mean	SD
Information	4.6	2.5
Output	4.0	3.1
User friendliness	3.7	2.5
Decision Support	2.4	1.9
Benefits	4.8	3.1
Satisfaction	3.5	3.0

Information and Output

Table 3.3.20 shows that information available from the system is relevant (3.8) accurate, timely etc. The respondents are also happy about the output in respect of volume and frequency.

Table 3.3.20 : Evaluation of System Outcomes–Information and Output

(N=14)

No.	Factors	Mean	SD
	Information :		
1.	Computer systems are capable	4.0	3.3
2.	Information is relevant	4.4	3.4
3.	Information is kept confidential when required	4.0	3.8
4.	Information provided by the system is accurate	4.6	3.6
5.	System provides timely information	4.6	3.6

[contd...]

[contd...]

No.	Factors	Mean	SD
6.	System furnishes exact information	4.2	3.8
7.	The information provided is reliable	4.2	4.2
8.	Current information is provided by the system	4.6	3.6
9.	The information is complete in all aspects	4.1	3.7
10.	It provides well designed formats	3.5	3.4
11.	Information furnished has clarity	4.2	2.4
	Total average :	3.8	3.9
Output			
1.	The reports and other information products are well scheduled	3.7	2.9
2.	Adequate volume of output is generated by the system	3.9	2.7
	Total Average :	3.8	2.8

User Friendliness

Table 5.2.21 shows the details about user friendliness of the system. The system is considered user friendly.

Table 3.3.21 : Evaluation of System Outcomes–User Friendliness (N=14)

Sl.No	Factors	Mean	SD
1.	Users are well trained to use the system	3.7	2.9
2.	The system is used by all concerned employees	3.7	2.4
3.	There is participation of users in the system development and instrumentation	3.5	1.9
4.	Users have confidence in the system	4.0	2.9
	Total average :	3.7	2.5

Decision Support

According to the respondents the system is less helpful on an average to the managers in making decisions relating to product, price and place. It is fairly helpful in the market analysis and forecasting and promotion decisions. Table 3.3.22 shows the details.

Table 3.3.22 : Evaluation of System Outcomes–Decision Support (N=14)

Factors	Mean	SD
Market analysis and forecasting	2.9	2.4
Product decisions	2.2	1.9
Price decisions	2.0	1.8
Place decisions	1.8	1.7
Promotion decisions	3.1	1.9
Average Total :	2.4	1.9

Benefits and Satisfaction

Table 3.3.23 shows that the respondents are benefited from the

Table 3.3.23 : Evaluation of System Outcomes–Benefits and Satisfaction (N=14)

No.	Factors	Mean	SD
1.	The system has tools to improve productivity of operations	3.2	1.7
2.	My job has become easy with the support of the system	3.7	3.8
3.	MKIS has improved the results of the organization	3.7	2.4
4.	MKIS is making the activities more efficient	3.7	2.9
4.	MKIS has boosted the profits of organisation	2.8	3.4
5.	My expectations of benefits of system are realised	4.4	3.4
	Total average	3.5	2.8
	Satisfaction :		
1.	The system is satisfactory to me	3.3	3.2

system. They have agreed very much with the statements. "The system has tools to improve productivity of operations." "Jobs have become easy and efficient" and "Making activity more efficient and boosted the profits." However, when rating the benefits they opined that the expectations are moderately realised. On the whole, the satisfaction with the system is moderate.

Overall Evaluation

The respondents are asked to evaluate the present marketing information system in the organisation on a 5-point scale of exceptional and poor. The system is considered average by majority of the respondents. Table 3.3.24 shows the details :

Table 3.3.24 : Overall Evaluation of Information System (N=14)

Factor	Mean	SD
Present marketing information system	3.1	4.6

3.4. SUMMARY

The three companies under study have established their marketing information systems in 1990s. "To make complex decisions easy" is the stated major goal supported by reasons like– "competitors have set up" and "for early adaptation of new technology." The systems are ERP, Net work and Oracle and SAP R3 ERP. Their future plans are focused on either completing the on going computerisation or maintenance of the designed systems to get the desired results.

As can be observed, various reports are generated. They broadly relate to markets, production and sales. An evaluation of the systems reveals that the respondents have rated their systems in the range of average to good. Systems management is appreciated by a majority of respondents in all the three companies. However, relatively, controls deserve much more attention as fewer respondents have rated them good. Comparatively, less number of respondents in ACC considered system management good.

Information system components (hardware, software, etc.) are rated 'above average' in all the three companies. Top management support and IS people are rated well in VSP. In all other cases the ratings are above average.

Quality of information and output are rated good in ACC. User friendliness is good in VSP. When it comes to benefits of the system, in ACC the respondents have given higher rating of 4.8. In all other cases, the ratings are above average. Only in VSP, one respondent opined information overload. Very few were of the opinion that there was "Information shortage."

The marketing intelligence sources are mainly around newspapers and journals, discussions with employees and others and TV. Internet is used in CPCL. Marketing research in considered important and used as and when necessary.

Evaluation by the spokespersons, indicate that in VSP and CPCL (incidentally, both are public enterprises), development requirements are not considered actively. Even the response to management requirements for modifications is slow and rigid.

4

Marketing Information System in Chemicals Sector

4.1 MARKETING INFORMATION SYSTEM IN NEULAND LABORATORIES LIMITED

Introduction

Neuland Laboratories Limited was established in 1984. The company is highly professional, has an illustrious board ably supported by a committed workforce, staff and managers who are keen to deliver.

Neuland believes the achievement of their goals depends on the results in the following key areas:

- Excellent customer interface.
- Ability to develop and launch innovative products that meet customer expectations.
- Value added solutions for customers.
- Optimise Neuland's product portfolio.
- Broad access to technology.
- A strong global presence.

Products

The product portfolio consists of Anti asthmatics (Albetuarol Sulphate (Salbutamol Sulphate), Terbutalene Sulphate, pratropium Maleate). Cardio-vascular (Enalpril Meleate, Sotalol Hcl, Labetalol Hc, Ramipril). Anti microbial (Ofloxacin, Ciprofloxacin, Enrofloxacin). Anti fungal (Itraconazole). Anti depressant (Mirtazapine) and Anti ulcerant (Ranitidine Hcl)

Marketing

In the last few years, the company received US FADA approvals for Albetural Sulphate and Ranitidine Hydrochloride Form I. Also on hand was European Certificate of suitability for Ranitidine Hydrochloride Form I. Neuland has developed new customers for Europe and USA.

The process of conversion of certificates and approvals into cash takes time. There are necessary formalities, but more important, the signals are encouraging. Customers are filing Abbreviated New Drug Applications (ANDA) with their products. The company hopes for fresh business in 2002–2003.

Discussions are going on for marketing of Albeturol Sulphate. There is encouraging response and samples are getting approved. Amongst other products, they have become the preferred and first supplier for Ciprofloxacin for many customers. The drug master file for this product was reviewed recently and queries were answered. Two customers prefer to use their product and have filed ANDAs in the USA. During the year, production volume was doubled compared to the previous year. Production was increased in 2001–02 for Ciprofloxacin HCL, Ranitidine HCl and Enalapril Maleate. They developed new customers for both the products. Sotalol has become one of their premium products. They are formulating definite business plans for further increasing the market for the products like Sotalol, Ipartropium Bromode, Itraconazole, Enalapril Maleate and Ofloxacin.

The operating profit for 2000–01 was about Rs. 7 crore. In the financial year 2001–02, its turnover went up to Rs. 106 crore, with the operating profit climbing to Rs. 10 crore.

It is the stated policy of the company to outsource early stage intermediates from the market, and use the plant facilities to produce value added products. They undertook several initiatives in R&D. The production and quality parameters were improved. The company has also invested in development work to improve internal process and operations. They developed technologies for Mirtazapine (anti depressant) Olanzapine (anti psychotic), Fluticasone (steroid) and Ramipril (cardio-vascular). Martazapine is being exported. Samples have been sent to test market Olanzapine and Ramipril.

Marketing Organisation

The marketing team of the company is led by General Manager (Marketing). He is assisted by Deputy General Manager who in turn supervises Senior Managers, Managers and Officers.

Marketing Information System

Marketing information system was computerised in the year 1994, for the following two reasons:

- The competitors like Reddy Labs, Biological E Ltd., and others have set up MIS.
- Demand from employees to expand computerisation to different areas.

Objectives Served

The identified principal benefits of marketing information system :

1. Help improve decision-making by furnishing quality information.
2. Help in better coordination by integrating various departments.
3. Help in generating a variety of reports that facilitate better decisions and actions.

The other benefits :

1. Keep a general database for access when required.
2. Make planning and controlling effective through analysis and reports.
3. Increase profits by improving performance.

The company is working on the packages developed by "FOCUS" which is built as per their requirements. The system helps in integrating marketing department with production, research and development, quality control and finance. It provides region-wise market potential and helps develop suitable marketing plan. Also it furnishes sales data analysis and credit control.

About the System

There are more than 25 computers with suitable configurations for implementing "Focus." The marketing information system wing has about 10 employees. Need based consultancy is sought from the local consulting firms. Users are trained to provide skills in using "Windows and Focus."

Reports

The main reports generated for decision-making include:

- Daily activity report
- Sales reports
- Country-wises and product-wise sales (past–present)
- Agent-wise sales (Comparison)
- Product-wise contribution.
- Inventory control reports
- Purchase and procurement report
- Market research report
- Distribution report
- Financial report.

Evaluation

The following inadequacies are identified:

1. The hardware is inadequate to the users
2. Development requirements are not considered actively

System Development (Future Plans)

Though the present system is considered well, it is decided to implement SAP to integrate the developments and meet future requirements.

Profile of Respondents

Table 4.1.1 describes the profile of the respondents from the organisation. The respondents include General Manager, Deputy General Manager, Senior Manager, two Managers, two Assistant Managers and three Officers. Experience-wise the respondent group consists of about 30% decision-makers with more than 10 years of experience, Level-wise; it can be observed that about 30% of them are at the senior management level. The remaining are managers and officers having less than 10 years of experience.

Table 4.1.1 : Profile of Respondents
(N = 10)

S.No.	Elements	F	%
1.	**Designation**		
	General Manager	1	10
	Deputy General Manager	1	10
	Senior Manager	1	10
	Manager	2	20
	Assistant Manager	2	20
	Officers	3	30
2.	**Experience (years)**		
	Less than 10 years	7	70
	10 years and above	3	30
3.	**Level in hierarchy**		
	Senior	3	30
	Junior	7	70

Table 4.1.2 shows the reporting relationships. General Manager (Marketing) reports to Managing Director; the Deputy Manager to General Manager, Senior Manager to Deputy General Manager,

Table 4.1.2 : Reporting Relationships of Respondents
(N = 10)

Reporting to :	F	%
Managing Director	1	10
General Manager	1	10
Deputy General Manager	1	10
Senior Manager	2	20
Manager	3	30
Assistant manager	3	30
Officer	0	0
Subordinate positions under Respondents :		
General Manager	9	90
Deputy General Manager	8	80
Senior Manager	7	70
Manager	5	50
Assistant manager	3	30
Officer	0	0

Managers report to Senior Manager, and officers and Assistant Managers report to Managers. All the respondents except officers have subordinate positions as shown in Table 4.1.2.

Role Clarity

The responses indicate that they are very much clear about their roles. A mean score of 4.8 to 4.6 on overall and item-wise statements as shown in Table 4.1.3.

Table 4.1.3 : Reporting Relationships of Respondents

(N = 10)

Reporting to :	F	%
Managing Director	1	10
General Manager	1	10
Deputy General Manager	1	10
Senior Manager	2	20
Manager	3	30
Assistant manager	3	30
Officer	0	0
Subordinate positions under Respondents :		
General Manager	9	90
Deputy General Manager	8	80
Senior Manager	7	70
Manager	5	50
Assistant manager	3	30
Officer	0	0

Decision Making

To what extent the decision-makers are dependent on superiors and subordinates? Table 4.1.4 shows that they are mostly dependant upon their superiors (4.0) and moderately on subordinates (3.0).

Table 4.1.4 : Dependency in Decision-Making and Implementation (N = 10)

Positions	Mean	SD
On superiors	4.0	3.0
On subordinates	3.0	2.0
On peers	--	--

The respondents have observed that they make use of mostly time series analysis techniques for key decisions as well as routine decisions.

Information Flow

The information flows to the different persons in the hierarchy of marketing is as follows:

- The General Manager receives information pertaining to future plans from the Managing Director on daily basis. He receives sales and competitors information daily from Deputy General Manager and Senior Manager.
- The Deputy General Manager receives from their superiors information inputs on target related information and current marketing strategies. He receives performance reports from his subordinates on a daily basis.
- The Senior Manager receives from their superiors information inputs on current marketing strategy as and when required. From their subordinates he receives day to day sales information.
- The Managers and Officers receive from their superior's information about demand, customer and inventory details. From their subordinates they receive customer orders and payment details.
- General Manager disseminates activity related information to the Managing Director frequently. He also sends frequently to the Deputy General Manager information pertaining to policy-related, objective-oriented and season-related information.

- Deputy General Manager reports to his superiors activity related information on daily basis. He also communicates daily performance expectations to his subordinates.

Reports

General Manager receives intelligence report from paper clippings, Pharma magazines and company agents. He receives inventory report and purchase reports from their respective departments i.e. stores and purchase. He receives daily report, sales report, market research report, distribution report from Deputy General Manager. He also receives financial report from finance department.

The General Manager sends daily report, (general information on performance and problems) daily sales report, intelligence report and market research report to the Managing Director. He sends inventory report to the stores and purchase department respectively. He sends distribution report to Deputy Manager, Finance Department and finance report to finance department as when necessary. He disseminates activity related information to the Managing Director daily. He also disseminates policy information to Deputy Manager frequently.

Deputy General Manager, Senior Manager and Managers submit sales report and other highlights to the General Manager. They inform their officer daily production programme and delivery schedules. The officers report frequently the information about market developments and submit daily sales reports.

Perception about Information

An inquiry about the availability of information in terms of sufficiency or overload or shortage has revealed that all the respondents with the exception of two managers have sufficient information for their effective functioning. Only two managers felt that there is information shortage. The shortage according to them relates to the external information about market development. Evidently, the information-related functions of the managers :

General Manager

- He forwards with remarks, reports on sales credits and discounts.

Table 4.1.5 : Perception about Information Received
(N = 10)

Perceptions	F	%
Information over-load	0	0
Information sufficiency	8	80
Information shortage	2	20

- He circulates performance reports.
- He approves list of customers and vendors.
- He collects information to provide status reports to the superiors.
- He receives sales reports from marketing section and he sends monthly sales reports to the superiors.
- He receives global production demand status reports, from region / country-wise government and research agencies.

Manager

Manager receives daily sales reports and monthly sales reports. They send monthly sales reports and quarterly sales report to their superiors.

Officers

Officers receive reports on product demand, credit collection and payments and customer feedback.

When asked about the necessity of the existing reports, the respondents felt that all of them are necessary. They opined that there is no need for any new reports.

Marketing Intelligence

What are the sources of marketing intelligence?

Table 4.1.6 shows the participation details of respondents in the conferences and workshops. From the table it can be observed that their participation is very low.

Table 4.1.7 shows the respondents use different sources of information viz. newspaper, journals, discussion with company personnel and also with persons belonging to other companies. The other sources are T.V. news and programmes, conferences and

Table 4.1.6 : Conferences / Workshops Attended by the Respondents.

(N = 10)

Year	Conference	Workshop	Seminar	Others	F	%
1998	---	---	---	----	---	----
1999	---	---	---	----	---	----
2000	1	1	---	---	2	20
2001	2	2	---	---	4	40

Table 4.1.7 : Sources of Information used to keep updated

(N = 10)

Source	F	%
Discussion with company personnel	10	100
Discussion with other company personnel	10	100
T. V. news and programs	10	100
Conference / Workshops / Seminars	10	100
News papers/ Journals	10	100
Internet	6	60

workshops / seminars. However, one medium that is less used is Internet. The non-users of it belong to lower management level.

Marketing Research

Marketing Research is considered very important for effective decision-making by the respondents. According to respondents, it is conducted frequently for the purpose of decision-making. Table 4.1.8 shows the details :

Table 4.1.8 : Use of Marketing Research in Decision-Making

N = 10

Factors	Mean	SD
Importance	5.0	4.0
Frequency	4.0	3.0

System Evaluation

The system effectiveness is evaluated based on the views of respondent managers as follows:

1. System management evaluation
2. Information system evaluation
3. People evaluation
4. Outcomes evaluation
5. Overall evaluation

Systems Management Evaluation

The system management is analysed with reference to five factors:

- Leadership
- Plans
- Controls
- Security and
- Change

Table 4.1.9 : Systems Management Evaluation

(N = 10)

S.No	Factor	Average Score	
		Frequency	%
1	Leadership	10	100
2	Plans	10	100
3	Controls	6.1	61
4	Security	10	100
5	Change	10	100

Table 4.1.9 shows the responses signifying system management factors. According to it, 100% of the respondents are of the view that the system is flexible and adaptive, plans are effective and leadership is good. About 100% of the respondents opined that security provisions of the system are good. Controls are effective according to 61% of the respondents.

Leadership

The marketing information system is supervised by a qualified manager. The management is motivating competently its personnels to provide effective information service. Training programs are conducted for employees to enhance usage.

Table 4.1.10 : Systems Management Evaluation – Leadership (N = 10)

No.	Factors	F	%
1.	Is the MKIS under the direction of qualified manager (specify)?	10	100
2.	Does management motivate its personnels to effectively provide desired information service?	10	100
3.	Is there a formal training program where deemed necessary?		
(i)	New employees?	10	100
(ii)	Transferred employees?	10	100
(iii)	Regular employees?	10	100

Plans

All the respondents have opined that master plan of marketing information system is well defined. Also it is integrated properly with departmental long range plans and organisational objectives. According to them the marketing information system plan is well established with defined procedures and standards. Top management, the management steering committee and information system management review the master plan periodically. Table 4.1.11 shows the details :

Table 4.1.11 : Systems management Evaluation–Plans

(N = 10)

No.	Factors	F	%
1.	Does the management have a well-defined master plan for MKIS?	10	1000
2.	Is the master plan an integrated?		
(i)	Objectives?	10	1000
(ii)	Strategies?	10	1000
(iii)	Projects?	10	1000
(iv)	Policies?	10	1000
(v)	Procedures?	10	1000
(vi)	Standards?	10	1000
3	Is department's long range plans related to organisational objectives?	10	1000
4.	Is the master plan subjected to periodic review?		
(i)	Top management?	10	1000
(ii)	Management steering committee?	10	1000
(iii)	Information systems management?	10	1000

Controls

The following IS control measures are considered effective by all the respondents:

- Management exercises the necessary control over its operations so that fraud, theft, and irregularities of IS methods and procedures can be detected.
- Management separated the functions of the department in order to minimise fraud, theft and irregularities.
- Management has segregated the functions of the department in order to minimise fraud, theft and irregularities.
- Provisions for back-up personnel in the key information systems positions are created.

- System has powerful air conditioning environment which is adequate.
- There are surprise audits (internal) to check irregularities.

However, the senior management has pointed out the following:

- There is no external, independent auditing of the system.
- The system procedures and documents are not kept current.

Table 4.1.12 : Systems Management Evaluation–Control (N = 10)

No.	Factors	F	%
1.	Does management exercise the necessary control over its operations so that fraud, theft, and irregularities of IS methods and procedures can be detected?	10	100
2.	Does management segregate the functions of the department in order to minimise fraud, theft, and irregularities?	10	100
3.	Is there a provision for back up personnel in key information systems positions?	10	100
4.	Does internal auditing periodically check on the operations of the information systems department?	10	100
5.	Is the information system audited periodically by an independent third party (outside auditors or consultants)?	10	100
6.	Is there a surprise audit of the information systems department for detecting?		
(i)	Fraud?	10	100
(ii)	Theft?	10	100
(iii)	Collusion?	0	0
(iv)	Embezzlement?	0	0
(v)	Sabotage?	0	0
(vi)	Irregularities?	0	0
(vii)	Does the computer system have adequately powered aircondition?	10	100
7.	Are systems and procedure manuals kept current?	0	0

Security

All the respondents felt that security controls are required by IS management. The security measures are well-designed and implemented in the organisation. There are security controls to ensure that all input data and corrections to them are processed properly and accurately. However, some of the respondents are of the view that security controls are not :

- fully understood and implemented, and
- security procedures manuals are not available.

Below is furnished the information Table 4.1.13 :

Table 4.1.13: Systems Management Evaluation–Security (N = 10)

No.	Factors	F	%
1	Are security controls required by information systems management?	10	100
2	Are security controls fully understood and implemented by systems and programming personnels?	10	100
3.	Are security controls sufficient to ensure that all input data and corrections to data have been processed properly and accurately?	10	100
4.	Are security controls written and contained in appropriate systems and procedure manuals for ready reference when necessary?	10	100

Change Management

The respondents are asked about the flexibility and adaptative capability of the system. The system is flexible and sensitive to change. A control mechanism with well-designed procedures is set up in the organisation. It functions by seeking approvals of top management. The change plans are well documented including the reasons for changes. The users are involved in the change process. Written memoranda are issued to appropriate personnel concerning changes. Auditors are also appraised of the important changes. During the change process effective control systems to prevent unauthorised changes in the master files and transactions files are also established. On the whole, the marketing information system is dynamic and adaptative.

Table 4.1.14 : System Management Evaluation–Change

(N = 10)

No.		Factors	F	%
49.		Is there a control mechanism for making appropriate information system changes?	10	100
50.		Does this control mechanism include a provision for approval?	10	100
51.		Are procedures established for making?		
	(i)	System changes	10	100
	(ii)	Program changes	10	100
	(iii)	Library (Program & file) changes	10	100
	(iv)	Computer operator changes	10	100
52.		Are all systems and programs changes immediately documented, including the reason for the changes?	10	100
53		Are written memoranda issued to the appropriate personnel concerning changes?	10	100
54.		Is the user involved in making changes where necessary?	10	100
55.		Are the internal and external auditors appraised of important changes?	10	100
56.		Are master files and transaction files controlled to prevent unauthorized changes during conversion?	10	100

Information System Evaluation

Table 4.1.15 system-related appraisal : The respondents have given positive scores for hardware, software, documentation, maintenance and integration of the system with other systems. The mean scores are in the range of 4.4 to 4.9. Element-wise evaluation of the system is provided in table 4.1.16.

Table 4.1.15 : Evaluation of Information System–System Elements (N=10)

Elements	Mean	SD
Hardware	4.4	3.3
Software	4.6	3.2
Documentation	4.4	3.5
Maintenance	4.9	2.7
Integration	4.6	2.7
Total average	4.5	3.0

Table 4.1.16 : Evaluation of Information System–System Details (N = 10)

No.	Factors	Mean	SD
	Hardware :		
1.	The response of the system is fast	5.0	4.0
2.	Accessing information is easy	5.0	4.0
3.	System security is very good	4.4	3.5
4.	In realisation of user needs, the system is the best	4.1	3.5
5.	The system has good flexibility	4.1	3.5
6.	Information processing is efficient	3.9	2.1
7.	Computer systems are adequate	4.8	2.0
	Total Average :	4.4	3.3
	Software :		
1.	Features used in programming languages are excellent	4.4	3.5
2.	Data analysis programs are updated	4.8	3.0
	Total Average :	4.6	3.25

[contd...]

No.	Factors	Mean	SD
	Documentation :		
1	Documentation if the system is completed	4.4	3.5
	Maintenance :		
2.	The system is well maintained	4.9	2.7
	Integrated :		
1.	The system is integrated with other systems.	4.8	3.0
2.	There is coordination between MKIS and other systems	4.4	2.5
	Total Average :	4.6	2.7

People Evaluation

Table 4.1.17 shows evaluation of effectiveness of people elements. The respondents have given an overall rating of 4.3. The aspects like top management support, I.T staff competence and

Table 4.1.17 : People Evaluation
(N=10)

Element	Mean	SD
Top management	3.7	2.7
IS staff	4.5	3.0
Total average	4.1	2.8

Table 4.1.18 : People Evaluation Details
(N=10)

No.	Factors	Mean	SD
	Top management :		
1.	Top management is involved in the development of the system	3.7	2.7
	IS Staff :		
1.	The staff in the organisation like to use the system	4.4	3.5
2.	IS staff are competent	4.6	2.5
	Total Average :	4.5	3.0

support and user involvement, training and utilisation of the system are rated good. Element-wise evaluation of the people is provided in table 4.1.18.

Outcomes Evaluation

The different outcomes of a system like Information quality, output, user friendliness, decision support, benefits and satisfaction are evaluated by respondents. The results are shown in table 4.1.19. According to it, the system is good in all respects, particularly, the benefits

Table: 4.1.19 : Evaluation of System Outcomes (N=10)

Aspect	Mean	SD
Information	4.6	2.5
Output	4.0	3.1
User friendliness	4.7	2.8
Decision Support	4.4	2.7
Benefits	4.8	3.0
Satisfaction	3.7	2.7

Information and Output

Table 4.1.20 shows that information available from the system is relevant (4.6), accurate, timely etc. The respondents are also happy

Table 4.1.20 : Evaluation of System Outcomes–Information and Output (N=10)

No.	Factors	Mean	SD
	Information		
1	Computer systems are capable	4.7	2.7
2	Information is relevant	4.9	3.5
3	Information is kept confidential when required	4.5	2.4

[contd...]

No	Factors	Mean	SD
	Information		
4	Information Provided by the system is accurate	4.6	2.5
5	System provides timely information	4.5	2.4
6	System furnishes exact information	4.5	2.4
7	The information provided is reliable	4.5	2.4
8	Current information is provided by the system	4.5	2.4
9	The information is complete in all aspects	4.6	2.5
10	It provides well designed formats	4.6	2.5
11	Information furnished has clarity	4.8	2.8
	Total average :	4.6	2.5
	Output		
1	The reports and other information products are well scheduled	4.4	3.5
2	Adequate volume of output is generated by the system	3.7	2.7
	Total Average :	4.0	3.1

about the output in respect of the volume, frequency and information products. Element-wise evaluation of the system is provided in table 4.1.20.

User Friendliness

Table 5.2.21 shows the user friendliness of the system. The system is perceived very much user friendly.

Table 4.1.21 : Evaluation of System Outcomes–User friendliness (N=10)

No.	Factor	Mean	SD
1	Users are well-trained to use the system	4.5	2.4
2	The system is used by all concerned employees	4.8	3.0
3	There is participation of users in the system development and instrumentation	4.8	3.0
4	Users have confidence in the system	4.8	3.0
	Total average :	4.7	2.8

Decision Support

According to the respondents, the system is fairly helpful on an average to the managers in making decisions. Table 4.1.22 shows the details.

Table 4.1.22 : Evaluation of System Outcomes–Decision Support
(N=10)

Factors	Mean	SD
Market analysis and forecasting	4.0	4.0
Product decisions	4.7	3.0
Price decisions	4.4	2.1
Place decisions	4.4	2.1
Promotion decisions	4.9	3.5
Overall	4.4	2.7

Benefits and Satisfaction

Table 4.1.23 shows that the respondents are benefited by the system. They have agreed very much with the statements–"The system has tools to improve productivity of operations." "Jobs have become easy and efficient", "making activities more efficient" and "boosted the profits." However, when rating the benefits they opined that the expectations are moderately realised. Accordingly, the satisfaction with the system is also moderate.

Table 4.1.23 : Evaluation of System Outcomes–Benefits and Satisfaction
(N=10)

No.	Factors	Mean	SD
	Benefits		
1	The system has tools to improve productivity of operations	4.6	2.5
2	My job has become easy with the support of the system	4.9	3.5

[contd...]

[contd...]

No.	Factors	Mean	SD
	Benefits :		
3	MKIS has improved the results of the organisation	4.9	3.5
4	MKIS is making the activities more efficient	4.9	3.5
5	MKIS has boosted the profits of the organisation	4.9	3.5
6	My expectations of benefits of system are realised	3.7	2.7
	Total average :	4.8	3.0
	Satisfaction :		
1	The system is satisfactory to me	3.5	2.7

Overall Evaluation

The respondents are asked to evaluate the present marketing information system in the organisation on a 5-point scale of exceptional and poor. The system is considered good by majority of the respondents. Table 4.1.24 shows the details :

Table 4.1.24 : Overall Evaluation of Information System

(N=10)

Factor	Mean	SD
Present marketing information system	4.0	4.0

4.2 MARKETING INFORMATION SYSTEM IN ERYTHRO PHARMA PRIVATE LIMITED

Introduction

Erythro Pharma Private Limited was incorporated as Lake View Labs Private Limited in 1991. It was started for the purpose of manufacturing various drugs and drug intermediates. However, the earlier promoters, after having acquired land and commenced civil works, did not take up the project. The company was then without any operations for a period of about 5 years. In late 1995 company was taken over by the new promoters, and renamed as "Erythro Pharma Private Limited."

The promoters have since invested over Rs. 100 lakhs in the company (including the price of purchase) and have made ready the manufacturing facilities for the production of certain chemical intermediates for exports. The facility commenced operations in March 1996.

Products

Erythro has been promoted for the purpose of manufacturing high value chemicals, mostly for use as intermediates in the fine chemicals and pharma industry. The products of Erythro include: 3, 5, 6 Trichloro Salicylic Acid, Quinzoline Phenyl Benzoxide, Phynyl acetylene, Pathalocyanine DYE 77, Green Dye, Yellow Green Dye, Chloro Pyridyl Piperizynil Imide, Dichloro Phynyl Benzoxide.

At present, the company is involved in manufacturing and exporting of 3, 5, 6 Tri Chloro Salicylic Acid. Tri Chloro Salicylic have an export market under a firm understanding with M/s Jame Fine Chemicals Inc. New Jersey, USA.

Marketing Organisation

The marketing organisation is headed by the Director. Vice President (Domestic and Exports) coordinates the domestic and international marketing and assists the Director. He is assisted by Senior Manager who in turn supervises a team consisting of Managers, Officers and an Assistant.

Marketing Information System

Marketing information system was computerised in the year 1999. The reasons for setting up of computerised marketing information system are :

- To make complex decisions easy
- As competitors have set up MIS
- It is an extension to computerisation in other departments.
- On the request of marketing managers.

Objectives Served

The identified principal benefits of marketing information system are :

1. Helps improve decision-making
2. Keeps a general database.

3. Helps in generating variety of reports
4. Helps planning and controlling effective
5. Helps better coordination and
6. Helps increase profits.

The other benefits are related to implementation

1. Updated information for implementation of decisions.
2. Improvement in implementation process.

About the System

The company has developed their information system through in-house package built as per their needs. The system helps in integrating marketing department with production, research, and development, quality control and finance. It provides region-wise data relating to market potential and helps develop suitable market plan. Also it furnishes sales data and analysis, and facilitates also credit control.

There are more than 20 computers with suitable configuration for implementing in-house developed packages. The marketing wing has about 9 employees. Users are trained to provide skill in using Windows and other packages.

Reports

The reports generated for decision-making include

- Details of execution of orders
- Time between orders receiving and its execution
- Performance evaluation of key areas
- New market information
- Distribution report
- Sales reports
- Country-wise product with sales report etc.

Evaluation

There are no inadequacies in the system. If any inadequacies are identified in the system, they immediately take steps to rectify the inadequacy or make alteration in the system to suit their needs and requirements. Thus, they keep improving their system performance.

Future Plans

Even though present system is alright they are interested in implementing ERP / SAP by the end by December 2002 to meet future requirements. They are also planning to decentralise the activities of the organisation.

Profile of Respondents

Table 4.2.1 describes the profile of the respondents from the organisation. The respondents include Vice-president (Domestic and Exports), two Senior Managers, two Managers and 4 Officers. Experience-wise, 55.5% of the respondents group have more than 10 years of experience, and are at the senior management level.

Table 4.2.1 : Profile of Respondents

(N =9)

S.No.	Elements	F	%
1.	**Designation :**		
	Vice President	1	11
	Senior Manager	2	22
	Manager	2	22
	Officers	4	44
2.	**Experience (years) :**		
	Less than 10	5	55.5
	10 & Above	4	44.5
3.	**Level in hierarchy :**		
	Senior	5	55.5
	Junior	4	44.5

Table 4.2.2 shows the reporting relationships. Vice-president reports to Managing Director, the Senior Managers to Vice President, Manager report to Senior Manager and Officers report to Managers. All the respondents except officers have subordinate positions as shown in Table 2.

Table 4.2.2 : Reporting Relationships of Respondents
(N =9)

Respondents	Reporting to
Vice-precedent	Director
Senior manager	Vice-precedent
Manager	Senior manager
Officer	Manager
Assistants	Officer
Subordinate positions under Respondents	**Subordinate positions**
Vice-precedent	Senior manager
Senior manager	Manager
Manager	Officer
Officer	Assistants

Role Clarity

Respondents were asked to identify their levels of clarity about the roles they play in the organisation. The responses as shown in

Table 4.2.3 : Perceived Role Clarity of Respondents
(N = 9)

Perceptions	Mean	SD
My role is clear to me	4.8	3.1
I do not have conflicts in my playing my role (No over lapping)	3.1	1.6
My authority is clear to me	4.8	3.1
My relations with others are well defined	4.8	3.1
I was told clearly about my responsibility (What I have to contribute)	4.8	3.1
Overall	4.4	2.8

Table 4.2.3 indicate that they are very much clear about their roles.

Decision Making

Table 4.2.4 shows that they are mostly depending upon their superiors (5.0) and moderately on subordinates (3.4) and less on peers.

Table 4.2.4 : Dependence in Decision Making and Implementation

(N = 9)

Positions	Mean	SD
On superiors	5.0	3.6
On subordinates	3.2	1.6
On peers	2.0	1.4

The respondents have observed that they make use of mostly statistical methods according to requirements. The statistical methods are used for key decisions as well as routine decisions.

Information Flow

The information that flows to the different persons in the hierarchy of marketing, is as follows :

- The Vice-President receives information pertaining to future outlook from the Managing Director. He receives sales and competitors' information from the Senior Managers.
- The Senior Managers receive from their superiors, information inputs on target related information and current market strategies. They receive performance reports from their subordinates on daily basis.
- The Managers receive from their superiors information inputs on current marketing strategy as and when required from their subordinates. They receive sales information on day to day basis. They receive customer payment details and orders.
- The officers receive from their superiors information about stock details.

Reports

Vice-President receives market target report from Managing Director. He also receives current sales reports, payment details report from the Senior Manager. The Senior Manager (Exports) receives export reports from the Manager. Senior Manager (Domestic) receives daily sales report, stock report, payment report, customers report from the Managers. The managers receive market targets from their superiors.

Perception about Information

All the respondents have sufficient information for their effective functioning.

Table 4.2.5 : Perception about Information Received
(N = 9)

Perceptions	F	%
Information over load	0	0
Information sufficiency	9	100
Information shortage	0	0

When asked about the necessity of the existing reports, the respondents felt that all of them are necessary. They felt that there is no need for any new reports.

Marketing Intelligence

Table 4.2.6 shows the participation details of respondents in the conferences and workshops. From the table, it can be observed that their participation is very less.

Table 4.2.6 : Conferences / Workshops Attended by the Respondents (N = 9)

Year	Conference	Workshop	Seminar	Others	F	%
1998	-	-	-	-	-	-
1999	-	-	-	-	-	-
2000	1	-	-	-	1	12.5
2001	1	-	-	-	1	12.5

Table 4.2.7 shows the different sources of information used by the managers to keep them updated. These are newspapers, journals, internet and discussion with company personnels and also with persons belonging to other companies. The other sources are T.V. news and programs. The nonusers of internet belong to lower management level.

Table 4.2.7 : Source of Information Used to Keep Updated

(N = 9)

Source	F	%
Discussion with company personnels	9	100
Discussion with other company personnels	6	66.6
T. V. news and programs	9	100
Conference / Workshops / Seminars	2	22.2
Newspapers/ Journals	9	100
Internet	4	44.4

Marketing Research

Marketing research is considered for effective decision-making by the respondents. It is conducted frequently for the purpose of decision-making. Table 4.2.8 shows the details:

Table 4.2.8 : Use of Marketing Research in Decision-Making

(N = 9)

Factors	Mean	SD
Importance	4.8	3.6
Frequency	3.6	2.4

System Evaluation

The system effectiveness is evaluated based on the views of the respondent managers as follows:

1. Systems management evaluation
2. Information systems evaluation

3. People evaluation
4. Outcome evaluation
5. Overall evaluation

System Management Evaluation

The system management is analysed with reference to the following factors:

- Leadership
- Plans
- Controls
- Security and
- Change

Table 4.2.9 shows the responses signifying system management factors. According to it, 61.7% of the respondents are of the view that the system is flexible and adaptive; plans are effective (66.6%) and leadership is good (71%). All the respondents expressed that security provisions of the system are excellent (52.7%). Controls are effective according to about 46.1 % of the respondents.

Table 4.2.9 : Systems Management Evaluation

(N = 9)

S.No	Factor	Average Score	
		F	%
1	Leadership	6.4	71
2	Plans	6	66.6
3	Controls	3.6	46.1
4	Security	4.7	52.7
5	Change	6.5	72.1

Leadership

The marketing information system is supervised by a qualified manager. The management is motivating competently its personnels to provide effective service. Training programmes are conducted for employees to encourage usage.

Table 4.2.10 : Systems Management Evaluation–Leadership (N = 9)				
No.		**Factors**	**F**	**%**
1.		Is the MKIS under the direction of qualified manager (specify)?	9	100
2.		Does management motivate its personnels to effectively provide the Desired information service?	7	77.7
3.		Is there a formal training program where deemed necessary?		
	(i)	New employees?	7	77.7
	(ii)	Transferred employees?	2	22.2
	(iii)	Regular employees?	7	77.7

Plans

All the respondents expressed that master plan of marketing information system is well-defined; also it is integrated properly with departmental long range plans and organisational objectives. According to them the marketing information system plan is well integrated with procedures and standards. Top management, the management steering committee and information system management periodically review the master plan. Table 4.2.11 shows the details.

Table 4.2.11 : Systems management Evaluation–Plans

(N =9)

No.		**Factors**	**F**	**%**
1.		Does the management have a well defined master plan for MKIS?	7	77.7
2.		Is the master plan integrated into?		
	(i)	Objectives?	6	66.6
	(ii)	Strategies?	4	44.4

[contd...]

[contd...]

No.		Factors	F	%
	(iii)	Projects?	3	33.3
	(iv)	Policies?	5	55.5
	(v)	Procedures?	8	88.8
	(vi)	Standards?	7	77.7
3		Are department long range plans related to organisational objectives?	7	77.7
4.		Is the master plan subjected to periodic review?		
	(i)	Top management?	9	100
	(ii)	Management steering committee?	5	55.5
	(iii)	Information systems management?	5	55.5

Controls

The following IS control measures are considered effective by all respondents. According to them:

- Management exercises the necessary control over its operations.
- Management has segregated the functions of the department in order to minimise fraud, theft and irregularities.
- Provision for back up personnel in key information systems positions is created.
- System has powerful air conditioning environment.
- There are surprise audits (internal) to check irregularities.

However, the management pointed out the following:

- There is no external, independent auditing of the system.
- The system procedures and documents are not kept current.

Table 4.2.12 shows the details:

Table 4.2.12 : Systems Management Evaluation–Control

(N =9)

No.		Factors	F	%
1.		Does management exercise the necessary control over its operations so that fraud, theft, and irregularities of IS methods and procedures can be detected?	6	66.6
2.		Does management segregate the functions of the department in order to minimise fraud, theft, and irregularities?	7	77.7
3.		Is there a provision for backup personnel in key information systems positions?	2	22.2
4.		Does internal auditing periodically check on the operations of the information systems department?	7	77.7
5.		Is the information system audited periodically by an independent third party (outside auditors or consultants)?	0	0
6.		Is there a surprise audit of the information systems department for detecting?		
	(i)	Fraud?	8	88.8
	(ii)	Theft?	6	66.6
	(iii)	Collusion?	0	0
	(iv)	Embezzlement?	0	0
	(v)	Sabotage?	0	0
	(vi)	Irregularities?	7	77.7
	(vii)	Does the computer system have adequately powered aircondition?	6	66.6
7.		Are systems and procedure manuals kept current?	5	55.5

Security

All the respondents opined that security controls are required by IS management. The security measures are well-designed, and implemented in the organisation. Security controls are designed to ensure that all input data and corrections to them are processed properly and accurately. Security controls are written and contained in manuals for ready reference when necessary.

Table 4.2.13 : Systems Management Evaluation–Security

(N = 9)

No.	Factors	F	%
1.	Are security controls required by information systems management?	7	77.7
2.	Are security controls fully understood and implemented by systems and programming personnel?	6	66.6
3.	Are security controls sufficient to ensure that all input data and corrections to data have been processed properly and accurately?	3	33.3
4.	Are security controls written and contained in appropriate systems and procedures manuals for ready reference when necessary?	3	33.3

Change Management

According to the respondents, the system is change-oriented. A control mechanism with well-designed procedures is set up in the organisation. It functions by seeking approvals of top management. The change plans are well documented including the reasons for changes. The users are involved in the change process. Written memoranda are issued to the personnel concerning changes. Auditors are also appraised of the important changes. During the change process effective control systems to prevent unauthorised changes in the master files and transactions files are also established.

Table 4.2.14 : System Management Evaluation–Change Management

(N =9)

No.		Factors	F	%
1.		Is there a control mechanism for making appropriate information systems changes?	8	88.8
2.		Does this control mechanism include a provision for approval?	5	55.5
3.		Are procedures established for making?		
	(i)	System changes?	4	44.4
	(ii)	Program changes?	8	88.8
	(iii)	Library (Program & file) changes?	0	0
	(iv)	Computer operator charges?	7	77.7
4.		Are all system and program changes immediately documented, including the reason for the changes?	7	77.7
5.		Are written memoranda issued to the appropriate personnel concerning changes?	6	66.6
6.		Is the user involved in making changes where necessary?	5	55.5
7.		Are the internal and external auditors apprised of important changes?	7	77.7
8.		Are master files and transaction files controlled to prevent unauthorised changes during conversion?	7	77.7

Information System Evaluation

Table 4.2.15 shows system related appraisal. The respondents have given positive scores for hardware, software, documentation, maintenance and integration of the system with other systems. The mean scores are in the range of 3.7 to 4.8. Element-wise evaluation of the system is provided in table 4.2.16

Table 4.2.15 : Evaluation of Information System–System Elements (N=9)

Elements	Mean	SD
Hardware	4.1	2.4
Software	4.3	3.0
Documentation	4.1	2.2
Maintenance	4.8	3.1
Integration	3.7	2.3
Total average	4.2	2.6

Table 4.2.16 shows evaluation of effectiveness of the people elements of system. The respondents have given rating of 3.9. The aspects like top management support, IT staff competence and support and user involvement and utilisation of the system are rated good.

Table 4.2.16 : Evaluation of information system–System Details (N = 9)

No.	Factors	Mean	SD
	Hard ware		
1.	The response of the system is fast	4.6	2.4
2.	Accessing information is easy	4.6	2.4
3.	System security is very good	4.1	2.2
4.	In realisation of user needs, the system is the best	4.1	2.2
5.	The system has good flexibility	4.6	2.4
6.	Information processing is efficient	4.0	3.6
7.	Computer systems are adequate	3.0	2.2
	Total Average :	4.1	2.4

[contd...]

[contd...]

No.	Factors	Mean	SD
	Software :		
1.	Features used in programming languages are excellent	4.6	2.4
2.	Data analysis programs are updated	4.0	3.6
	Total Average :	4.3	3.0
	Documentation :		
1.	Documentation if the system is completed	4.1	2.2
	Maintenance :		
1.	The system is well maintained	4.8	3.1
	Integrated :		
1.	The system is integrated with other systems.	4.6	2.4
2.	There is coordination between MKIS and other systems	2.8	2.2
	Average Total :	3.7	2.3

People Evaluation

Table 4.2.17 shows that the information available from the system is relevant (4.1), accurate, timely etc. The respondents are also happy about the output in respect of the volume and frequency. Element-wise people evaluation is provided in table 4.2.18.

Table 4.2.17 : People Evaluation

(N=9)

Element	Mean	SD
Top management	4.2	2.7
IS staff	4.2	2.7
Total average	4.2	2.7

Table 4.2.18 : People Evaluation Details

(N=9)

No.	**Factors**	**Mean**	**SD**
	Top Management :		
1	Top management is involved in the development of the system	4.2	2.7
	IS Staff :		
1	The staff in the organisation like to use the system	3.8	2.1
2	IS staff are competent	4.6	2.4
	Total Average :	4.2	2.7

Outcomes Evaluation

The different outcomes of a system like Information quality, output, user friendliness, decision support, benefits and satisfaction are evaluated by respondents. The results are shown in table 4.2.19. According to it, the system is good.

Table: 4.2.19 : Evaluation of System Outcomes

(N=9)

Aspect	**Mean**	**SD**
Information	4.1	2.5
Output	4.0	2.7
User friendliness	3.9	2.9
Decision Support	3.4	2.5
Benefits	3.7	2.9
Satisfaction	4.0	3.6

Information and Output

Table 4.1.20 shows that information available from the system is relevant (4.6), accurate, timely etc. The respondents are also happy about the output in respect of the volume, frequency and information products. Element-wise evaluation of the system is provided in table 4.1.20.

Table 4.2.20 : Evaluation of System Outcomes–Information and Output

(N=9)

No.	Factors	Mean	SD
	Information		
1	Computer systems are capable	3.0	2.2
2	Information is relevant	4.6	2.4
3	Information is kept confidential when required	4.6	2.4
4	Information provided by the system is accurate	4.6	2.4
5	System provides timely information	4.6	2.4
6	System furnishes exact information	4.6	2.4
7	The information provided is reliable	4.6	2.4
8	Current information is provided by the system	4.0	2.6
9	The information is complete in all aspects	4.0	2.6
10	It provides well designed formats	3.3	2.4
11	Information furnished has clarity	4.0	3.6
	Total average :	4.1	2.5
	Output		
1	The reports and other information products are well scheduled	4.8	3.1
2	Adequate volume of output is generated by the system	3.3	2.4
	Total Average :	4.0	2.7

User Friendliness

According to Table 5.2.21 user friendliness of the system is high.

Table 4.2.21 : Evaluation of System Outcomes–User friendliness (N=9)

No.	Factors	Mean	SD
1	Users are well trained to use the system	4.0	3.6
2	The system is used by all concerned employees	4.0	3.6
3	There is participation of users in the system development and instrumentation	3.1	2.2
4	Users have confidence in the system	3.1	2.2
	Total average	3.5	2.9

Decision Support

According to the respondents the system is fairly helpful on an average to the managers in making decisions relating to product and price. It is also helpful in the market analysis and forecasting, place and promotion decisions. Table 4.2.22 shows the details

Table 4.2.22 : Evaluation of System Outcomes – Decision Support (N=9)

Factors	Mean	SD
Market analysis and forecasting	3.6	2.6
Product decisions	3.8	3.3
Price decisions	4.0	1.8
Place decisions	2.2	2.7
Promotion decisions	3.4	2.2
Overall	3.4	2.5

Benefits and Satisfaction

Table 4.2.23 shows that the respondents are pleased with the benefits of the system. They considered it beneficial (3.9). They agreed with the statement–"The system has tools to improve productivity of operations". They have also accepted that 'their jobs have become easy and efficient'. The respondents have expressed satisfaction with the system (3.8) :

Table 4.2.23 : Evaluation of System Outcomes–Benefits and Satisfaction

(N=9)

No.	Factors	Mean	SD
	Benefits :		
1	The system has tools to improve productivity of operations	4.0	3.6
2	My job has become easy with the support of the system	4.0	3.6
3	MKIS has improved the results of the organisation	3.7	3.1
4	MKIS is making the activities more efficient	3.4	1.9
5	MKIS has boosted the profits of organisation	4.0	3.6
6	My expectations of benefits of system are realised	3.5	1.9
	Total average :	3.7	2.9
	Satisfaction :		
1	The system is satisfactory to me	4.0	3.6

Overall Evaluation

The system is considered good by majority of the respondents. Table 4.2.24 shows the mean score on this aspect :

Table 4.2.24 : Overall Evaluation of Information System

(N=9)

Factor	Mean	SD
Present marketing information system	4.0	3.6

4.3 MARKETING INFORMATION SYSTEM IN BIOLOGICAL E. LIMITED

Introduction

Biological E. Limited was incorporated in 1953. Its sales revenue for the year 2000 touched Rs. 132 crores and profit before tax was Rs. 65.2 million. The company emphasises on R & D. By the emphasis on R & D, the following benefits are achieved.

Products

- New products and formulations were introduced.
- Development of formulations specific to export market.
- Brand line extensions to expand the market share.
- Safe and environment friendly processes.

Marketing Organisation

The marketing team of the company is led by Director Marketing for domestic operations. He is assisted by General Manager-Marketing, General Manager–Sales. General Manager–Marketing supervises Group Product Manager, who supervises four Product Managers and Zonal Managers, sixteen National Sales Managers and Zonal Managers, Divisional Managers, Area Managers and Territory Managers, around 350 members with various designations.

International operations are headed by Vice President–Marketing. He is assisted by Manager–International Marketing. Manager supervises the Assistant Manager.

Marketing Information System

Marketing information system was computerised in the year 1998.

Objectives

- The main reason for setting up of computerised marketing information system is:
- To make complex decisions easy.

The other benefits that the systems are expected to provide are:

- It keeps a general database.
- It generates a variety of reports.

- It makes planning and controlling effective.
- It helps improve decision-making.
- It helps in better coordination.
- It helps increase profits.

In a short span of 1998–99 to 2001 the company developed its own IT strengths. The company had full fledged EDP department and IT company called Vasistatha Technology.

About the System

The computerised system integrates Marketing, Purchase, Production, Quality Control, R & D, Finance and HRM Departments. The company has EDP section and planning to have better rapport with IT industry for continuous upgradation.

Reports

The main reports generated for decision-making include:

- Daily activity report — Production, R&D / QC, Monthly
- Sales Report — Weekly, Quarterly
- Inventory control report
- Purchase and procurement report
- Personnel appraisal report
- Market research and analysis report
- Distribution report — Location-wise, Department-wise
- Financial report

Evaluation

The one inadequacy pointed out is that the 'Distribution report' needs some improvement to improve collection and profitability.

Profile of Respondents

Table 4.3.1 shows the profile of the respondents from the

organisation. The respondents include Vice President–International Marketing, Manager–International Marketing, Assistant Manager–International Marketing and General Manager–Marketing Domestic, Group Product Manager and two product managers. Experience-wise the respondent group consists of about 42.8% decision-makers with more than 10 years of experience. Level-wise, it can be observed that about 28.5% of them are at senior management level and most of them have less than 10 years of experience.

Table 4.3.1 : Profile of Respondents
(N = 7)

S.No.	Elements	F	%
1.	**Designation :**		
	Vice President - International Marketing	1	14.2
	Manager – International Marketing	1	14.2
	Assistant Manager – International Marketing	1	14.2
	General Manager – Marketing	1	14.2
	Group Product Manager	1	14.2
	Product Manager (2)	2	28.5
2.	**Experience (years) :**		
	Below 10 years	4	57.7
	10 years and above	3	42.8
3.	**Level in hierarchy :**		
	Senior	2	28.5
	Middle	2	28.5
	Junior	3	42.8

Table 4.3.2 shows the reporting relationships. Vice President–International Marketing reports to Director Marketing, Manager to Vice President, Assistant Manager to Manager and General Manager–Marketing to Director Marketing, Group Product Manager–All the respondents have subordinate positions as shown in Table 4.3.2.

Table 4.3.2 : Reporting Relationships of Respondents (N = 7)

Respondents	Reporting to
Vice President - International Marketing	Director - Marketing
Manager - International Marketing	Vice President - International Marketing
Assistant Manager - International Marketing	Manager - marketing
General Manager - Marketing	Director - Marketing
Group Product Manager	General Manager - Marketing
Product Manager (2)	Group Product Manager
Subordinate positions under Respondents	**Subordinate positions**
Vice President - International Marketing	Manager - Marketing
Manager - International Marketing	Assistant Manager
Assistant Manager - International Marketing	Executives
General Manager - Marketing	Group Product Manager
Group Product Manager	Product Manager
Product Manager (2)	Product Executives

Role Clarity

Respondents were asked to identify their levels of clarity about the roles they play in the organisation. The responses indicate that they have reasonably good role clarity (4.4). They have clear view about their relationships (4.0), authority (4.4) and responsibility (4.0). They don't have role conflicts (3.8). Table 4.3.3 shows the details.

Table 4.3.3 : Perceived Role Clarity of Respondents (N = 7)

Perceptions	Mean	SD
My role is clear to me	4.4	1.4
I do not have conflicts in my playing my role (No over lapping)	4.7	1.9
My authority is clear to me	4.4	1.4
My relations with others are well defined	4.0	1.2
I was told clearly about my responsibility	4.0	1.4
(What I have to contribute)		
Overall	4.3	1.4

Decision-Making

Table 4.3.4 shows that they are mostly depending upon their peers (4.2) subordinates (4.1) and finally superiors (3.8).

Table 4.3.4 : Dependence in Decision-Making and Implementation (N = 7)

Positions	Mean	SD
On superiors	3.8	1.2
On subordinates	4.1	1.4
On peers	4.2	1.4

The respondents have observed that they make use of mostly standard methods for key decisions as well as routine decisions.

Information Flow

The information flows to the different persons in the hierarchy of marketing is as follows:

- Vice President–International Marketing receives information pertaining to future plans, marketing proposals and policy related information from the Director. He sends activity related information to the Manager.
- Manager receives from the Vice-President policy related information that helps in decision-making. He sends activity, policy, objective and decision related information to Assistant Manager.
- Assistant Manager receives information pertaining to all work related matters from the Manager. He sends the same information as above to the Manager.
- General Manager–Marketing receives information pertaining to all activities of marketing from the Director–Marketing. He sends activity related and product related information to Group Product Manager.
- Group Product Manager receives information regarding product management from General Manager. He sends the same to Product Managers.

Perception about Information

An inquiry about the availability of information in terms of sufficiency or overload or shortage has revealed that about 42% of the respondents have information sufficiency and 42% of the respondents have shortage of information for their effective functioning. However, one manager has information overload in his functioning. The shortage according to him relates to the external information on market developments. Table 4.3.5 furnishes the details:

Table 4.3.5 : Perception about Information Received

(N = 7)

Perceptions	F	%
Information over- load	1	14
Information sufficiency	3	42
Information shortage	3	42

Reports

Vice President–International Marketing receives intelligence report, and sales report from the Manager. He sends summary and exception reports to the Director.

Manager receives daily report and sales reports from the Assistant Manager, inventory report from stores, purchase report from purchase department, market research report from assistant manager, distribution report from domestic, and finance report from finance department. Manager sends daily report and sales reports to Vice President, inventory report to stores, purchase report to purchase department, market research report to Vice President.

General Manager–Marketing receives intelligence report from his subordinates. He receives inventory, purchase report from respective departments. He receives daily sales report, marketing research report, distribution report, product related reports from the Group Product Manager. He also receives collections and payment report from finance department. General Manager sends all summary reports to the Director.

Group Product Manager receives product reports from Product Executives. They send product summary reports to Group Product Manager.

The respondents felt that all existing reports are necessary. When inquired about the need for any new reports, they said the existing reports are adequate to meet their present as well as future requirements of their work.

Marketing Intelligence

Marketing intelligence requires exposure to mass media and attendance at seminars and conferences and workshops. Table 4.3.6 shows the particulars:

Table 4.3.6 : Conferences / Workshops Attended by the Respondents.

(N = 7)

Year	Conference	Workshop	Seminar	Others	F	%
1998	1	-	-	-	1	14.2
1999	1	-	-	-	1	14.2
2000	2	-	-	-	2	28.5
2001	2	-	-	-	2	28.5

Table 4.3.7 shows the different sources of information used by the managers to keep them updated. These are newspapers, journals, internet, discussion with company personnel and persons belonging to other companies. The other sources are T.V. news and programs, conferences and workshop/ seminars.

Table 4.3.7 : Source of Information Used to Keep Updated

(N = 7)

Source	F	%
Discussion with company personnel	7	100
Discussion with other company personnel	7	100
T. V. news and programs	5	71.4
Conference / Workshops / Seminars	7	100
News papers/ Journals	7	100
Internet	3	42

Marketing Research

Marketing research is viewed as an important source of information for effective decision-making. It is conducted frequently for the purpose of decision-making. Table 4.3.8 shows the details.

Table 4.3.8 : Use of Marketing Research in Decision-Making

(N = 7)

Factors	Mean	SD
Importance	4.2	1.4
Frequency	3.4	1.2

System Evaluation

The system effectiveness is evaluated based on the views of respondent managers as follows:

1. System management evaluation
2. Information system evaluation
3. People evaluation
4. Outcomes evaluation
5. Overall evaluation

System Management Evaluation

The system management is analysed with reference to the following factors:

- Leadership
- Plans
- Controls
- Security and
- Change

Table 4.3.9 shows the responses signifying system management factors. According to it, 95% of the respondents are of the view that system is flexible and adaptive; leadership is good (88.4%) and plans are effective (80.1%). About 85.5% of the respondents opined that security of the system is very good. Controls are effective according to 86% of the respondents. System possesses change characteristics according to 90.9% of the respondents.

Table 4.3.9 : Systems Management Evaluation

(N = 7)

S.No	Factor	Average Score	
		Frequency	%
1	Leadership	6.2	88.42
2	Plans	5.6	80.18
3	Controls	6.2	88.6
4	Security	6.0	85.5
5	Change	6.4	90.9

Leadership

The marketing information system in the organisation is under the direction of a qualified manager. The management is ably motivating its personnel to effectively provide information service. There are training programs for employees which they considered necessary. Table 4.3.10 shows the details:

Table 4.3.10 : Systems Management Evaluation–Leadership

(N = 7)

No.	Factors	F	%
1.	Is the MKIS under the direction of qualified manager (specify)?	7	100
2.	Does management motivate its personnels to effectively provide a desired information service?	7	100
3.	Is there a formal training program where deemed necessary		
(i)	New employees?	5	71.4
(ii)	Transferred employees?	6	85.7

Plans

According to 80.1% of the respondents, the master plan of marketing information system is well-defined and integrated into departmental long range plans and organisational objectives. Also the marketing information system plan is well integrated into procedures and standards. Top management, the management steering committee and information system management periodically review the master plan. Table 4.3.11 shows the details.

Table 4.3.11 : Systems Management Evaluation–Plans

(N = 7)

No.		Factors	F	%
1.		Does the management have a well-defined master plan for MKIS?	5	71
2.		Is the master plan integrated into?		
	(i)	Objectives?	7	100
	(ii)	Strategies?	4	57
	(iii)	Projects?	5	71
	(iv)	Policies?	6	85
	(v)	Procedures?	6	85
	(vi)	Standards?	7	100
3		Is departments long range plans related to organisational objectives?		
4.		Is the master plan subjected to periodic review?	6	85
	(i)	Top management?	7	100
	(ii)	Management steering committee?	4	57
	(iii)	Information systems management?	5	71

Controls

The following IS controls measures are considered effective by all the respondents. According to them :

- Management exercises the necessary control over its operations.
- Management has segregated the functions of the department in order to minimise fraud, theft and irregularities.

- Provision for back-up personnel in key information systems positions is created.
- Internal auditing periodically checks operations of IS department.
- System has powerful air-conditioning environment which is adequate.
- There is an external, independent activity of the system.
- The system procedures and documents are kept current.

Table 4.3.12 shows the details:

Table 4.3.12: Systems Management Evaluation – Control
(N = 7)

No.	Factors	F	%
1.	Does management exercise the necessary control over its operations so that fraud, theft, and irregularities of IS methods and procedures can be detected?	6	85
2.	Does management segregate the functions of the department in order to minimise fraud, theft, and irregularities?	7	100
3.	Is there a provision for back-up personnel in key information systems positions?	7	100
4.	Does internal auditing periodically check on the operations of the information systems department?	6	85
5.	Is the information system audited periodically by an independent third party (outside auditors or consultants)	5	71
6.	Is there a surprise audit of the information systems department for detecting?		
(i)	Fraud?	7	100
(ii)	Theft?	6	85
(iii)	Collusion?	7	100
(iv)	Embezzlement?	5	71
(v)	Sabotage?	6	85
(vi)	Irregularities?	6	85
(vii)	Does the computer system have adequate powerful airconditioning?	6	85
7.	Are systems and procedure manuals kept current?	7	100

Security

All the respondents felt that security controls are required by IS management. The security measures are well-designed and implemented in the organisation. About 71% of the respondents feel that the security controls are sufficient to ensure that all input data and corrections to them are processed properly and accurately and security controls are documented. Table 4.3.13 furnishes the information:

Table 4.3.13 : Systems Management Evaluation–Security

(N = 7)

No.	Factors	F	%
1	Are security controls required by information systems management?	7	100
2	Are security controls fully understood and implemented by systems and programming personnel?	7	100
3.	Are security controls sufficient to ensure that all input data and corrections to data have been processed properly and accurately?	5	71
4.	Are security controls written and contained in appropriate systems and procedures manuals for ready reference when necessary?	5	71

Change Management

According to Table 4.3.14 the system is perceived by respondents as change-oriented. A control mechanism with well-designed procedures is set up in the organisation. It functions by seeking approvals of top management. The change plans are well documented including the reasons for changes. The users are involved in the change process. Written memoranda are issued to the appropriate personnel concerning changes. Auditors are also appraised of the important changes. During the change process, effective control systems to prevent unauthorised changes in the master files and transactions files are also established. On the whole, the marketing information system is dynamic and flexible.

Table 4.3.14 : System Management Evaluation–Change Management

(N = 7)

No.	Factors	F	%
1.	Is there a control mechanism for making appropriate information systems changes?	7	100
2.	Does this control mechanism include a provision for approval?	7	100
3.	Are procedures established for making–		
(i)	System changes?	6	85
(ii)	Program changes?	5	71
(iii)	Library (Program and file) changes?	6	85
(iv)	Computer operator changes?	4	57
4.	Are all system and program changes immediately documented, including the reason for the changes?	6	85
5.	Are written memoranda issued to the appropriate personnel concerning changes?	6	85
6.	Is the user involved in making changes where necessary?	5	71
7.	Are the internal and external auditors appraised of important changes?	6	85
8.	Are master files and transaction files controlled to prevent unauthorised changes during conversion?	6	85

Information System Evaluation

Table 4.3.15 shows system related appraisal. The respondents have given positive scores for system, software, documentation, maintenance and integration. Element-wise evaluation of the system is provided in table 4.3.16.

Table 4.3.15 : Evaluation of Information System–System Elements

(N=7)

Elements	**Mean**	**SD**
Hardware	3.9	1.4
Software	3.9	2.3
Documentation	3.7	1.3
Maintenance	4.4	1.4
Integration	4.0	2.0
Total Average	3.9	1.7

Table 4.3.16 : Evaluation of Information System-System Details

(N = 7)

No.	**Factors**	**Mean**	**SD**
	Hard ware		
1.	The response of the system is fast	3.8	1.4
2.	Accessing information is easy	4.0	1.8
3.	System security is very good	4.1	2.3
4.	In realisation of user needs, the system is the best	4.0	1.8
5.	The system has good flexibility	3.7	1.3
6.	Information processing is efficient	4.0	1.8
7.	Computer systems are adequate	3.8	1.4
	Total Average :	3.9	1.7

[contd...]

[contd...]

No.	Factors	Mean	SD
	Software :		
1.	Features used in programming languages are excellent.	4.1	2.3
2.	Data analysis programs are updated.	3.8	2.3
	Total Average :	3.9	2.3
	Documentation :		
1.	Documentation if the system is completed.	3.7	1.3
	Maintenance :		
1.	The system is well maintained.	4.4	1.4
	Integrated :		
1.	The system is integrated with other systems.	4.0	2.8
2.	There is coordination between MKIS and other systems.	4.0	1.2
	Total Average :	4.0	2.0

People Evaluation

Table 4.3.17 shows people element of system evaluation, the respondents have rated good various aspects like top management support, IT staff competence and support and end-user involvement of the system. Element-wise evaluation of the system is provided in table 4.3.18.

Table 4.3.17 : People Evaluation

(N=7)

Element	Mean	SD
Top management	4.0	2.8
IS staff	4.2	1.4
Total average	4.1	2.1

Table 4.3.18 : People Evaluation Details
(N=7)

No.	Factors	Mean	SD
	Top Management :		
1	Top management is involved in the development of the system.	4.0	2.8
	IS Staff :		
1	The staff in the organisation like to use the system.	4.4	1.7
2	IS staff are competent.	4.1	1.2
	Total Average :	4.2	1.4

Outcome Evaluation

Table 4.2.19 shows that the system is good in all the respects, particularly, the benefits. Element-wise evaluation of the system is provided in table 4.3.20.

Table 4.2.19 : System Evaluation Outcomes
(N=9)

Aspect	Mean	SD
Information	3.9	1.4
Output	4.0	1.4
User friendliness	3.9	1.6
Decision Support	4.1	1.5
Benefits	3.9	1.3
Satisfaction	4.1	1.9

Information and Output

Table 4.3.20 shows that information available from the system is good by itself, relevant, accurate, timely etc. However, the respondents are less happy about the output in respect of the volume, though they are happy that the reports and other information products are well scheduled.

Table 4.3.20 : Evaluation of System Outcomes–Information and Output

(N=7)

No.	Factors	Mean	SD
	Information		
1.	Computer systems are capable	3.8	1.2
2.	Information is relevant	3.8	1.2
3.	Information is kept confidential when required	4.2	1.9
4.	Information provided by the system is accurate	4.4	1.4
5.	System provides timely information	4.2	1.3
6.	System furnishes exact information	4.0	1.8
7.	The information provided is reliable	4.0	1.8
8.	Current information is provided by the system	3.8	1.4
9.	The information is complete in all aspects	3.7	1.2
10.	It provides well-designed formats	3.8	1.0
11.	Information furnished has clarity		
	Total average :		
	Output		
1.	The reports and other information products are well scheduled	4.2	1.9
2.	Adequate volume of output is generated by the system	3.8	1.0
	Total Average :	4.0	1.4

User Friendliness

Table 4.3.21 shows the system is very much user friendly.

Table 4.3.21 : Evaluation of System Outcomes–User Friendliness (N=9)

No.	Factors	Mean	SD
1.	Users are well trained to use the system	4.0	1.1
2.	The system is used by all concerned employees	4.1	1.2
3.	There is participation of users in system development and instrumentation	4.0	2.8
4.	Users have confidence in the system	3.8	1.4
	Total average :	3.9	1.6

Decision Support

According to the respondents, the system is on an average helpful to the managers in making decisions. Table 4.3.22 shows the details:

Table 4.3.22 : Evaluation of System Outcomes-Decision Support (N=7)

Factors	Mean	SD
Market analysis and forecasting	4.1	1.2
Product decisions	4.0	1.8
Price decisions	4.2	1.9
Place decisions	4.4	1.4
Promotion decisions	3.8	1.2

Benefits and Satisfaction

Table 4.3.23 shows that the respondents are pleased with the benefits of the system. They consider it beneficial (3.9). They agree with the statements. "The system has tools to improve productivity of operations." They have also accepted that 'their jobs have become easy and efficient'. The respondents have expressed satisfaction with the system (4.1).

Table 4.3.23 : Evaluation of System Outcomes–Benefits and Satisfaction

(N=7)

No.	Factors	Mean	SD
	Benefits		
1.	The system has tools to improve productivity of operations	4.4	1.4
2.	My job has become easy with the support of the system	4.2	1.4
3.	MKIS has improved the results of the organisation	4.1	1.9
4.	MKIS is making the activities more efficient	3.4	1.0
5.	MKIS has boosted the profits of organisation	3.4	1.0
6.	My expectations of benefits of system are realised	4.0	1.0
	Total average :	3.9	1.3
	Satisfaction :		
1.	The system is satisfactory to me	4.1	1.9

Overall Effectiveness

The respondents are asked to evaluate the present marketing information system in the organisation on a 5-point scale representing exceptional and poor at the polar points. The system is considered good by majority of the respondents. Table 4.3.24 shows the details:

Table 4.3.24 : Overall Evaluation of information System

(N=7)

Factor	Mean	SD
Present marketing information system	3.5	1.4

4.4 SUMMARY

Neuland and Erythro Pharma have set up MKIS to gain competitive edge and meet employee demands. Biological E has set up MKIS 'to make complex decisions easy'. The systems in the three organisations are at present, less sophisticated, within-house developed packages. The future plans for the three organisations focus on SAP / ERP. All the organisations generate several reports. The reports can be broadly classified into sales, purchase, inventory and finance. While marketing research is considered important and used to meet special requirements, marketing intelligence is created through discussions, TV, conferences, newspapers and journal. Only respondents of Erythro pharma reported the use of internet.

The evaluations of effectiveness of the systems indicate that the systems in Neuland and Erythro Pharma are rated good whereas in Biological E, it is rated above average. Component–wise evaluation shows that system management is more effective in Neuland than in other two companies. Information system is considered very good in Neuland and Erythro Pharma and good in Biological E. 'People' component is rated very good in the three companies, only exception is 'top management' supporting Neuland.

When it comes to outcome evaluation, respondents of Neuland rated it very good. So is the case of Erythro Pharma. Relatively the system in Biological E is rated less beneficial. Overall ratings are also in the same pattern. Information shortages are reported by a few respondents in Neuland and Bilogical E. According to the spokes persons of Neuland and Bilogical E, their systems have inadequacies. In Neuland hardware is inadequate and development requirements are not actively considered. In Biological E, the distribution report needs modification.

5

Marketing Information System in Service Sector

5.1 MARKETING INFORMATION SYSTEM IN ANTRIX CORPORATION LIMITED

Introduction

Antrix Corporation Limited was incorporated in September 1992 by the Government of India to market space products and services. Indian Space Programme, over the past three decades, set a fine example for development of state-of-the-art technologies related to outer space and their applications in a variety of fields like telecommunications, TV broadcasting and satellite aided search and rescue, meteorology and remote sensing of natural resources.

Antrix Corporation Limited is an apex marketing agency (Fig. 5.1 and Fig. 5.2) that devotes its efforts and energies to sharing this rich bank of space expertise with the world. Antrix has access to the resources of ISRO, DOS and more importantly, to the vibrant Indian industry that has geared itself to handle high-technology projects. Antrix draws upon the heritage of the Indian Space Programme and ISRO's vast experience and proven scientific talent which span over two decades.

Antrix offers a rainbow of versatile and varied resources. From manpower training to software, subsystems and components for satellites, fabrication of satellites to user requirements, launch services and tracking facilities, Antrix has the total systems of capability. This indicates that the level of integration Antrix can provide is unrespectedly high.

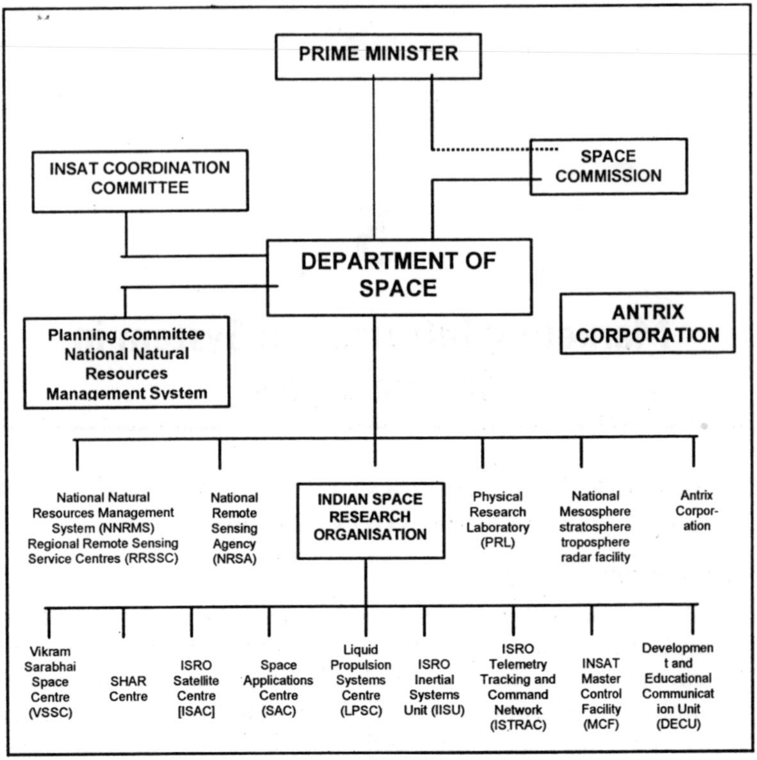

Fig. 5.1.1 Organisation Chart

Marketing Organisation

The marketing organisation is headed by the Executive Director. The Executive Director coordinates the whole marketing activity. He is assisted by Director–International Marketing Scientist 'F' (SF) business development. The Director, international marketing, supervises Manager of Business Development.

Marketing Information System

Antrix Corporation would like to have an information management system with a repository of the information, contract and order tracking facility and a decision support data base system. This application will cover the following major requirements / issues:

1. *A repository of*
   - All the enquiries received from various customers and enquiries to the vendors from ANTRIX

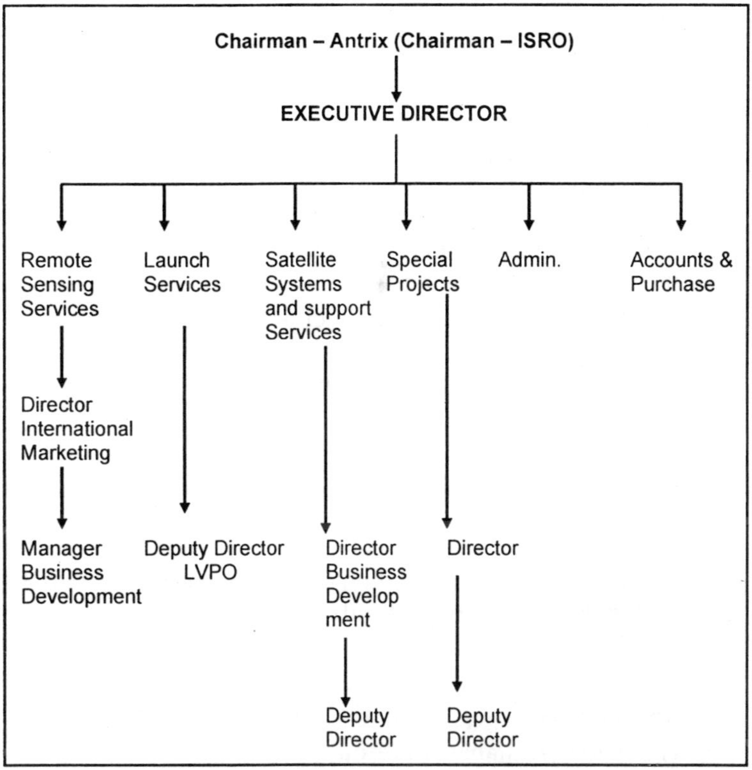

Fig. 5.1.2 Organisation chart of ANTRIX

- Communication with subcontractors/suppliers before and after quoting to the customers
- Quotations to the customers and the communication
- Details of the contract/purchase order signed either for the purchase / sale of products and services
- General office administration and office expenditure management including telephone/communication service charges, visitor entry records, payroll, travel management, tracking the incoming and outgoing postal mail/couriers and inventory of items etc.
- A database and link to the EXIM (Export, Import) documents and policies.

2. Status monitoring / tracking facilities for all the contracts and orders that are completed or that are currently working on.
3. A two-way communication with Tally S/W: Tracking the status of payments, deliverables / receivables and notifying the identified authority through email and system POP UP message as decided with the creation of online invoice and reminder formats. A link to the data base of resources available that can be user updated.
4. Validating the payments/deliveries based on the terms and conditions of the contract/order including—alerting the Accounts department. Prior to the payment deadlines or milestones, for raising invoices or receivable deadlines.
5. Online View–Provide hard copy reports of different formats like contract status, payment received, receivables ageing (Outstanding figures on a Monthly, Yearly or Contract basis), and the status of invoices, categorised according to different parameters. The published reports to be compatible with the ISO-9000 certification standards defined with graphing capability.
6. Repository of all the contracts completed or important documents with a provision to import and edit if required.
7. A link to the database of resources available that can be user updated.
8. Provision for an electronic bulletin board with auto announcement prompts to all connected users.
9. Audit Trail and Investment decision support and search facility on key words, reference numbers.
10. Other user defined interfaces for a full-fledged automation of the information.

The system developed should have the ability to route contracts and orders for approval including multiple routing stops and customisable routing paths with concurrent connectivity to multiple users to access live data and high leveled inbuilt data security.

About the System

The company is at present using VB front end software, Windows 2000 Internet and Internet Spread sheets and other necessary software packages as and when necessary.

The company is using sufficient computer systems with suitable configuration (Pentium III Network enabled) to use the application software. The company has about 10 employees. Users are trained to provide skill for using windows, Oracle and other necessary packages. The IS people were trained. The key aspects covered in training were:

- Use of the system
- Data security, integrity soon.
- Troubleshooting.

Reasons for setting up of computerised marketing information system are:

- To make complex decisions easy
- It is an extension to computerisation made already in other departments.
- Creates information availability for an effective as efficient decision-making
- To assess the demand, and competition in a better way.
- On request of marketing managers
- To improve the efficiency of information sharing
- For updating information.

Reports

Various reports are generated. The key reports are:

- Customer satisfaction
- Customer profile and needs
- Customer loyalty
- Future plans of customer which demand produces
- Demand and elasticity
- Competitors' pricing and product features and product strategies etc.
- Brand image, influence
- Substitute technology and alternative technology
- Government policies affecting the market
- Legal reports etc.

Evaluation

MKIS is not yet fully computerised as the required software is not yet available. They are in the process of developing their own software suited to their requirements. They are of the view that the following developments in the system are necessary :

- System should be close ended
- It can be constantly updated
- It must be highly secured

Future Plans

Bread board systems are planned for development.

Profile of Respondents

Table 5.1.1 describes the profile of the respondents from the organisation. The respondents include Executive Director, Director International Marketing, 'Scientist F' Business Development, Manager Business Development and Assistant manager. Experience-wise the respondent group consists of about 80% decision-makers with more than 10 years of experience. Level-wise it can be observed that about 40% of them are at senior and middle management levels.

Table 5.1.1: Profile of Respondents
(N = 5)

S.No.	Elements	F	%
1.	**Designation**		
	Executive Director	1	20
	Director International Marketing	1	20
	SF	1	20
	Manager	1	20
	Assistant Manager	1	20
2.	**Experience (years)**		
	Below 10 years	1	20
	10 years and above	4	80
3.	**Level in hierarchy**		
	Senior	2	40
	Middle	2	40
	Junior	1	20
4.	**Department :** Marketing	5	100

Table 5.1.2 shows the reporting relationships and subordinate positions under the respondents:

Table 5.1.2 : Reporting Relationships of Respondents

(N = 5)

Respondents	Reporting to
Executive Director	Chairman
Director International Marketing	Executive Director
SF	Executive Director
Manager	Director
Assistant Manager	Manager / SF
Subordinate positions under Respondents	**Subordinate positions**
Executive Director	Director, SF, Manager
Director International Marketing	Manager - SD
SF	Assistant Manager
Manager	Assistant Manager
Assistant Manager	-

The respondents revealed their main job concerns as follows:

- Executive Director–All activities pertaining to marketing
- Director–International Marketing
- Scientist 'F'–Marketing, Business Development, Preparation of proposals, contract management and execution etc.
- Manager–Business development and marketing of IRS services globally, advertising, marketing research, response to enquiries, website content management
- Assistant Manager–Assisting Scientist 'F' / Manager. Preparation of day to day payments and receivables, liaison with middle management

Role Clarity

The responses indicate that they have reasonably good role clarity (4.8). They have clear view about their relationships (5.0), authority (4.4) and responsibility (4.2). They don't have role conflicts (4.6). The measurement of role clarity on the four dimensions also established an average score of (4.5) which is near to the overall score of (4.6). Table 5.1.3 shows the details.

Table 5.1.3 : Perceived Role Clarity of Respondents

(N = 5)

Perceptions	Mean	SD
My role is clear to me	4.8	1.5
I do not have conflicts in my playing my role (No over lapping)	4.6	1.2
My authority is clear to me	4.4	1.2
My relations with others are well defined	5.0	2.0
I was told clearly about my responsibility (What I have to contribute)	4.2	1.5
Overall	4.4	1.4

Decision-Making

Table 5.1.4 shows that the respondents are mostly depending upon their seniors (4.2), and very less on subordinates and peers.

Table 5.1.4 : Dependence in Decision-Making and Implementation

(N = 5)

Positions	Mean	SD
On superiors	4.2	1.54
On subordinates	2.4	1.54
On peers	2.6	1.09

What methods do the decision-makers employ in data analysis? The respondents have observed that they make use of mostly standard methods for key decisions as well as routine decisions.

Information Flow

The information flows to the different persons in the hierarchy of marketing is as follows:

- The Executive Director receives policy related and target related future plans from the Chairman. He sends the same to his subordinates. He also sends performance related information to the Chairman.
- The Director International Marketing receives market-related, business-related, and customer-related information from his subordinates. From the government, he receives export-import policy related information.
- Scientist 'F' receives market-related, business performance and customer details from his superiors and also sends reports to superiors as often.
- The Manager receives enquiries, responses and reports from the Director international Marketing on real time basis. He also receives documents and typing work done from his subordinates on real time basis.
- The Manager receives proposals and market information from the Executive Director and Director on real time basis.

Perception about Information

An inquiry about the availability of information in terms of sufficiency or overload or shortage has revealed that all the respondents with the exception of two managers have information shortage for their effective functioning. Only one manager felt that the information is sufficient and another one felt that there is information overload. The shortage according to him relates to external information.

Table 5.1.5 : Perception about Information Received

(N = 5)

Perceptions	F	%
Information over load	1	20
Information sufficiency	1	20
Information shortage	3	60

Reports

Executive Director receives management system reports which include customer satisfaction, competitors' pricing and product features and product strategies, substitute technology and alternative trends, customer profile and needs, demand and elasticity, future plans of customer, customer loyalty, brand image and influence, government policies etc. from various levels of the organisation and government. Executive Director sends summary reports, detailed reports and exception reports to the chairman.

Director-International Marketing receives satellite news, business and launch reports from the Manager. The Director sends business reports to his subordinates.

Scientist 'F' receives financial performance reports from account section. SF sends reports relating to performance of the company, customer satisfaction, customer complaints, and other miscellaneous reports to all concerned.

The **Manager** receives Asia Sat News from the World Wide Web space news from space.com, design news from satnews.com, monthly operation report from ISRO, updates notes from Library and product brochures from manufacturers. The Manager sends 'satnews' and business and launch reports to his superiors. He also sends the same information to his colleagues in Antrix / ISRO.

The respondents felt that all reports are highly necessary. Further, they said there is no need for any new reports.

Marketing Intelligence

Table 5.1.6 shows details of means of marketing intelligence:

Table 5.1.6 : Conferences / Workshops Attended by the Respondents.

(N = 5)

Year	Conference	Workshop	Seminar	Others	F	%
1998	2	-	-	-	2	33
1999	2	1	-	-	3	50
2000	2	1	-	-	2	33
2001	3	-	-	-	3	50

Table 5.1.7 shows the different sources of information used by the managers to keep them update. They are newspaper, journals, discussion with company personnel and TV news and programs The other sources are conferences and workshop/ seminars

Table 5.1.7 : Source of Information Used to Keep Updated

(N = 5)

Source	F	%
Discussion with company personnel	5	100
Discussion with other company personnel	1	20
T. V. news and programs	5	100
Conference / Workshops / Seminars	4	80
News papers/ Journals	5	100
Internet	1	20

Marketing Research

The importance of marketing research as an aid for effective decision-making is recognised by the respondents. It is conducted as and when necessary for the purpose of decision-making. Table 5.1.8 shows the details.

Table 5.1.8 : Use of Marketing Research in Decision-Making

(N =5)

Factors	Mean	SD
Importance	4.4	1.1
Frequency	3.0	1.1

SYSTEM-EVALUATION

The system effectiveness is evaluated based on the views of respondent managers as follows:

1. System management evaluation
2. Information system evaluation
3. People evaluation
4. Outcomes evaluation

System Management Evaluation

The system management is analysed with reference to the following factors:

- Leadership
- Plans
- Controls
- Security, and
- Change

Table 5.1.9 shows the responses signifying system management factors. According to it, 65% of the respondents are of the view that, system is flexible and adaptive; leadership is good (64%) and plans are effective (72.7%). About 80% of the respondents opined that security of the system is very good. Controls are effective according to 74.7% of the respondents. System has changed characteristics according to 72.7% of the respondents.

Table 5.1.9 : Systems Management Evaluation

(N = 5)

S.No	Factor	Average Score	
		Frequency	%
1	Leadership	3.2	64.0
2	Plans	3.6	72.7
3	Controls	2.7	39.7
4	Security	4.0	80.0
5	Change	3.6	72.7

Leadership

The marketing information system in the organisation is under the direction of a qualified manager. The management is ably motivating its personnel to effectively provide information service. There are training programs for employees which they considered necessary. Table 5.1.10 shows the details.

Table 5.1.10 : Systems Management Evaluation - Leadership (N = 5)

No.	Factors	F	%
1.	Is the MKIS under the direction of qualified manager (specify)?	4	80
2.	Does management motivate its personnels to effectively provide a desired information service?	5	100
3.	Is there a formal training program where deemed necessary		
(i)	New employees?	3	60
(ii)	Transferred employees?	1	20
(iii)	Regular employees?	3	60

Plans

According to 76.6% the respondents the master plan of marketing information system is well-defined and integrated with departmental long range plans and organisational objectives. Also the marketing information system plan is well integrated with procedures and standards. Top management, the management steering committee and Information system management periodically review the master plan. Table 5.1.11 shows the details.

Table 5.1.11 : Systems management Evaluation–Plans (N = 5)

No.	Factors	F	%
1.	Does the management have a well-defined master plan for MKIS?	5	100
2.	Is the master plan integrated into–		
(i)	Objectives?	5	100
(ii)	Strategies?	5	100
(iii)	Projects?	2	40
(iv)	Policies?	4	80
(v)	Procedures?	5	100
(vi)	Standards?	2	40
3	Is department's long range plans related to organisational objectives?	5	100
4.	Is the master plan subjected to periodic review?		
(i)	Top management?	2	40
(ii)	Management steering committee?	2	40
(iii)	Information systems management?	3	60

Controls

The following IS control measures are considered effective by all the respondents. According to them :

- Management exercises the necessary control over its operations.
- Management has segregated the functions of the department in order to minimise fraud, theft and irregularities.
- Provision for backup personnel in key information system positions is created.
- Internal auditing periodically checks operations of IS department.
- System has powerful air conditioning environment which is adequate.
- The system procedures and documents are not kept current.

However, the senior management has pointed out the following:

- There is no external, independent auditing of the system.
- There are no surprise audits (internal) to check irregularities.

Table 5.1.12 shows the details:

Table 5.1.12 : Systems Management Evaluation–Control

(N = 5)

No.	Factors	F	%
1.	Does management exercise the necessary control over Its operations so that fraud, theft, and irregularities of IS methods and procedures can be detected?	4	80
2.	Does management segregate the functions of the department in order to minimise fraud, theft, and irregularities?	4	80
3.	Are there provisions for back up personnel in key information systems positions?	5	100
4.	Does internal auditing periodically check on the operations of the information systems department?	4	80

[contd...]

No.	Factors	F	%
5.	Is the information system audited periodically by an independent third party (outside auditors or consultants)?	2	40
6.	Is there a surprise audit of the information systems department for detecting–		
(i)	Fraud?	1	20
(ii)	Theft?	1	20
(iii)	Collusion?	1	20
(iv)	Embezzlement?	1	20
(v)	Sabotage?	1	20
(vi)	Irregularities?	1	20
(vi)	Does the computer system have adequate power air condition?	4	80
7.	Are systems and procedure manuals kept current?	4	80

Security

About 80% of the respondents felt that security controls are required by IS management. The security measures are well-designed and implemented in the organisation. The security controls are sufficient to ensure that all input data and corrections to them are processed properly and accurately. However, some of the respondents are of the view that security measures are not available. Table 5.1.13 furnishes the information :

Table 5.1.13 : Systems Management Evaluation–Security
(N = 5)

No.	Factors	F	%
1	Are security controls required by information systems management?	4	80
2	Are security controls fully understood and implemented by systems and programming personnel?	4	80
3.	Are security controls sufficient to ensure that all input data and corrections to data have been processed properly and accurately?	4	80
4.	Are security controls written and contained in appropriate systems and procedured manuals for ready reference when necessary?	4	80

Change Management

According to Table 5.1.14, the system is perceived by respondents as change-oriented. A control mechanism with well-designed procedures is set up in the organisation. It functions by seeking approvals of top management. The change plans are well documented including the reasons for changes. The users are involved in the change process. Written memoranda are issued to the appropriate personnel concerning changes. Auditors are also appraised of the important changes. During the change process effective control systems to prevent unauthorised changes in the master files and transactions files are also established.

Table 5.1.14 : System Management Evaluation–Change

(N = 5)

No.	Factors	F	%
1.	Is there a control mechanism for making appropriate information systems changes?	4	80
2.	Does this control mechanism include a provision for approval?	1	20
3.	Are procedures established for making–		
(i)	System changes?	4	80
(ii)	Program changes?	4	80
(iii)	Library (Program & file) changes?	4	80
(iv)	Computer operator changes?	4	80
4.	Are all system and program changes immediately documented, including the reason for the change?	4	80
5.	Are written memoranda issued to the appropriate personnel concerning changes?	4	80
6.	Is the user involved in making changes where necessary?	4	80
7.	Are the internal and external auditors apprised of important changes?	4	80
8.	Are master files and transaction files controlled to prevent unauthorised changes during conversion?	3	60

Information System Evaluation

Table 5.1.15 shows system related appraisal. The respondents have given positive scores for system, software, documentation, maintenance and integration of the system with other systems. The mean scores are in the range of 3.0 to 3.8. Element-wise evaluation of the system is provided in table 5.1.16.

Table 5.1.15 : Evaluation of Information System

(N=5)

Elements	Mean	SD
Hardware	3.7	1.47
Software	3.8	1.21
Documentation	3.8	1.09
Maintenance	3.0	1.09
Integration	3.3	1.31
Total Average	3.52	1.23

Table 5.1.16 : Evaluation of Information System–System Details

(N = 5)

No.	Factors	Mean	SD
	Hardware		
1.	The response of the system is fast	4.2	1.5
2.	Accessing information is easy	4.2	1.5
4.	System security is very good	3.8	1.5
5.	In realisation of user needs, the system is the best	3.4	1.0
6.	The system has good flexibility	3.0	2.0
7.	Information processing is efficient	3.2	1.0
8.	Computer systems are adequate	4.2	1.5
	Average	3.7	1.4

[contd...]

[contd...]

No.	Factors	Mean	SD
	Software :		
9.	Features used in programming languages are excellent	3.6	1.34
10.	Data analysis programs are updated	4.0	1.0
	Average	3.8	1.2
	Documentation :		
11	Documentation if the system is completed	3.8	1.0
	Maintenance :		
12.	The system is well maintained	3.0	1.0
	Integrated :		
13.	The system is integrated with other systems.	3.0	1.0
14.	There is coordination between MKIS and other systems	3.6	1.54
Total		3.3	1.35

People Evaluation

Table 5.1.17 shows evaluation of effectiveness of overal rating of 3.5. The aspects like top management support, IT staff competence and support and user involvement, training and utilisation of the system are rated good. Element-wise evaluation of the system is provided in table 5.1.18.

Table 5.1.17 : People Evaluation

(N=5)

Element	Mean	SD
Top management	3.0	2.0
IS staff	3.6	1.1
Average	3.3	1.5

Table 5.1.18 : People Evaluation Details

(N=5)

No.	Factors	Mean	SD
	Top Management :		
15	Top management is involved in the development of the system	3	2
	IS Staff :		
16.	The staff in the organisation like to use the system	2.8	1.0
17.	IS staff are competent	4.4	1.2
	Average :	3.6	1.1

Outcomes Evaluation

The different outcomes of a system like Information quality, output, user friendliness, decision support, benefits and satisfaction are evaluated by respondents. The results are shown in Table 5.2.19. According to it, the system is good in all respects including, the benefits:

Table 5.1.19 : Evaluation of System Out-comes

(N=5)

Aspect	Mean	SD
Information	3.8	1.4
Output	3.5	1.0
User friendliness	4.1	1.3
Decision Support	3.3	1.4
Benefits	4.1	1.3
Satisfaction	3.8	1.5

Information and Output

Table 5.1.20 shows that information available from the system is good by itself, relevant, accurate, timely etc. However, the respondents are less happy about the output in respect of the volume, though they are happy that the reports and other information products are well scheduled.

Table 5.1.20 : Evaluation of System Outcomes–Information and Output

(N=5)

No.	Factors	Mean	SD
	Information :		
1.	Computer systems are capable	4.2	1.5
2.	Information is relevant	4.4	1.6
3.	Information is kept confidential when required	4.4	1.2
4.	Information provided by the system is accurate	3.8	1.2
5.	System provides timely information	4.2	1.5
6.	System furnishes exact information	4.0	1.0
7.	The information provided is reliable	4.2	1.5
8.	Current information is provided by the system	3.6	1.0
9.	The information is complete in all aspects	3.0	2.0
10.	It provides well designed formats	3.0	2.0
11.	Information furnished has clarity	3.8	1.5
	Average :	3.8	1.4
	Output :		
1.	The reports and other information products are well scheduled	3.0	1.0
2.	Adequate volume of output is generated by the system	4.0	1.0
	Average :	3.5	1.0

User Friendliness

Table 5.2.21 shows the user friendliness of the system in respect of training, user involvement in system development and implementation, and user confidence of the system.

Table 4.2.21 : Evaluation of System Outcomes – User friendliness (N=9)

No.	Factors	Mean	SD
1.	Users are well trained to use the system	3.0	2.0
2.	The system is used by all concerned employees	4.2	1.5
3.	There is participation of users in the system development and implementation	4.0	1.0
4.	Users have confidence in the system	4.2	1.54
	Total average :	4.1	1.39

Decision Support

According to the respondents the system is fairly helpful on an average to the managers in making decisions relating to product and price. It is also helpful in the market analysis and forecasting, place and promotion decisions. Table 5.1.22 shows the details.

Table 5.1.22 : Evaluation of System Outcomes – Decision Support (N=5)

Factors	Mean	SD
Market analysis and forecasting	2.8	1.5
Product decisions	3.6	1.5
Price decisions	2.8	1.0
Place decisions	3.6	1.5
Promotion decisions	3.8	1.5

Benefits and Satisfaction

Table 5.1.23 shows that the respondents are satisfied with the benefits of the system. They have agreed very much with the statements. "The system has tools to improve productivity of operations." 'Jobs have become easy and efficient making activities more efficient' and 'boosted the profits'. However, when rating the benefits they opined that the expectations are well-realised. Accordingly, the satisfaction with system is high.

Table 5.1.23 : Evaluation of System Outcomes–Benefits and Satisfaction

(N=5)

No.	Factors	Mean	SD
	Benefits :		
1.	The system has tools to improve productivity of operations	4.2	1.5
2.	My job has become easy with the support of the system	4.4	1.2
3.	MKIS has improved the results of the organisation	4.4	1.2
4.	MKIS is making the activities more efficient	3.6	1.2
5.	MKIS has boosted the profits of organisation	4.0	1.0
6.	My expectations of benefits of system are realised	4.2	1.54
	Total average :	4.1	1.3
	Satisfaction :		
41.	The system is satisfactory to me	3.8	1.5

Overall Evaluation

The respondents are asked to evaluate the present marketing information system in the organisation on a 5-point scale representing exceptional and poor at the polar points. The system is considered good by majority of the respondents. Table 5.1.24 shows the details:

Table 5.1.24 : Overall Evaluation of Information System

(N=5)

Factor	Mean	SD
Present marketing information system	2.8	1.54

5.2 MARKETING INFORMATION SYSTEM IN MEDINOVA DIAGNOSTIC SERVICE LIMITED

Introduction

Medinova Diagnostic Service Limited was established in the year 1987 in Andhra Pradesh, under the companies act with the main objective of rendering diagnostic services. Apart from rendering diagnostic services through its four diagnostic centres at Hyderabad, Bangalore, Pune and Kolkata it is also providing technical expertise to set up diagnostic centres on turn key basis under franchise arrangements throughout the country under the name of Medinova. The company has been held mainly by M/s Standard Medical and Pharmaceuticals Ltd.

Medinova Diagnostic is a novel concept in diagnostics offering cost-effective health care-a comprehensive range of diagnostic services, all under one roof. It cuts down prolonged investigative hospitalisation or delays in diagnosis. The emphasis will be on speed and accuracy. It is equipped with the latest state-of-the -art diagnostic instruments. Medinova is managed by a team of highly trained professionals.

SERVICES

Medinova has been providing 1000 plus diagnostic services under two types as follows:

1. Radiology and Imaging Services

CT scan, Ultra monograph and 2D Color Doppler, Diagnostic Radiology, Special procedures by appointment

2. Laboratory Services

Endoscope procedures, Clinical Chemistry, Endocrinology, Hematology, Histopathology, Microbiology, Serology and Immunology, Collagen Disorder Profile, Drug Assay, Lipid Profile, Diabetic Profile, Hepatic Profile, Liver Function Tests, Renal Profile, Coronary Profile, Cardiac Injury Profile, Hypertension Profile, Oncology Profile, Total Body Profile, Metabolic Profile, Pre-operative Profile, Prenatal Profile, Anemia Package, Arthritis Package, Bones / Joint Package, Cardiac Risk Evaluation Package, Respiratory Package, Pancreatic Package, Fluid Balance Package, Urology Urinary Tract Disease, Urinary Stones Package, Neurology Stroke Package, Coagulation Screen , Hemolytic Profile, Kidney Function Test, Renal Allograft Profile, Fertility Profile (female / male) , Laser Health checkup.

Marketing Organisation

The marketing organisation is headed by General Manager. He supervises Assistant General Manager, Marketing Manager. Marketing Manager supervises a team of Marketing Executives.

Marketing Information System

Marketing information system was computerised in the year 1990. The main reason for setting up of computerised marketing information system is to make complex decisions easy.

The identified principal benefits of MKIS are:

- Helps improve decision-making
- Generates a variety of reports
- Makes planning and controlling effective
- Increases profits
- Keeps a general database.

About the System

The company is using Clipper Software which is built as per their requirements. The system helps integrating marketing department with Finance, Human Resource Development, Production, and Research and Development. It provides branch-wise market potential and helps develop suitable marketing plan. Also it furnishes sales data and analysis and credit controls. There are more than 15 computers with suitable configuration. Formal Training has been provided as and when necessary.

Reports

The main reports generated for decision-making include :

- MIS reports (Daily analysis)
- Corporate business report
- Collection and payment report
- Client reporting report
- Client feed back report
- Doctor's report on perception on services

Evaluation

The following inadequacies are identified:

1. System has poor security.
2. Old database and its updating
3. Chances of corrupting data
4. Some untrained users because of old software still in use.

System Development Plans

The future plans centre around high system security, and developing latest database. Develop system controls to protect from computing data provide training for EDP people. They are planning for SAP / ERP future requirements.

Profile of Respondents

Table 5.2.1 describes the profile of the respondents from the organisation. The respondents include General Manager, five Marketing Managers. Experience-wise the respondent group consists of about 17% decision-makers with more than 10 years of experience. Level-wise, it can be observed that about 17% of them are at the senior management level. The remaining are managers and officers having less than 10 years of experience.

Table 5.2.1 : Profile of Respondents

(N = 6)

S.No.	Elements	F	%
1.	**Designation :**		
	General Manager	1	17
	Marketing Manager	5	83
	Assistant Manager	--	---
2.	**Experience (years) :**		
	Less than 10 years	5	83
	10 years and above	1	17
3.	**Level in hierarchy :**		
	Senior	1	17
	Junior	5	83

Table 5.2.2 shows the reporting relationships. General Manager reports to Managing Director. Marketing Manager reports to General Manager. All the respondents except officers have subordinate positions as shown in Table 5.2.2 :

Table 5.2.2 : Reporting Relationships of Respondents

(N = 6)

Respondents	Reporting to
General Manager	Director
Marketing Manager	General manager
Subordinate positions	
General Manager	Marketing Manager
Marketing Manager	Assistant Manager

Role Clarity

Respondents were asked to identify their levels of clarity about the roles they play in the organisation. The responses indicate that they are very much clear about their roles. A mean score of 4.8 to 4.6 on overall and item-wise statements as shown in Table 5.2.3.

Table 5.2.3 : Perceived Role Clarity of Respondents

(N = 6)

Perceptions	Mean	SD
My role is clear to me	4.6	1.6
I do not have conflicts in my playing my role (No over lapping)	4.0	1.4
My authority is clear to me	4.8	1.9
My relations with others are well-defined	5.0	2.4
I was told clearly about my responsibility (What I have to contribute)	4.5	1.9
Overall	4.5	1.8

Decision-Making

Table 5.2.4 shows that they are mostly dependant upon their superiors (4.8) and moderately on subordinates (3.0).

Table 5.2.4 : Dependence in Decision-Making and Implementation (N = 6)

Positions	Mean	SD
On superiors	4.8	1.9
On subordinates	3.0	0.9
On peers	1.5	1.4

The respondents have observed that they make use of mostly time series analysis techniques for key decisions as well as routine decisions.

Information Flow

The information flows to the different persons in the hierarchy of marketing is as follows:

- The General Manager receives information pertaining to business targets and future plans from the Director. The General Manager also receives business performance reports from marketing managers area-wise.
- The General Manager sends information regarding business strategies to marketing managers. The General Manager also sends performance summaries to the Director.
- The Marketing Managers receive target activity and strategy related information from General Manager.
- The Marketing Manager shares with colleagues regarding daily business
- The Marketing Manager sends day-to-day performance to the General Manager.

Perception about Information

All the respondents with the exception of two managers have sufficient information for their effective functioning. Only two managers felt that there is information shortage.

Table 5.2.5 : Perception about Information Received

(N = 6)

Perceptions	F	%
Information over load	1	16
Information sufficiency	3	50
Information shortage	2	33

Reports

General Manager receives summary reports from Marketing Managers. General Manager sends all summary reports to the Director. Marketing Managers receives daily analysis report from EDP, target report from General Manager, customer information from PRO, sales reports from Managing Director. Marketing managers send customer information reports and sales repots to General Manager.

When asked about the necessity of the existing reports, the respondents felt that all of them are necessary. The respondents opined that there is no need for any new reports.

Marketing Intelligence

Table 5.2.6 shows the participation details of respondents in the conferences and workshops. From the table it can be observed that their participation is very low.

Table 5.2.6 : Conferences / Workshops Attended by the Respondents

(N = 6)

Year	Conference	Workshop	Seminar	Others	F	%
1998	1	---	---	---	1	17.0
1999	1	---	---		1	17.0
2000	1	---	---	1	2	33.3
2001	1	---	---	1	2	33.3

Table 5.2.7 shows the respondents use different source of information viz. newspapers, journals, discussion with company

personnel and also with persons belonging to other companies. The other sources are T.V. news and programmes, conferences and workshops / seminars. However, one medium that is less used is internet. The non-users of it belong to lower management level.

Table 5.2.7 : Source of Information Used to Keep Updated
(N = 6)

Source of information	F	%
Discussion with company personnel	6	100
Discussion with other company personnel	6	100
T. V. news and programs	6	100
Conference / Workshops / Seminars	6	100
News papers/ Journals	6	100
Internet	4	66

Marketing Research

Marketing research is considered very important for effective decision-making by the respondents. According to the respondents, it is conducted frequently for the purpose of decision-making. Table 5.2.8 shows the details:

Table 5.2.8 : Use of Marketing Research in Decision-Making
(N = 6)

Factors	Mean	SD
Importance	4.5	1.4
Frequency	4.5	1.4

System Evaluation

The system effectiveness is evaluated based on the views of respondent managers as follows:

1. System management evaluation
2. Information system evaluation
3. People evaluation
4. Outcomes evaluation

Systems Management Evaluation

The system management is analysed with reference to 5 factors;

- Leadership
- Plans
- Controls
- Security and
- Change

Table 5.2.9 shows the responses signifying system management factors. According to it, about 81% of the respondents are of the view that system is flexible and adoptive, plans (89.1%) are effective and leadership (76.4%) is good. About 83% of the respondents opined that security provisions of the system are good. Controls are effective according to 81% of the respondents. About 75.3% respondents have opined that system is change oriented.

Table 5.2.9 : Systems Management Evaluation

(N = 6)

S.No	Factor	Average Score	
		F	%
1	Leadership	4.6	76.4
2	Plans	5.3	89.1
3	Controls	4.9	81.3
4	Security	5.0	83.0
5	Change	4.5	75.3
Total average		4.8	81.0

Leadership

The marketing information system is supervised by a qualified manager. The management is motivating competently its personnel, to provide effective information service. Training programs are conducted for employees to enhance usage.

Table 5.2.10 : Systems Management Evaluation–Leadership

(N = 6)

No.	Factors	F	%
1.	Is the MKIS is under the direction of qualified manager (specify)?	6	100
2.	Does management motivate its personnels to effectively provide the Desired information service?	6	100
3.	Is there a formal training program where deemed necessary?		
(i)	New employees?	4	66
(ii)	Transferred employees?	4	66
(iii)	Regular employees?	3	50

Plans

All the respondents opined that the master plan of marketing information system is well-defined. Also it is integrated properly with departmental long range plans and organisational objectives. According to them, the marketing information system plan is well established with defined procedures and standards. Top management, the management steering committee and information system management review the master plan periodically. Table 5.2.11 shows the details:

Table 5.2.11 : Systems management Evaluation–Plans

(N = 6)

No.	Factors	F	%
1.	Does the management have a well defined master plan for MKIS?	6	100
2.	Is the master plan integrated into–		
(i)	Objectives?	6	100
(ii)	Strategies?	6	100
(iii)	Projects?	6	100

[contd...]

[contd...]

No.		Factors	F	%
	(iv)	Policies?	4	66
	(v)	Procedures?	6	100
	(vi)	Standards?	5	83
3		Is departments long range plans related to organisational objectives?	5	83
4.		Is the master plan subjected to periodic review?		
	(i)	Top management?	5	83
	(ii)	Management steering committee?	5	83
	(iii)	Information systems management?	6	100

Controls

The following IS controls measures are considered effective by all the respondents:

- Management exercises the necessary control over its operations so that fraud, theft, and irregularities of IS methods and procedures can be detected.
- Management separated the functions of the department in order to minimise fraud, theft and irregularities.
- Management has segregated the functions of the department in order to minimise fraud, theft and irregularities.
- Provision for backup personnel in the key information systems positions is created.
- System has powerful air conditioning environment which is adequate.
- There are surprise audits (internal) to check irregularities.

However, the senior management has pointed out the following:

1. There is no external, independent auditing of the system.
2. The system procedures and documents are not kept current.

Table 5.2.12 : Systems Management Evaluation – Control

(N = 6)

No.	Factors	F	%
1.	Does management exercise the necessary control over Its operations so that fraud, theft, and irregularities of IS methods and procedures can be detected?	4	66
2.	Does management segregate the functions of the department in order to minimise fraud, theft, and irregularities?	4	66
3.	Is there a provision for backup personnel in key information systems positions?	6	100
4.	Does internal auditing periodically check on the operations of the information systems department?	6	100
5.	Is the information system audited periodically by an independent third party (outside auditors or consultants)?	4	66
6.	Is there a surprise audit of the information systems department for detecting?		
(i)	Fraud?	6	100
(ii)	Theft?	6	100
(iii)	Collusion?	4	66
(iv)	Embezzlement?	4	66
(v)	Sabotage?	4	66
(v)	Irregularities?	5	83
(vi)	Does the computer system have adequate power air condition?	6	100
7.	Are systems and procedure manuals kept current?	5	83

Security

All the respondents felt that security controls are required. The security measures are well-desiesigned and implemented in the organisation. There are sufficient security controls to ensure that all input data and corrections to them are processed properly and accurately. However, some of the respondents are of the view that security controls are not fully understood and implemented. Security procedures manuals are not available (Table 5.2.13).

Table 5.2.13 : Systems Management Evaluation – Security

(N = 6)

No.	Factors	F	%
1	Are security controls required by information systems management?	5	83
2	Are security controls fully understood and implemented by systems and programming personnel?	5	83
3.	Are security controls sufficient to ensure that all input data and corrections to data have been processed properly and accurately?	5	83
4.	Are security controls written and contained in appropriate systems and procedures manuals for ready reference when necessary?	5	83

Change Management

The system is flexible and sensitive to change. A control mechanism with well-designed procedures is set up in the organisation. It functions by seeking approvals of top management. The change plans are well documented including the reasons for changes. The users are involved in the change process. Written memoranda are issued to the appropriate personnel concerning changes. Auditors are also appraised of the important changes. During the change process effective control systems to prevent unauthorised changes in the master files and transactions files are also established. On the whole, the marketing information system is dynamic and adaptative.

Table 5.2.14 : System Management Evaluation–Change
(N = 6)

No.	Factors	F	%
1.	Is there a control mechanism for making appropriate information systems changes?	6	100
2.	Does this control mechanism include a provision for approval?	6	100
3.	Are procedures established for making?		
(i)	System changes?	4	66
(ii)	Program changes?	5	83
(iii)	Library (Program and file) changes?	3	50
(iv)	Computer operator changes?	4	66
4.	Are all system and program changes immediately documented, including the reason for the change?	5	83
5	Are written memoranda issued to the appropriate personnel concerning changes?	4	66
6.	Is the user involved in making changes where necessary	5	83
7.	Are the internal and external auditors apprised of important changes?	4	66
8.	Are master files and transaction files controlled to prevent unauthorised changes during conversion?	4	66

Information System Evaluation

Table 5.2.15 shows system related appraisal. The respondents have given positive scores for hardware, software, documentation, maintenance and integration of the system with other systems. The mean scores are in the range of 3.6 to 4.3. Element-wise evaluation of the system is provided in table 5.2.16.

Table 5.2.15 : Evaluation of Information System – System Elements (N=6)

Elements	Mean	SD
Hardware	4.2	1.1
Software	4.3	1.1
Documentation	4.1	1.1
Maintenance	3.6	1.1
Integration	4.0	1.3
Total average	4.0	1.1

Table 5.2.16 : Evaluation of information system–System Details (N = 6)

No.	Factors	Mean	SD
	Hardware :		
1.	The response of the system is fast	4.3	1.1
2.	Accessing information is easy	3.8	1.1
3.	System security is very good	4.3	1.6
4.	In realisation of user needs, the system is the best	4.1	1.1
5.	The system has good flexibility	5.1	1.4
6.	Information processing is efficient	4.3	1.1
7.	Computer systems are adequate	4.0	0.9
	Total Average :	4.2	1.1
	Software :		
1.	Features used in programming languages are excellent	4.6	1.6
2.	Data analysis programs are updated	4.1	1.9
	Total Average :	4.3	1.7

[contd...]

[contd...]

No.	Factors	Mean	SD
	Documentation :		
1	Documentation if the system is completed	4.1	1.1
	Maintenance :		
2.	The system is well maintained	3.6	1.1
	Integrated :		
1.	The system is integrated with other systems.	4.3	1.6
2.	There is coordination between MKIS and other systems	3.8	1.1
Total Average :		4.0	1.3

People Evaluation

Table 5.2.17 shows evaluation of effectiveness of people elements. The respondents have given an overall rating of 4.0. The aspects like top management support, I.T staff competence and support and user involvement, training and utilisation of the system are rated good. Element-wise evaluation of the people is provided in tables 5.2.18.

Table 5.2.17 : People Evaluation
(N=6)

Element	Mean	SD
Top management	4.1	1.1
IS staff	4.0	1.3
Total average	4.5	1.2

Table 5.2.18 : People Evaluation Details
(N=6)

No.	Factors	Mean	SD
	Top management :		
1.	Top management is involved in the development of the system	4.1	1.1
	IS Staff :		
1.	The staff in the organisation like to use the system	4.3	1.6
2.	IS staff are competent	3.8	1.1
Total Average :		4.0	1.3

Outcomes Evaluation

The different outcomes of a system like Information quality, output, user friendliness, decision support, benefits and satisfaction are good (Table 5.2.19):

Table: 5.2.19 : Evaluation of System Outcomes
(N=6)

Aspect	Mean	SD
Information	4.1	1.2
Output	4.6	1.6
User friendliness	4.1	1.5
Decision Support	4.2	1.2
Benefits	3.9	1.4
Satisfaction	4.3	1.1

Information and Output

Table 5.2.20 shows that information available (4.1) from the system is relevant, accurate, timely etc. The respondents are also happy about the output in respect of the volume, frequency and information products are well-scheduled.

Table 5.2.20 : Evaluation of System Outcomes-Information and Output
(N=6)

No.	Factors	Mean	SD
	Information		
1.	Computer systems are capable	3.6	1.1
2.	Information is relevant	4.0	0.9
3.	Information is kept confidential when required	3.6	0.9
4.	Information provided by the system is accurate	3.8	1.1
5.	System provides timely information	4.0	0.9

[contd...]

[contd...]

No.	Factors	Mean	SD
6.	System furnishes exact information	4.5	1.4
7.	The information provided is reliable	4.3	1.1
8.	Current information is provided by the system	4.5	1.4
9.	The information is complete in all aspects	4.3	1.6
10.	It provides well designed formats	4.8	1.9
11.	Information furnished has clarity	4.3	1.1
	Total average :	4.1	1.2
	Output :		
1.	The reports and other information products are well-scheduled	4.6	1.6
2.	Adequate volume of output is generated by the system	4.6	1.6
	Total Average :	4.6	1.6

User Friendliness

Table 5.2.21 shows the user friendliness of the system. In aspects like training, user involvement in system development and implementation, and user confidence of the system is friendly.

Table 5.2.21 : Evaluation of System Outcomes–User friendliness (N=9)

No.	Factors	Mean	SD
1.	Users are well trained to use the system	3.8	1.1
2.	The system is used by all concerned employees	4.3	1.1
3.	There is participation of users in the system development and implementation	4.6	1.6
4.	Users have confidence in the system	4.0	2.4
	Total average :	4.1	1.5

Decision Support

According to the respondents, the system is fairly helpful to the managers in making decisions relating to product and price. It is also helpful in the market analysis and forecasting, place and promotion decisions. Table 5.2.22 shows the details:

Table 5.2.22 : Evaluation of System Outcomes–Decision Support System

(N=6)

Factors	Mean	SD
Market analysis and forecasting	4.1	1.1
Product decisions	4.3	1.6
Price decisions	4.5	1.4
Place decisions	4.1	1.1
Promotion decisions	4.3	1.1

Benefits and Satisfaction

Table 5.2.23 shows that the respondents are benefited by the system. They have agreed very much with the statements–"The system has tools to improve productivity of operations." 'Jobs have become easy and efficient,' 'making activities more efficient' and 'boosted the profits'. When rating the benefits they opined that the expectations are realised. Accordingly, the satisfaction with system is high.

Table 5.2.23 : Evaluation of System Outcomes–Benefits and Satisfactory

(N=6)

No.	Factors	Mean	SD
1.	The system has tools to improve productivity of operations	4.0	2.4
2.	My job has become easy with the support of the system	4.5	1.4
3.	MKIS has improved the results of the organisation	4.6	1.6
4.	MKIS is making the activities more efficient	3.6	1.1

[contd...]

[contd...]

No.	Factors	Mean	SD
5.	MKIS has boosted the profits of organisation	3.6	0.9
6.	My expectations of benefits of system are realised	3.6	1.1
	Total average	3.9	1.4
	Satisfaction :		
1.	The system is satisfactory to me	4.3	1.1

Overall Evaluation

The system is considered good by majority of the respondents. Table 5.2.24 shows the details:

Table 5.2.24 : Overall Evaluation of Information System

(N=6)

Factor	Mean	SD
Present marketing information system	4.0	0.9

5.3. SUMMARY

Antrix had established MKIS in 1972 and Medinova 1993. Both the organisations have set-up MKIS for the same purpose of making complex decisions easy.

Antrix is presently using Oracle, VB and Internet facility whereas Medinova is dependent on Clipper and Oracle. The system in Antrix is yet to be fully computerised. Antrix is planning for bread-board system, whereas Medinova is set out for SAP/ERP. Both the organisations use reports generated by the system. Marketing intelligence sources are primarily discussions, TV and print media. Marketing research is considered important and used as and when necessary.

Information system is rated below average in Antrix and good in Medinova. The poor rating in Antrix may be because the system is not yet completed and brought to full use. In respect of system, people and outcomes also the scores of Medinova system are on higher side, excepting in two cases viz., user friendliness and benefits. In these cases, the ratings are almost similar to those of Amtrix.

Information overload and shortages are reported in both the organisations Information shortage is reported only in Antrix. According to the spokesperson of Medinova, the following inadequacies exist :

- System has poor security
- Maintenance of old database and updating it
- Chances of corrupting data
- Some untrained users (EDP) because of old software.

6

Summary of Findings and Suggestions

In this final chapter, an attempt is made to summarise the findings and provide suggestions to make systems effective from the user point of view.

Need for the Study

In India, many organisations have set up marketing information systems (MKIS) for various reasons. However, due to lack of publicity and research, the status of the MKIS, its configuration, its applications, and its effectiveness are less known to the management world of practitioners, researchers, teachers and students.

A review of studies on marketing information systems indicates that research was mostly carried out in developed countries like USA and UK. The studies focused on concept and components [*Banks 1968, Uhl 1968, McCann 1986, Burke 1994, Shigeru Yagi 1994 and Jane 1995*], importance [*Buckland and Brancheau 1998, Ing and Mitchell 1993, Deighton and Others 1994*], development [*Cox and Good 1967, Iangle 1988, Somenda 1997*] and evaluation [Ackoff 1967, *Brien 1968, Li 1997, Cortada 1995 and Malik and Goyal 2000*]. In India, research on information systems is still at a nascent stage. Few researchers like [*Sharma 1990, Goyal 2001 and Vittal 1999*] studied information systems in Indian organisations. The studies examined the general information systems and information resource management practices.

A comprehensive research on marketing information systems is yet to take place. The available literature comprises mostly conceptual explorations and journalistic descriptions of existing marketing information systems. As such, there is a need to undertake a systematic study on the status, working and effectiveness of the marketing information systems.

Research Problem

In view of the above, the study is undertaken to find answers to the questions:

- What is the state of the art of marketing information systems in Indian organisations?
- How well are they performing?
- Do they need improvements? If yes, what kind of measures are needed?

Objectives of the Study

Following are the objectives of the study :

- To describe marketing information systems in select organisations
- To evaluate the effectiveness of the systems based on :
  - (i) Comparative study of information systems in similar organisation(s)
  - (ii) Users' opinions
- To identify measures to improve the effectiveness of the systems.

Research Model

An analytical model representing system effectiveness variables under study is shown in Fig. 6.1.

Propositions

The study examines the following propositions:

- Design / Technological effectiveness

The information systems represent the state of the art

- Functional effectiveness

The information systems are effective in serving the functional needs of marketing.

- Change effectiveness

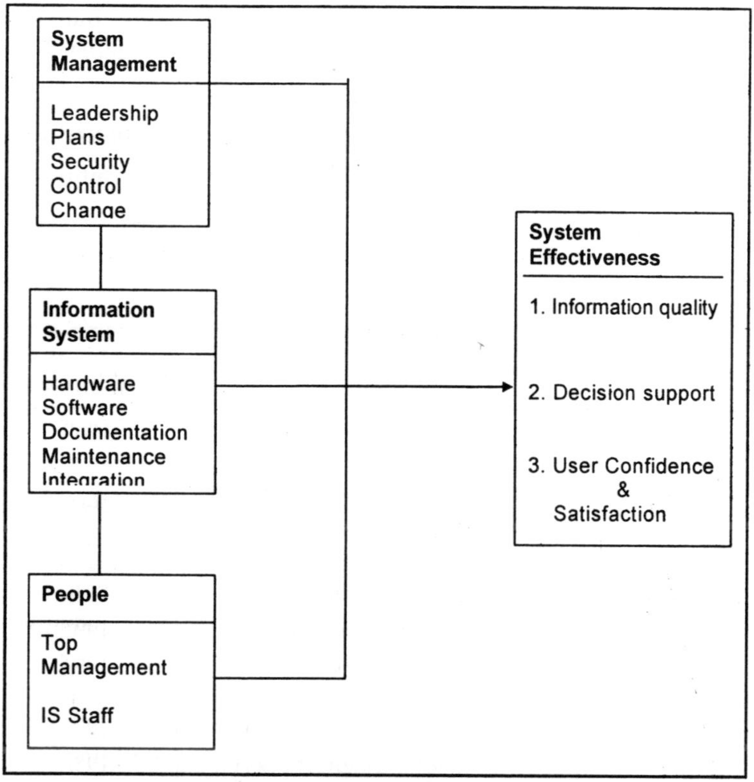

Fig. 6.1: An Analytic Model of Information System Effectiveness.

The information systems are change-oriented :

- Use effectiveness

The information systems are user friendly

- Cost effectiveness

The information systems are cost effective.

- System management effectiveness

The information systems have effective leadership, plans, security and controls.

Research Site

In all eight organisations are studied representing three important sectors of industry–core, chemicals and services. The inclusion of the organisations is influenced by their acceptance to take part in the study. However, care is taken to select organisations:

- Which organisation have minimum of 10 years of existence
- Which organisation are progressive and facing competitors
- Which organisation are classified as large organisations by Indian standards

The selected organisations are as follows :

Exhibit 6.1 : Research Organisations

Sector	Organisation	Year of Establishment
Core	➢ Chennai Petroleum Corporation Limited	1969
	➢ Viskhapatnam Steel Plant	1982
	➢ ACC Cement	1936
Chemical	➢ Neuland Laboratories Limited	1984
	➢ Erythro Pharma Limited	1991
	➢ Biological E Limited	1953
Services	➢ Antrix Corporation Limited	1972
	➢ Medinova Diagnostic Services Limited	1987

Data are also collected from all the managers in the marketing department of the participant organisations. The managers have designations like Vice-president, General Manager, Deputy General Manager, Assistant General Manager, Senior Manger, Manager and Officers. The number of marketing managers varied from 6 to 14 in the corporate or regional offices of select organisations.

Profile of the Respondents

The respondents represent a mix of senior and junior management levels, who are experienced more than 10 years and less. All of them have good role clarity. All of them are dependent on superiors in decision-making. Some of them reported dependence on peers and subordinates. Exhibit 6.2 shows particulars.

Exhibit 6.2 : Profile of the Respondents

Sector	Organisation	Experience (>10 Years) (%)	Level Senior management (%)	Role clarity (Mean Scores)	Decision Dependence on (Mean Scores)		
					Superiors	Subordinates	Peers
Core Sector	CPCL	63.6	63.6	3.9	4.4	1.4	1.9
	VSP	81.8	81.8	4.2	4.3	3.3	3.9
	ACC	14.2	14.2	4.1	3.5	2.3	2.2
Chemical Sector	Neuland	30.0	30.0	4.7	4.0	3.0	-
	Erythro Pharma	44.5	44.5	4.4	5.0	3.2	2.0
	Biological	42.8	42.8	4.3	3.8	4.1	4.2
Service Sector	ANTRIX	80.0	80.0	4.4	4.2	2.4	2.6
	Medinova	17.0	17.0	4.5	4.8	3.0	1.5

Findings

The findings of the study sector-wise are presented providing a comparative picture.

Core Sector

Exhibits 6.3, 6.4 and 6.5 present a comparative analysis of the findings. The three companies under study have established their marketing information systems in 1990s. "To make complex decisions easy" is the stated major goal supported by reasons like– "Competitors have set up" and "for early adaptation of new technology."

The systems are ERP, Network and Oracle and SAP R3 ERP. Their future plans are focused either on completing the on-going computerisation or maintenance of the designed systems to get the desired results. As can be observed, various reports are generated. They broadly relate to markets, production and sales.

An evaluation of the systems reveals that the respondents have rated their systems in the range of average to good. Systems management is appreciated by a large majority of respondents in all the three companies. However, relatively, controls deserve much more attention as fewer respondents have rated them good. Comparatively, less number of respondents in ACC considered system management good.

Information system components (hardware, software, etc.) are rated 'above average' in all the three companies. Top management support and IS people are rated well in VSP. In all other cases the ratings are above average.

Quality of information and output are rated good in ACC. User friendliness is good in VSP. When it comes to benefits of the system, in ACC the respondents have given higher rating of 4.8. In all other cases, the ratings are above average. Only in VSP, one respondent felt information overload. Very few felt "Information shortage."

The tapping of marketing intelligence sources is centered around newspapers and journals, discussions with employees and others and TV. Internet is used in CPCL. Marketing research is considered important and used as and when necessary in all the organisations.

Evaluation by the spokesperson, indicate that in VSP and CPCL (incidentally, both are public enterprises), development requirements are not considered actively. Even the response to management requirements for modifications is slow and rigid.

Exhibit 6.3 : Comparative Analysis of MKIS in Core Sector

Sl No	Aspect	CPCL (N=11)	VSP (N=11)	ACC (N=14)
1.	Year of Setting up	1995	1998	1998
2.	Purpose	➢ Make complex decision easy ➢ As competitors have setup	➢ Make complex decisions easy	➢ Make complex decisions easy ➢ Early adaptation of new technology ➢ To monitor global business
3.	System Details	ERP	Network and Oracle	SAP R3 ERP
4.	Future Plans	Completion of ERP	SAP	--
5.	Information Overload	-NO-	9%	- NO-
	Information Shortage	9.1%	18%	21.4%
6.	Marketing Intelligence	➢ Newspapers and Journals ➢ Discuss-ions ➢ Internet	➢ Newspapers ➢ TV ➢ Discussions	➢ Newspapers ➢ TV ➢ Discussions
7.	Marketing Research	➢ Viewed significantly ➢ Used occasionnally	➢ Viewed significantly ➢ Used occasionnally	➢ Viewed significantly ➢ Used occasionally

Exhibit 6.4 : Reports in Core Sector–Company- Wise

	CPCL	VSP	ACC
1.	Product demand	Market research report	Daily activity report
2.	Customer feed back		Sales report
3.	Sales report	Price movement	Competition report
4.	Collection and payments	Gross sales realisation Stock	Daily collection report
5.	Industry performance report	Sales credits and discounts	Distribution report Price trend
6.	ICIS - LOR (London oil report		Analysis report
7.	for lubes)	Performance reports	Dealers report
8.	Internet sites Petroleum Bazaar Analysis by specialists /	Customer reports	Daily retailers report
9.	experts in the field Quality control	Status reports	Daily site report
10.	Laboratory report Tank Dip Statement	Sales reports (D / W / M / QTY / HY / YY)*	Previous day stock report
11.	-	Production demand	Previous day out - standing report
12.	-	Exceptional report	Agent-wise and Region-wise sales report
13.	-	Materials management report	Agent-wise sales Purchase and procurement repost
14.	-	Production report	Market research report
15.	-	Mill stock report	Distribution report
16.		BSY stock report	Financial report.
17.	-	JCP report	-
18.	-	DCIS report	-
19.	-	Ministerial	-
	-	report	-
20.	-	Inventory report	-
	-	Dispatch	
21.		planning report	

Exhibit 6.5 : Comparative Evaluation of MKIS in Core Sector			
Aspects	**CPCL**	**VSP**	**ACC**
System Management Evaluation*	(87.4)	(85.4)	(72.3)
Leader ship	90.9	81.8	69.9
Plans	92.7	89.2	62.9
Controls	74.0	74.1	76.4
Security	86.3	93.1	69.8
Change	93.1	98.2	82.6
Information System Evaluation**	(3.40)	(3.94)	(3.26)
Hardware	3.4	3.7	3.0
Software	3.4	3.8	3.3
Documentation	3.4	3.8	3.1
Maintenance	3.3	4.5	3.3
Integration	3.5	3.9	3.6
People Evaluation**	(3.6)	(4.0)	(3.85)
Top management	3.6	4.0	4.1
IS people	3.6	4.0	3.6
Outcomes Evaluation**	(3.50)	(3.67)	(3.75)
Information	3.5	3.5	4.6
Output	3.3	3.3	4.0
User friendliness	3.5	4.0	3.7
Decision support system	3.5	3.5	2.4
Benefits	3.7	3.9	4.8
Satisfaction	3.5	3.8	3.5
Overall Evaluation*	(3.6)	(3.7)	(3.1)

* Percentages ** Mean values

Exhibits 6.6, 6.7 and 6.8 summarise the findings in the chemicals sector pertaining to marketing information systems. Of the three companies, two have established marketing information systems in 1999. Neuland and Erythro pharma have set up MKIS to gain

Exhibit 6.6 : Comparative Evaluation of MKIS in Chemical Sector

Sl. No	Aspect	Neuland (N=10)	Erythro Pharma (N=9)	Biological (N=7)
1.	Year of Setting up	1994	1999	1999
2.	Purpose	➢ As competitors has setup ➢ Demand for employees	➢ As competitors has setup ➢ Demand for employees ➢ Make complex decisions easy An extension of other systems.	➢ Make complex decisions easy ➢ An extension of other systems.
3.	System Details	Networks & FOCUS	In-house developed package	In-house developed package
4.	Future Plans	SAP	SAP – ERP	--
5.	Information Overload	-NO-	-NO-	14%
	Information Shortage	20%	-NO-	42%
6.	Marketing Intelligence	➢ Discussions ➢ TV ➢ Conference ➢ Newspapers and Journals	➢ Discussions ➢ TV ➢ Conference ➢ Newspapers and Journals ➢ Internet	➢ Discussions ➢ TV ➢ Conference ➢ News-papers and Journals
7.	Marketing Research	➢ Viewed significantly ➢ Used occasionally	➢ Viewed significantly ➢ Used occasionally	➢ Viewed significantly Used occasionally

Exhibit 6.7 : Reports in Chemicals Sector- Company-Wise

Sl. No.	Neuland	Erythro Pharma	Biological E
1	Daily activity report	Details of execution orders	Daily activity report (production, R&D/QC.)
2	Sales report	Time between orders receiving and its execution	Sales report (weekly, monthly, quarterly)
3	Country-wise, product-wise sales (past-present)	Performance evaluation of key areas	Inventory control report
4	Agent-wise sales (comparison)	New market information	Purchase and Procurement report
5	Product-wise contribution	Distribution report	Personnel appraisal report
6	Inventory control reports	Sales report	Market research and analysis report
7	Purchase and procurement report	Country-wise product with sales report etc.	Distribution report (location-wise, Department-wise)
8	Market research report	Market target report	Financial report
9	Distribution report	Current sales report	Product summary report
10	Financial report	Payment details report	Collection and payments report
11	--	Export report	--
12	--	Stock report	--
13	--	Customers report	--

Exhibit 6.8 : Comparative Evaluation of MKIS in Chemical Sector

Aspects	Neuland(10)	Erythro Pharma(9)	Biological E. (7)
System Management Evaluation*	(92.2)	(84.8)	(86.8)
Leadership	100	80	88.4
Plans	100	100	80.8
Controls	61	54	88.6
Security	100	100	85.5
Change	100	90	90.9
Information System Evaluation**	(4.5)	(4.2)	(3.9)
Hardware	4.4	4.1	3.9
Software	4.6	4.3	3.9
Documentation	4.4	4.1	3.7
Maintenance	4.9	4.8	4.4
Integration	4.6	3.7	4.0
People Evaluation**	(4.1)	(4.2)	(4.1)
Top management	3.7	4.2	4.0
IS people	4.5	4.2	4.2
Outcomes Evaluation**	(4.3)	(3.4)	(3.9)
Information	4.6	3.5	3.9
Output	4.0	3.3	4.0
User friendliness	4.7	3.9	3.9
Decision support system	4.4	3.4	4.1
Benefits	4.8	3.7	3.9
Satisfaction	3.5	4.0	4.0
Overall Evaluation*	(4.0)	(4.0)	(3.5)

* Percentages ** Mean values

competitive edge and meet employee demands. Biological E has set up to MKIS 'to make complex decisions easy'.

The systems in the three organisations have at present, less sophisticated and in-house developed packages. The future plans for the three organisations focus on SAP / ERP. All the organisations generate several reports as shown in Exhibit 6.7. The reports can be broadly classified into sales, purchase, inventory and finance. While marketing research is considered important and used to meet special requirements, marketing intelligence is created through discussions, TV, conferences, newspapers and journals. Only respondents of Erythro pharma reported the use of internet.

The evaluation of effectiveness of the systems indicates that the systems in Neuland and Erythro Pharma are rated good whereas in Biological E, it is rated above average. Component-wise evaluation shows that system movement is more effective in Neuland than in other two companies. Information system is considered very good in Neuland and Erythro Pharma and good in Biological E. 'People' component is rated very good in the three companies, only exception is 'top management' support in Neuland.

When it comes to outcomes evaluation, respondents of Neuland rated it very good. So is the case of Erythro Pharma. Relatively, the system in Biological E is rated less beneficial. Overall ratings are also in the same pattern. Information shortages are reported by a few respondents in Neuland and Bilogical E.

According to the spokesperson of Neuland and Bilogical E, their systems have inadequacies. In Neuland hardware is inadequate and, development requirements are not actively considered. In Biological E, the distribution report needs modification.

Exhibits 6.9, 6.10 and 6.11 assemble the findings on marketing information systems in the service sector. Antrix had established MKIS in 1972 and Medinova 1993. Both the organisations have set up MKIS for the same purpose of making complex decisions easy.

Antrix is presently using Oracle, VB and Internet facility whereas Medinova is dependent on Clipper and Oracle. The system in Antix is not yet to be fully computerised. Antrix is planning for bread-board system, whereas Medinova is set out for SAP/ERP. Both the organisations use reports generated by the system (Exhibit 6.10).

Exhibit 6.9 : Comparative Analysis of MKIS in Service Sector

No	Aspect	Antrix (N=5)	Medinova (N=6)
1.	Year of Setting up	1972	1995
2.	Purpose	Make complex decisions easy	Make complex decisions easy
3.	System Details	Oracle, VB, Internet	Clipper and Oracle
4.	Future Plans	Bread-board system	SAP – ERP
5.	Information Overload	20%	16%
	Information Shortage	60%	33%
6.	Marketing Intelligence	➢ Discussions ➢ TV ➢ Newspapers and Journals	➢ Discussions ➢ TV ➢ Conference
7.	Marketing Research	➢ Viewed significantly ➢ Used occasionally	➢ Viewed significantly ➢ Used occasionally

Exihibit 6.10 : Reports in Services Sector-Company-Wise

Sl.No.	Antrix	Medinova
1	Customer satisfaction report	MIS report Daily
2	Competitors pricing and product features	Corporate business repot
3	Substitutes Technology and alternative technology	Collection and payment report
4	Customer profiles and needs	Client reporting report
5	Demand and elasticity	Client feed back report
6	Future plans of customer which demand produces	Doctor's report on perception on services
7	Customer loyalty	Sales reports.
8	Brand image, influence	--
9	Government polices affecting the market	--
10	Legal reports	--
11	Satillite news	--
12	Business and launch report	--

Exhibit 6.11 : Comparative Evaluation of MKIS in Services Sector

Aspect	Antrix (5)	Medinova (6)
System Management Evaluation*	(65.8)	(80.1)
Leader ship	64.0	76.4
Plans	72.7	89.1
Controls	39.7	81.3
Security	80.0	83.0
Change	72.7	75.3
Information System Evaluation**	(3.5)	(4.2)
Hardware	3.7	4.2
Software	3.8	4.3
Documentation	3.8	4.1
Maintenance	3.0	3.6
Integration	3.3	4.0
People Evaluation**	(3.3)	(4.5)
Top management	3.0	4.1
IS people	3.6	4.0
Outcomes Evaluation**	(3.7)	(3.5)
Information	3.8	4.1
Output	3.5	4.6
User friendliness	4.1	4.1
Decision support system	3.3	4.2
Benefits	4.1	3.9
Satisfaction	3.8	4.3
Overall Evaluation*	(2.8)	(4.0)

* Percentages ** Mean values

Marketing intelligence sources are primarily discussions, TV and print media. Marketing research is considered important and used as and when necessary.

Information system is rated below average in Antrix and good in Medinova. The poor rating in Antrix may be because the system is not yet completed and brought to full use. In respect of System, People and Outcomes also the scores of Medinova system are on higher side. In case of user friendliness and benefits the ratings are almost the same.

Information overload and shortages are reported by some in both the organisations.

According to the spokesperson of Medinova, following inadequacies exist:

- System has poor security
- Maintenance of old database, and its updating
- There are chances of corrupting data
- There are some untrained users (EDP) because of old software.

Propositions Examined

The six propositions developed for studying marketing information systems are examined here.

1. The information systems represent the state of the art technology.

Many organisations have SAP / ERP, Net Work, Oracle and VB representing the state of the art MKIS. In future, all the organisations will have SAP / ERP. Excepting VSP, all the organisation uses marketing research frequently. Marketing intelligence sources for all the companies include the traditional means like newspapers, journals, and discussions besides TV and internet, the latest information exploder. (Exhibit 6.12)

2. The information systems are effective in serving the functional needs of marketing.

The major purposes of MKIS (Exhibit 6.13) are :

- To make complex decisions easy
- To match competitors' information capabilities

The decision support provided by MKIS is rated good (score of 3.3 to 4.4) in all the organisations excepting Antrix (2.4) which is

Exhibit 6.12 : Marketing Information Systems–A Comparative view

Sector	Organis-ations	Existing System	Use of Mark-eting Rese-arch Frequ-ency (Mean Score)	Mark-eting Intell-igence	Future Plans
Core	CPCL	ERP	3.5	Tradit-ional & Internet	Com-pletion of ERP
	VSP	Network and Oracle	2.2	DO	SAP
	ACC	SAP R2 ERP	3.2	DO	-
Chem-ical	Neuland	Network & 'FOCUS'	4.0	DO	SAP
	Erythro Pharma	In-house develop-ped Package	3.6	DO	SAP – ERP
	Biological	In-house develop-ped Package	3.4	DO	-
Services	Antrix	Oracle, VB, Internet	3.0	DO	Bread Board System
	Medinova	Clipper and Oracle	4.5	DO	SAP - ERP

Exhibit 6.13 : Functional Effectiveness of MKIS

Sector	Organisations	Decision Support by MKIS (Mean Score)	Benefits of MKIS (Mean Score)	Purpose
Core	CPCL	3.5	3.7	Make complex decisions easy
	VSP	3.5	3.9	-DO-
	ACC	2.4	4.8	-DO-
Chemical	Neuland	4.4	4.8	As competitors have set up
	Erythro Pharma	3.4	3.7	-DO-
	Biological	4.1	3.9	Make complex decision easy
Services	Antrix	3.3	4.1	-DO-
	Medinova	4.2	3.9	-DO-

still evolving its MKIS. Further the benefits of MKIS which include improving productivity, ease in doing job, and making activities efficient are rated very good (3.7 to 4.8) by the respondents. From this, it can be concluded that that the evolving MKIS of the organisations under study are enhancing functional effectiveness of the organisations.

3. The information systems are change-oriented.

A probe is made into change orientation on aspects like whether there is a control mechanism for making appropriate changes. Exhibit 6.14 shows that all the organisations other than those in services have very high change orientation (82.6 to 100%). Even in case of services also the perceived change orientation is above 70% (72.7–75.3 %). Hence, it can be said that information system are change-oriented

Exhibit 6.14 : Change Orientation of MKIS

Sector	Organisations	Change Orientation (%)
Core	CPCL	93.1
	VSP	98.2
	ACC	82.6
Chemical	Neuland	100.0
	Erythro Pharma	90.0
	Biological	90.9
Services	Antrix	72.7
	Medinova	75.3

4. *Information systems are user friendly*

The marketing information systems are considered user friendly. The mean scores on the 5-point agreement scale ranged between 3.5 to 4.7 (Exhibit 6.15). The overall score represents agreement on aspects like training to users, participation of users in system development, use of the system and user confidence.

Exhibit 6.15 : User friendliness of MKIS

Sector	Organisations	Mean Score
Core	CPCL	3.5
	VSP	4.0
	ACC	3.7
Chemical	Neuland	4.7
	Erythro Pharma	3.9
	Biological	3.9
Services	Antrix	4.1
	Medinova	4.1

Exhibit 6.16 : Cost Effectiveness of MKIS

Benefits	Core Sector			Chemicals			Services	
	CPCL	VSP	ACC	Neu-land	Erythro	Biological	Antrix	Medinova
Has tools to Productivity	4.0	3.9	3.2	4.6	4.0	4.4	4.2	4.0
Improved Results	4.8	4.0	3.7	4.9	3.7	4.1	4.4	4.6
Boosted Profits	3.7	3.9	2.8	4.9	4.0	3.4	4.0	3.6
Expectations realised	3.4	4.0	4.4	3.7	3.5	4.0	4.2	3.6

Exhibit 6.17 : Information System Management Effectiveness

(Percentages)

Sector	Organisations	Leadership	Plans	Controls	Security
Core	CPCL	90.9	92.7	74.0	86.3
	VSP	81.8	89.2	74.1	93.1
	ACC	69.9	62.9	76.4	69.8
Chemical	Neuland	100.0	100.0	61.0	100.0
	Erythro Pharma	80.0	100.0	54.0	100.0
	Biological	88.4	80.8	88.6	85.5
Services	Antrix	64.0	72.7	39.7	80.0
	Medinova	76.4	89.1	81.3	83.0

Based on this finding, it can be concluded that systems are user friendly.

5. Information systems are cost effective

Cost effectiveness is measured by the results obtained like productivity, improved results, and expectations realised. Exhibit 6.16 shows the benefit of MKIS in the select organisations. On the whole, respondents of various organisations have given a rating above 3, and confirmed cost effectiveness of MKIS.

6. Information systems have effective leadership, plans, controls and security

The information system management evaluation in the select organisation reveals that leadership, plans, controls, security are effective. Exhibit 6.17 presents the evaluation in percentage scores by the respondents. Relatively, leadership and controls in Antrix are rated effective by less number of respondents.

System Inadequacies

The inadequacies in the MKISs of the select organisations as identified by the organisational representatives and respondents of the study are summarised here:

CPCL

By the views of the representative

- ➢ Hardware is inadequate to the users
- ➢ Development needs are not considered actively
- ➢ Response to requests for modifications is slow

By the views of the respondents :

- ➢ No surprise audit of the information systems department for detecting fraud, theft, collusion etc.

VSP

By the views of the representative :

- ➢ Hard ware is inadequate
- ➢ Development requirements are not considered actively.

ACC

By the views of the representative :

- The present system is considered good as it meets even future requirements

By the views of the respondents :

- Features used in programming languages are not excellent
- The decision support is less.

Neuland

By the views of the representative :

- The hardware is inadequate to the users
- The responses to management requests for modifications are slow

By the views of the respondents:

- There is no surprise audit of the information system department for detecting embezzlement, sabotage, irregularities.

Erythro Pharma

According to the representative, there are no inadequacies in the system

By the views of the respondents:

- Provision for backup personnel in key positions required
- No surprise audit of the IS department for detecting collusion, embezzlement and sabotage
- Security controls are not sufficient to ensure that all input data and corrections to data have been processed properly and accurately
- Procedures for system changes and library changes are to be well established.

Biological E.

By the representative:

- Distribution report needs some improvement to improve collection and profitability.

Antrix

By the views of the representative:

- MKIS is not yet fully computerised

By the views of the respondents:

- There is no surprise audit of the information department for detecting fraud, theft, collusion, embezzlement, sabotage, irregularities.

Medinova

By the views of the representative :

- System has poor security
- Maintenance of old database and its updating
- There is a chance of corrupting data
- There are some untrained users because of old software

Conclusions

From the above summary of findings, the following conclusions emerge :

1. Information systems in the select organisations are developed to make complex decisions easy and match with the competitor's abilities.
2. Information systems represent the latest developments in the technology. They are evolving with technology.
3. The major elements in MKIS are reporting system supported by marketing research and intelligence systems. Managers use both quantitative as well as qualitative models in decision-making.
4. Information overloads or shortages are less.
5. Information systems are effective in serving the functional needs of marketing.
6. Information systems are change-oriented.
7. Information systems are user friendly; users are satisfied with the system.
8. Information systems are cost effective.
9. Information systems have effective leadership, plans, controls, and security.
10. Few inadequacies are also reported, they relate to hardware, audit, user training, data base, security, and response to development requests.

Suggestions

What do the findings and conclusions mean to the organisations under study? What kind of approaches and actions are required in the light of them?

1. ***Adopt IRM Concept***

   Of the few inadequacies mentioned, the important one that deserves careful consideration is the response of management to development needs. Other points relate to user training, audit, data base maintenance, security and hardware. To overcome all these deficiencies IRM concept is recommended.

   In IRM concept, Information is viewed as a key resource and investment in information technology is made to gain competitive advantage. It helps streamline system management establish functional authority for effective performance and results, and integrating IS management with enterprise functions.

2. ***Design Comprehensive Information Systems and appoint qualified staff to bridge gap between IS staff and users.***

   To complete and emerge successfully, Indian companies have to adopt a quick but logical approach in decision-making. Information is the vital and necessary input in any decision-making of a manager. To provide each level of authority with appropriate information in the right form and at the right time a systems approach is inevitable. A comprehensive management information system not only will help to collect, discriminate, select, relate, classify and interpret the information according to the needs of the user but also integrates organisational functions. The finding that organisations under study are moving to ERP / SAP is healthy, judged in this perspective.

   Mc. Nevin (1968) identified that coco cola company bridge the gap between expectations of IS people and the state of the art in business by setting MIS department at corporate level and carrying out developmental research and continuing research to build models and solve predictable marketing problems.

   Richard H. Brein (1968) found in one company two new positions–information system manager and operations research manager were created before the acquisition of a larger, more sophisticated computer system and it was successful.

3. *Provide adequate Hardware Facilities*

   In case of CPCL, VSP, and Neuland, the inadequacy of hardware systems is felt. However, the respondents have agreed with the view that it is a passing problem in the period of transition to computerisation. However, steps may be initiated to overcome this problem by providing capabilities for operation and backup.

4. *Strengthen Auditing Systems*

   The lack of surprise audit of the information system department was identified in CPCL, Neuland, Eritro Pharma, and Antrix. The other four organisations under study reported that they have surprise auditing. In view of the significance of systems audit, the 'surprise' approach may also be adopted by these companies to detect and prevent irregularities.

5. *Security*

   In Erythro Pharma and Medinova, security concerns are voiced. Proper controls are to be set-up to ensure that all input data and corrections to data are processed properly and accurately. Also procedures for systems changes are to be well established to avoid any loss of data.

6. *User Training*

   In all the organisations excepting one, user training was considered satisfactory. However, steps should be initiated to continue the training process as user needs are dynamic and skills require upgradation. The threat of obsolescence is to be thwarted by periodical training programmes.

Directions for Future Research

Research on information systems in India is a recent phenomenon for obvious reasons. On an average, Indian companies spent only around 0.75 % of their revenues on IT. Very few companies have adopted Information Resource Management concept (IRM). The scope for empirical research on information systems is thus abundant.

In case of marketing information systems, a systematic study is not made so far. As such this study is made exploratory to provide a stimulus for in depth studies and a platform for discussions on further probe. The following studies may be undertaken (Cross-sectional and longitudinal) in future in Indian organisations industry-wise.

- Marketing mix elements and MKIS
- Product development and MKIS
- Integration of MKIS with other functional ISs
- Marketing efficiency and MKIS
- Performance and satisfaction of marketing personnel and MKIS
- E-Commerce
- Internet Selling.

Appendices
Questionnaire-1

QUESTIONNAIRE TO THE ORGANISATION (MARKETING MANAGERS)

The study is undertaken as a part of the doctoral research of the investigator. It proposes to describe and evaluate the MKIS in select organisations. You are requested to cooperate and furnish required information to enable us in making a meaningful study, which will be mutually beneficial. In case it is necessary we assure you, the information will be kept **strictly confidential.**

PART - A

1. Name of the organisation:
2. Date of establishment:
3. Details of the ownership and collaboration:
4. Product of the company:
5. Divisions / Branches and location:
6. Organisational structure details:
   (Kindly provide chart)
7. Company performance over the last five years:
   (i) Sales turnover:
   (ii) Profit after taxes:
   (iii) Total number of employees:

PART–B

Marketing Organisation

1. Details of organisation structure:
2. Employee profile:

Level	Function	Designation	Number

PART - C

Marketing Information System

1. When was MKIS computerised:
2. Trace the reasons for computerising of MKIS:
3. Outline the development of MKIS in your organisation
4. What is the total outlay so far?
5. Details of MKIS Budget and expenditures for the last 5 years?

Year	1997	1998	1999	2000	2001
Budget					
Expenditure					

PART - D

System Description

1. Furnish details of present MKIS.
   (a) Hardware configuration:

   (b) Software availability :

2. Give detail of IS people presently involved in MKIS:

3. What kind of training is provided to users of MKIS?

4. Mention the type of reports which are generated for decision-making?

PART–G

Evaluation

1. What are the identified inadequacies of the present system?

2. Even if the present system is alright, what developments do you think are necessary?

3. Details of the future plans for the development of MKIS

Questionnaire-2

Given below questions which require you to answer :

(i) By writing information in the space provided against / below the questions

(ii) By checking or circling a number on a 5-point scale against the statement.

PART-A

PERSONAL PROFILE

1. Designation:
2. Experience in the organisation:
3. Level in hierarchy:
4. Department:
5. You report to:
6. Subordinate positions under you:
7. Indicate major areas of responsibilities:

   (Advertising, Marketing search, and Brand Management)
8. Role clarity: About your role in the organisation?

	Very Much				Very Less
My role is clear to me	5	4	3	2	1
I do not have conflicts in playing my Role (no overlapping)	5	4	3	2	1
My authority is clear to me	5	4	3	2	1
My relations with others are well defined	5	4	3	2	1
I was told clearly about my responsibility (What I have to contribute)	5	4	3	2	1

9. I depend in my decision-making and implementation on the following :

	Very Much				Very Less
Superiors	5	4	3	2	1
Subordinates	5	4	3	2	1
Peers	5	4	3	2	1

PAR T- B

Data Analysis Methods

10. **What data analysis methods do you use at present to make *key decisions*?** Which methods do you prefer to use in future?

Sl. No.	**Key decisions**	**Methods**		
		In use	**Do not prefer to use**	**Prefer to use**

PART-C

Information Flow (Input and Output)

12. What kind of information do you get and from which source?

Source	Designation	Information	Frequency
Superior			
Subordinates			
Peers			

13. What kind of information do you disseminate and to whom?

To	Designation	Information	Frequency
Superior			
Subordinates			
Peers			

14. By the information I get. I feel I have

Information overload ()

Information sufficiency ()

Information shortage ()

PART–D

Transactions and Reporting

15. List the reports you receive, name the source, and identify whether they are necessary? If necessary write Y otherwise N against the report?

S.No.	Title of the report	Receive from	Y/N

16. List the reports, you send to whom, and identify whether they are necessary? If necessary, write Y otherwise N against the report?

S.No.	Title of the report	Receive from	Y/N

PART –E

Intelligence

17. List the dailies, magazines and journals that you get and read and that you want to get and read?

Presently getting	Reading	Want to get	Want to read

18. Are you a member of professional organisations? Please specify?

19. Your participation in conference workshops, during the last 4 years ?

Year	Conference	Workshops	Seminars	Any other
1998				
1999				
2000				
2001				

20. To keep yourself informed what source of information do you use?

Discussion with company personnel []
Discussion with other company personnel []
TV news and programmes []
Conference / Workshops / Seminars []
Newspapers / Journals []
Any other, please specify []

PART–F

Marketing Research

21. How important marketing research is in your decision-making?

Very Important Unimportant

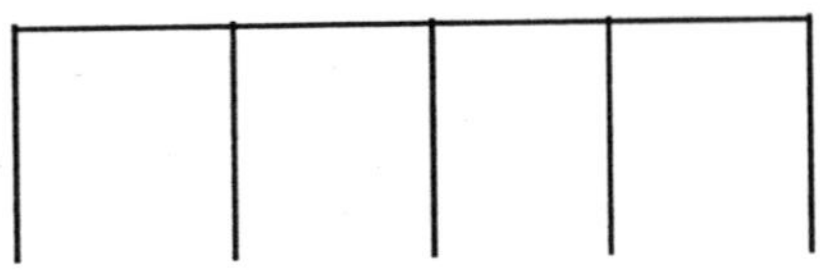

5 4 3 2 1

22. How frequently you have used Marketing Research to make decisions in the last three years?

Very much Never

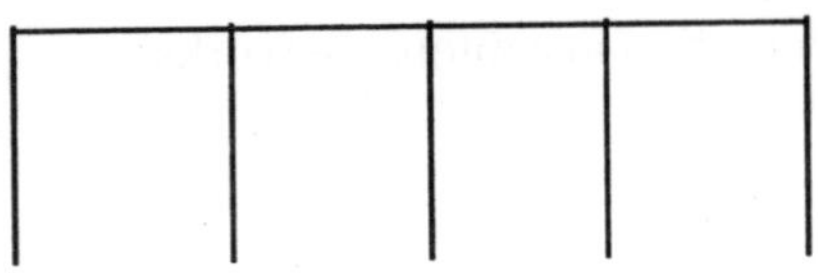

5 4 3 2 1

PART–G

System Management

(a) Leadership

23. Is the MKIS under the direction of qualified manager (Specify) Yes / No

24. Does management motivate its personnel's to effectively provide a desired information service Yes / No

25. Is there a formal training program where deemed necessary for

    1. New employees? Yes / No
    2. Transferred employees? Yes / No
    3. Regular employees? Yes / No

(b) Plans

26. Does the management have a well-defined master plan for MKIS Yes / No

27. Is the master plan integrated with

    1. Objectives? Yes / No
    2. Strategies? Yes / No
    3. Projects? Yes / No
    4. Policies? Yes / No
    5. Procedures? Yes / No
    6. Standards? Yes / No

28. Are departments long range plans related to organisational Objectives? Yes / No

29. Is the master plan subjected to periodic review?

    1. Top management? Yes / No
    2. Management steering committee? Yes / No
    3. Information systems management? Yes / No

(1) Controls

30. Does management exercise the necessary control over Its operations so that fraud, theft, and irregularities of IS methods and procedures can be detected? Yes/ No

31. Does management segregate the functions of the Department in order to minimise fraud, theft, and irregularities? Yes / No

32. Are there provisions for backup personnel in key Information Systems Positions? Yes / No

33. Does internal auditing periodically check on the operations of the information systems department? Yes / No

34. Is the information system audited periodically by an independent third party? (Outside auditors or consultants)? Yes / No

35. Is there a surprise audit of the information systems department for detecting?

    1. Fraud? Yes / No
    2. Theft? Yes / No
    3. Collusion? Yes / No
    4. Embezzlement? Yes / No
    5. Sabotge? Yes / No
    6. Irregularities? Yes / No
    7. Does the computer system have adequate powerful air-conditioning? Yes / No

36. Are systems and procedure manuals kept current? Yes / No

(2) Security

37. Are security controls required by information systems management? Yes / No

38. Are security controls fully understood and implemented by systems and programming personnel? Yes / No

39. Are security controls sufficient to ensure that all input data and corrections to data have been processed properly and accurately? Yes / No

40. Are security controls written and contained in appropriate systems and procedures manuals for ready reference when necessary? Yes / No

(3) Change

41. Is there a control mechanism for making appropriate information systems changes? Yes / No

42. Does this control mechanism include a provision for approval? Yes / No
43. Are procedures established for making:
    1. System changes? Yes / No
    2. Program changes? Yes / No
    3. Library (program and file) changes? Yes / No
    4. Computer operator changes? Yes / No
44. Are all system and program changes immediately documented, including the reason for the changes? Yes / No
45. Are written memoranda issued to the appropriate personnel concerning changes? Yes / No
46. Is the user involved in making changes where necessary? Yes / No
47. Are the internal and external auditors appraised of important changes? Yes / No
48. Are master files and transaction files controlled to prevent unauthorised changes during conversion? Yes / No

PART–H

Evaluation of Information system

49. How do you rate the present marketing information system of your organisation?

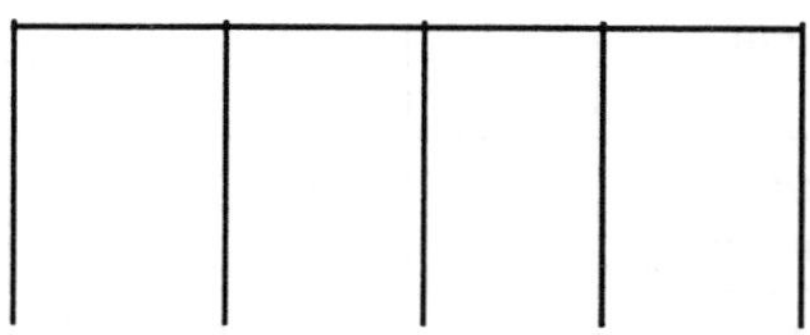

5 4 3 2 1

Exceptional Unsatisfactory

50. How do you rate the support of the information system to the following?

	Excellent				Poor
1. Market analysis and forecasting	5	4	3	2	1
2. Product decisions	5	4	3	2	1
3. Price decisions	5	4	3	2	1
4. Place decisions	5	4	3	2	1
5. Promotion decisions	5	4	3	2	1

51. To what extent the following are true in your organisation?

Sl. No.	Aspects	Very much	Much	Uncertain	Less	Very less
1.	The response of the system is fast	5	4	3	2	1
2.	Accessing information is easy	5	4	3	2	1
3.	Features used in programming languages are excellent	5	4	3	2	1
4.	System security is very good	5	4	3	2	1
5.	In realisation of user needs, the system is the best	5	4	3	2	1
6.	Documentation of the system is complete	5	4	3	2	1
7.	The system has good flexibility	5	4	3	2	1
8.	The system is integrated with other systems	5	4	3	2	1
9.	The staff in the organisation like to use the system	5	4	3	2	1

Sl. No.	Aspects	Very much	Much	Unce-rtain	Less	Very less
10.	The reports and other information products are well scheduled	5	4	3	2	1
11.	The system is well maintained	5	4	3	2	1
12.	Users are well trained to use the system	5	4	3	2	1
13.	Information processing is efficient	5	4	3	2	1
14.	Data analysis programs are updated	5	4	3	2	1
15.	Computer systems are adequate	5	4	3	2	1
16.	Computer systems are capable	5	4	3	2	1
17.	Information is relevant	5	4	3	2	1
18.	Information is kept confidential when required	5	4	3	2	1
19.	Is staff are helpful?	5	4	3	2	1
20.	Information provided by the system is accurate	5	4	3	2	1
21.	System provides timely information	5	4	3	2	1
22.	System furnishes exact information	5	4	3	2	1

Sl. No.	Aspects	Very much	Much	Unce-rtain	Less	Very less
23.	The information provided is reliable	5	4	3	2	1
24.	Current information is provided by the system	5	4	3	2	1
25.	The information is complete in all aspects	5	4	3	2	1
26.	It provides well designed formats	4	3	2	1	
27.	Information furnished has clarity	5	4	3	2	1
28.	Adequate volume of output is generated by the system	5	4	3	2	1
29.	The system is used by all concerned employees	5	4	3	2	1
30.	Top management is involved in the development of the system	5	4	3	2	1
31.	There is participation of users in the system development and implementation	5	4	3	2	1
32.	Users have confidence in the system	5	4	3	2	1

Sl. No.	Aspects	Very much	Much	Unce-rtain	Less	Very less
33.	The system has tools to improve productivity of operations	5	4	3	2	1
34.	My job has become easy with the support of the system	5	4	3	2	1
35.	My expectations of the benefits of system are realised	5	4	3	2	1
36.	The system is satisfactory to me	5	4	3	2	1
37.	There is coordination between MKIS and other systems	5	4	3	2	1
38.	MKIS has improved the results of the organisation	5	4	3	2	1
39.	MKIS is making the activities more efficient	5	4	3	2	1
40.	MKIS has boosted the profits of organisation	5	4	3	2	1

Index

A

Abbreviated New Drug Application, 176

ACC cement, 95, 151, 282

Accounting Information System, 92

Ackoss, 66, 67, 82, 92, 279

Activity Management, 47, 49

Adler, 27

Agra, 128

Ahmedabad, 128

Allan Fletcher Gillman, 73, 90

Ambler Tim, 55

Analytic Model, 281

Angdew A. Mitchell, 60, 76

Antrix Corporation Limited, 95, 237-39, 277, 282, 288-91, 296-97, 301

Asian Paints, 51

Asset Management System, 51

B

Bangalore, 128, 152, 259

Barmes James H. Jr., 65

Bernadetta Agatha Szajna, 72, 89

Bernhardt, 25

Bharat Petroleum, 51

Bhopal, 152

Bhubaneswar, 128

Biological E. Limited, 95, 216, 235, 282, 288-91, 295-97, 301

Blattberg, 27

Bonnle K. Burkland, 59, 76, 92, 279

Brancheau, 92

Brand Management, 156

Brand Promotion, 156

Brein and Stafford Model, 28

Brien, 92, 279

Burk, 92, 279

Business Organisation, 25, 54

Byong-Do-Kim, 63, 79

C

Capital Management, 53

Cartada, 92, 279

Case Method, 95

Chang Liu, 65, 80

Change Management, 208, 227, 232, 270

Channel Management, 156

Charles D. Schewe, 68, 84
Chennai Petroleum Corporation Limited, 95, 103, 282
Chennai, 128
Claggett, 33
Claire Maureen Forrest, 67, 83
Clipper Software, 260
Cognitive Dissonance Theory, 72
Coimbatore, 128, 152
Comparative Evaluation, 285, 287, 288, 290
Contact Management, 47, 49
Contingency Model, 63
Cox and Good Model, 29
Cox and Good, 92, 279

D

D.P. Goyal, 68, 84
Daniel Robey, 73, 91
Data Quest, 49, 53, 54, 55
Daviding, 60, 76
Dealer Management, 156
Decision Making, 157, 160, 177-80
Decision Support System, 62, 67, 171
Delghton, 279
Delhi, 128, 152
Department of Space, 238
Desantis, 72, 90
Don Peppers, 60, 76
Donald F. Cox, 62, 79
Donald R. Lehman, 68, 84
Dr. Anand Teltembole, 51, 55

E

Economic Reforms, 25
Edward Philip Bovich, 62, 73
Eldon Y. Li, 69, 85
Electronic Data Interchange, 72, 73
Elena, 71, 88
Engineers India Limited, 103
Enterprise Resource Planning, 151
Erik Brynroffon, 70, 86
Erythro Pharma Limited, 95, 196, 282, 288, 289-91, 295-97, 301
Executive Information System, 47
Extended Technology Acceptance Model, 71

F

Faridabad, 128
Finance Information System, 47

G

Gallyan Cook, 61, 78
General Marketing Information System, 34, 92
Georgeday, 61, 67
Gernot Bernhand Langle, 62
Ghaziabad, 128
Ginzberg, 72, 90
Glazer, 27
Glenn Edward Maples, 71, 87

Global Marketing, 27
Globalisation, 25, 27
Goyal, 92, 279

H

H. Su Cheng, 63, 79
Hero Honda
Hotakata Katahera, 59, 75
Human Resource Information System, 47
Hyderabad, 128, 259

I

Iangle, 92
IBM, 105
Indian Oil Corporation, 106
Indian Space Programme, 237
Indian Space Research Organisation, 238
Indore, 128
Information Flow, 134, 181, 201, 220, 245, 263
Information System Component, 172
Information System Evaluation, 120-21, 145, 161, 166, 190, 203, 209, 223, 229, 253, 265, 271
Information System Management, 119, 141, 163, 186-87, 189, 206, 208, 225, 227, 238, 247, 249, 253, 270
Information Technology, 25, 28, 151
Integrated Refinery Information System, 104-105
International Marketing, 197, 218-21, 238-39, 242-43, 245-46
Inventory Management, 53

J

Jaipur, 128
Jam Fine Chemical Inc New Jersy, USA, 197
James C. Brancheau, 59, 76
James Edward Turner, 72, 89
James L Wiek, 68, 84
James Tegan, 63, 80
James Wo Cortada, 70, 71, 87
Jane Fedoerowich, 59, 75
Jane, 92, 279
Jeanne Wenzel Ross, 64, 80
Jiangming ye, 63
Jiro Kokuryo, 61, 77
Johannes Marie Lucien, 61, 77
John D. Johnson, 65
John Delighton, 60, 76
John M. Uhl, 57, 74
Julian W. Riehl, 72, 89

K

Kamna Mallik, 68, 84
Kanpur, 152
Karahanna, 71, 88
Kate M. Kaisar, 64, 80
Kenneth D. Une, 57, 74
Kinnear, 25
Kirloskar, 52
Kochi, 128

Kolkata, 128, 137, 152, 259
Korea Longterm Bank, 63
Kotler, 29, 30
Kotler Model, 29

L

Langle, 279
Lazer, 27
Leo Ramesh, 73, 91
Leon R. Price, 66, 82
Liberalisation, 25
Logistic Information System, 47
Longitudinal Casual Research Techniques, 67
Ludhiana, 128

M

Malcolm, A. Mc Nevin, 67, 83
Management Information System, 68
Maratha Pogers, 60, 76
Mark Donald, 77, 87
Marketing Case Based Reasoning System, 32
Marketing Creativity Enhancement Program, 32
Marketing Decision Support, 32
Marketing Encyclopaedia System, 47, 49
Marketing Expert System, 32
Marketing Information Revolution, 27
Marketing Information System (MKIS), 25-27, 29, 32, 39, 54, 57, 68, 92, 94, 96, 103, 107, 115-16, 120, 126, 133, 140-41, 150-51, 153, 162, 172, 175, 177, 186, 190, 196-97, 204-05, 216, 224-25, 234, 237-38, 241, 248-49, 251, 258-60, 266, 279-80, 284, 308
Marketing Information System, 129, 130, 205
Marketing Intelligence, 138, 159, 173, 183, 202, 222, 235, 246, 264, 284-85, 291
Marketing Knowledge Based System, 32
Marketing Management Support System, 30
Marketing Mix, 35, 305
Marketing Neural Nets, 32
Marketing Organisation, 129, 152, 177, 197, 216, 238, 260, 307
Marketing Problem Solving Mode, 30
Marketing Research and Analysis, 133
Marketing Research, 160, 184, 185, 203, 217, 221, 223, 235, 243, 247, 265, 284, 285, 294, 316
Maruti Udyog, 52, 53
Mc Lean, 69, 85
Mecann, 92, 279
Medinova Diagnostic Service Limited, 95, 259, 282, 292-97, 302
Microsoft, 125
Miller, 71, 87

Ministry of Surface Transport, 105
Mitcheell, 92, 279
Model of Individual Choice, 68
Motler Model, 29
Motor Sprit, 104
Multi nominal Logic model, 65
Multimedia Marketing Plan, 58
Mumbai, 128, 152
Mune, 27
Murdick, 33
Myingoong Cheon, 63, 80

N

Nagpur, 128
National Informatics Centre, 105
National Iranian Oil Corporation, 103
Nevland Laboratories, 95, 175, 235, 282, 288-91, 295-97, 301
Nysolick, Ross and Claggett Model, 33

O

Opportunity Management System, 46, 49
Oracle Sales Analysis, 48, 49
Oracle, 105, 130, 172, 284

P

Patna, 128, 152
P.G. Kulkarni, 70, 186
Point of Sale Marketing System, 59
Prime Minister, 238
Privatisation, 25
Prospect Management, 79
Pune, 128, 159
Push Model, 63

R

R. Kelly Jr. 71, 87
Rashi Glazer, 61, 77
Ray Joseph Blankenship, 65, 81
Raymond R. Burke, 58, 75
Reddy Labs Biological E. Limited, 177
Redington, 53
Reffference Model, 63
Relational Data Base Management System, 105
Research Model, 67, 280
Research Problems, 280
Richard B. Roseckey, 61, 77
Richard H. Brien, 66, 82
Robert C. Blattberg, 63, 79
Robert E. Good, 69, 79
Ross, 33

S

S. Balu, 55
S. Chandrashekhran, 52
S. Gopal Krishnan, 52
S.H. Delone, 69, 85
S.R. Bala Subramanian, 55
Sales Force Automation Software, 48
Sales Information System, 41, 44-47

Samsung, 53, 63

Secunderabad, 152

Seymour Banks, 57, 74

Sharma, 279

Shiguru Yagi, 59, 75, 92, 279

Somendra Pant, 63, 79, 92, 279

Space Commission, 238

Standard Medical and Pharmaceuticals, 259

Stephan, 27

Supply Chain Management, 51, 156

System Evaluation, 139, 161

System Management Evaluation, 142-45, 161, 166, 185-90, 203-05, 207-09, 223-24, 226-28, 247-52, 265-67, 269-71, 290

T

Team Sales Solution, 47

Tech Pacific, 53

Technology Acceptance Model, 71

Timo Sorimen, 69, 85

Timothy Peter Shea, 59, 75

Trade Matrix, 51

Traditional Marketing Information System, 58

V

Van Engelen, 61, 77

Varun Grover, 63, 80

Vasistha Technology, 217

Videsh Sanchar Nigam Limited, 105

Vijaya Sarathy, 73, 91

Vishakhapatnam Steel Plant, 95, 126, 282

Vittal, 279

Vizag, 128

W

Warren Lee Dickson, 66, 82

W.H. Delone, 69-85

Wierenga and Bruggen Model, 30